YALE AGRARIAN STUDIES SERIES
James C. Scott, Series Editor

The Agrarian Studies Series at Yale University Press seeks to publish outstanding and original interdisciplinary work on agriculture and rural society—for any period, in any location. Works of daring that question existing paradigms and fill abstract categories with the lived experience of rural people are especially encouraged.

—James C. Scott, *Series Editor*

James C. Scott, *Seeing Like a State: How Certain Schemes to Improve the Human Condition Have Failed*

Steve Striffler, *Chicken: The Dangerous Transformation of America's Favorite Food*

Parker Shipton, *The Nature of Entrustment: Intimacy, Exchange, and the Sacred in Africa*

Alissa Hamilton, *Squeezed: What You Don't Know About Orange Juice*

Parker Shipton, *Mortgaging the Ancestors: Ideologies of Attachment in Africa*

Bill Winders, *The Politics of Food Supply: U.S. Agricultural Policy in the World Economy*

James C. Scott, *The Art of Not Being Governed: An Anarchist History of Upland Southeast Asia*

Benjamin R. Cohen, *Notes from the Ground: Science, Soil, and Society in the American Countryside*

Parker Shipton, *Credit Between Cultures: Farmers, Financiers, and Misunderstanding in Africa*

Paul Sillitoe, *From Land to Mouth: The Agricultural "Economy" of the Wola of the New Guinea Highlands*

Sara M. Gregg, *Managing the Mountains: Land Use Planning, the New Deal, and the Creation of a Federal Landscape in Appalachia*

Michael R. Dove, *The Banana Tree at the Gate: A History of Marginal Peoples and Global Markets in Borneo*

Patrick Barron, Rachael Diprose, and Michael Woolcock, *Contesting Development: Participatory Projects and Local Conflict Dynamics in Indonesia*

Edwin C. Hagenstein, Sara M. Gregg, and Brian Donahue, eds., *American Georgics: Writings on Farming, Culture, and the Land*

Timothy Pachirat, *Every Twelve Seconds: Industrialized Slaughter and the Politics of Sight*

Andrew Sluyter, *Black Ranching Frontiers: African Cattle Herders of the Atlantic World, 1500–1900*

Brian J. Gareau, *From Precaution to Profit: Contemporary Challenges to Environmental Protection in the Montreal Protocol*

For a complete list of titles in the Yale Agrarian Studies Series, visit www.yalebooks.com.

From Precaution to Profit

Contemporary Challenges to
Environmental Protection in
the Montreal Protocol

BRIAN J. GAREAU

Yale UNIVERSITY PRESS

New Haven and London

Yale University Press books may be purchased in quantity for educational,
business, or promotional use. For information, please e-mail sales.press@yale.edu
(U.S. office) or sales@yaleup.co.uk (U.K. office).

Set in Minion type by
IDS Infotech Ltd., Chandigarh, India.
Printed in the United States of America.

Library of Congress Cataloging-in-Publication Data

Gareau, Brian, 1973–
From precaution to profit: contemporary challenges to environmental
protection in the Montreal Protocol/Brian J. Gareau
pages cm.—(Yale agrarian studies series)
Includes bibliographical references and index.
ISBN 978-0-300-17526-4 (hardback)
1. Ozone-depleting substances—Government policy. 2. Air—Pollution—
Government policy. 3. Environmental policy—International cooperation.
4 Globalization. I. Title
TD887.O95G37 2013
363.73—dc23
2012035607

A catalogue record for this book is available from the British Library.

This paper meets the requirements of ANSI/NISO Z39.48–1992 (Permanence
of Paper).

10 9 8 7 6 5 4 3 2 1

For
Tara, my wife.
And for our children,
Delphine, Beatrix, and Leonel.

Contents

Preface

For most people, global environmental problems like global climate change and ozone-layer depletion are "out there," far removed from our daily lives. We know that it is our choices, our collective ways of life, that are contributing to these immense problems, but they often seem out of our control, out of our reach. This book shows that global environmental problems are not always out of our control, are not always "out there" in some far-away place. Instead, they are very often strongly, materially connected to our communities, to our food production choices, to debates over scientific knowledge that take place at our universities, and to struggles over political power in which our governments participate. Sometimes these connections are strongest in places we might least suspect, such as in a field of strawberries. This local rootedness of global environmental problems in social life is not always obvious to us.

When I first started investigating the worker livelihoods, environmental conditions, and political economic aspects of strawberry production in Central Coast California, I never imagined that what I was really doing was gaining insight into the local conditions of production upon which major debates over certain ozone-depleting chemicals were taking place at

one of the most famously successful global environmental
agreements in history, the Montreal Protocol on Substances
That Deplete the Ozone Layer. In 2002, my wife, an agroecolo-
gist, conducted research for the Center for Agroecology and
Sustainable Food Systems at the University of California at
Santa Cruz to interview growers about the various choices that
they make with regard to chemical use versus more sustainable
pest-management strategies. I had recently begun investigating
strawberry production, and I had learned about the heated
debates that were about to erupt between the U.S. government,
environmental groups, and other countries over the scheduled
phaseout, in 2005, of methyl bromide, an ozone depleter that
virtually made strawberry production possible on a large scale
in California. I asked my wife if she would be willing to ask
strawberry growers in her sample what they planned to do
once methyl bromide was phased out under the Montreal
Protocol. On the whole, strawberry growers did not know what
they would do, but they trusted that the California Strawberry
Commission and their pest-control advisers would simply
make sure that things would be all right. At first, this seemed
puzzling to me, and I wondered whether strawberry growers
might be unaware of or a bit indifferent about their futures.

I was wrong. These growers knew, intuitively perhaps,
that they were a part of a very powerful production complex
that would make sure that they were secure, that they would
have methyl bromide until it was undoubtedly clear that some
alternative chemical could replace it without any unforeseen
risk to their profits. The California Strawberry Commission
and other powerful agro-industrial institutions have the
capability to "jump" from the local scale (e.g., Central Coast
California) to the global scale (e.g., Montreal Protocol
meetings) in order to influence the outcomes of global

environmental politics. The fact that such "jumping" happens with the support of the U.S. government, which historically has always strongly supported its agro-industry, makes these institutions incredibly influential in the global arena. The Montreal Protocol had never had to deal with this sort of influence before, and it would soon find it very disrupting. Whether California growers needed methyl bromide or not (and this is an intense debate that I pursue in this book), the ability to have their needs and wants jump scale to influence ozone politics shows how global environmental agreements can be deeply rooted in local conditions of production.

The strawberry fields had found their way into global debates surrounding the depletion of the ozone layer. But very few people were aware of this, fewer still understood it, and even fewer found it or current disruptions in the Montreal Protocol to be a problem. One delegate for the European Union, an expert on the methyl bromide issue from political and legal standpoints, asked me in 2003, "Do California straw-berry growers really need all that methyl bromide?" At the time I could not answer the question, but it struck me as very odd for an expert on the topic to ask such a basic question. At the same meeting, a methyl bromide scientist told me that he would be interested in reading my book when it became avail-able so that he "could see how politics affect science" in the methyl bromide debates. It seemed that strawberry growers intuitively knew some things that the ozone experts were not entirely sure of. The central purpose of this book is to illustrate why this shift in the Montreal Protocol is a serious problem marking a larger shift in global environmental governance that we should all be concerned about.

This book challenges the oft-cited belief that the Montreal Protocol remains an exemplary global environmental agreement. Through an analysis of the political decision-making process and controversies generated at Montreal Protocol meetings (which I attended from 2003 through 2007), the book documents new ways global environmental governance is organized based on neoliberal ideals. It shows how neoliberalism—as a dominant discourse and economic practice—has become increasingly embedded in the Montreal Protocol and how global powers are able to act protectionist amid that discourse. It demonstrates how recent controversies in the Protocol involve much more than just economic protectionism per se; they also involve the protection of the legitimacy of certain forms of scientific knowledge. It traces the rise of a new form of disagreement in the Protocol among global powers, members of the scientific community, and civil society and agro-industry groups, signaling the negative impact of neoliberal policies on ozone politics and global environmental governance more broadly. The book also reveals how global civil society groups involved in the Protocol are affected by the neoliberal discourse, which has left them relatively ineffective in influencing states to place environmental protection above economic interests. With scholars and policymakers increasingly looking to the Montreal Protocol for guidance on dealing with the issue of global climate change, it is imperative that we recognize its drawbacks before any synthesis across treaties is attempted.

The book is written primarily for scholars, graduate and advanced undergraduate students, and an educated general audience interested in globalization, international politics, environmental studies, global environmental governance, environmental sociology, and the sociology of science and technology. As such, I trust that the book will be of interest in a number of academic fields. Indeed, it is my hope that the

book will attract a readership among my colleagues in sociology, but also in geography, political science, and anthropology,
as well as others interested in continuing the hard work of
bridging the theoretical spaces that divide our disciplines. I
have made a conscious effort to present my work at academic
conferences both inside and outside my academic discipline,
and this book reflects many of the helpful comments I
received during those exciting excursions.

Acknowledgments

It goes without saying that without the assistance I received from many excellent people, this book would have never materialized. While the research herein is based on my dissertation, which I completed at the University of California at Santa Cruz, this book also benefits immensely from subsequent research, graduate student seminars, undergraduate lecture discussions, research assistant investigations, and comments from colleagues at Boston College and professional meetings in the United States and internationally. Hence, I am grateful for the assistance of many people from the Pacific to the Atlantic and beyond.

Wally Goldfrank provided inexhaustible support on my research. I am very grateful for his ruthless honesty in critiquing my work, as it has made me a better scholar and writer than I would otherwise be. Melanie DuPuis first approached me with the idea of researching strawberries. What started out as a project investigating how farmers planned to handle a non–methyl bromide strawberry world turned into a much larger endeavor that took me around the world to Montreal Protocol meetings in Montreal, Dakar, Prague, Nairobi, and Geneva. I am grateful for the years of interest Melanie put into my work.

Many more people have provided me with their time, energy, and input. Ben Crow and Ronnie Lipschutz provided very helpful suggestions on earlier drafts in dissertation form. John Borrego, Michael Goldman, and Andy Szasz also commented on my work and helped me clarify my arguments. Many people have been very helpful during my time at Boston College, not least Julie Schor, Sarah Babb, Eve Spangler, and students Rachel Weed and Joseph Manning. Others that contributed to my work as research assistants are Kelly Workman and Margeaux Schmerler from UC–Santa Cruz. My interviews at Montreal Protocol meetings would not have been possible without the guidance, time, and friendship of several very kind and important ozone advocates: Stephen O. Andersen, Melanie Miller, Martin Barel, Jim Wells, David Doniger, Sally Schneider, Ian Porter, Michelle Marcotte, Tom Land, Hodayah Finman, and many government delegates worldwide. For those I forgot to mention, my sincere apologies.

Research funding was provided by the University of California's Chancellor's Dissertation Fellowship, the University of California Institute on Global Conflict and Cooperation (IGCC), the UC–Santa Cruz STEPS Institute for Innovation in Environmental Research, the UC–Santa Cruz Center for Agroecology and Sustainable Food Systems, the UC Pacific Rim Research Program, and the UC–Santa Cruz Department of Sociology. Boston College offered generous support to complete this work through several sources, including two Research Expense Grants provided by the Boston College Committee on Research and Publication of the University Research Council, a grant from the Boston College Institute for the Liberal Arts, and a Boston College Faculty Research Incentive Grant. This project benefitted from conference exposure due in part to two grants from the National Science Foundation's Award for U.S.

Participants in the International Sociological Association (SES-0548370 and SES-0852624). Parts of this book have appeared, in earlier forms, in the journals *Antipode* (vol. 40 [2008]: 102–130), *Environmental Politics* (vol. 21 [2012]: 88–107), *Environment and Planning A* (vol. 41 [2009]: 2305–2323), *Social Sciences Quarterly* (vol. 89 [2008]: 1212–1229), and *International Environmental Agreements* (vol. 10 [2010]: 209–231), as well as in the *Routledge Handbook of World-Systems Analysis* (2012).

Additionally, I am very grateful for the time, energy, and support of the staff at Yale University Press. Jean Thomson Black is an exceptionally helpful editor, as well as being very positive and all around a pleasure to work with. Very special thanks to Jean, her assistant Sara Hoover, senior production editor Ann-Marie Imbornoni, copyeditor Bojana Ristich, three anonymous reviewers for exceptional advice, and all the staff at Yale University Press. And special thanks to James C. Scott for including this book in the Yale Agrarian Studies Series.

Most of all, I wish to thank my family for their support. My wife, Tara, has been a loving partner and best friend through this whole process, as she is always. I am very grateful to have her with me. My parents, Joe and Pauline, and siblings, Lynn and Keith, have been extremely supportive and excited about this project.

I dedicate this book to Tara and also to our children, for whom I would do almost anything, even sit through hundreds of hours of often extremely boring plenary session meetings, wearing a suit and tie, in order to try to help make the world a better place for them.

Of course, at the end of the day, I am the sole author, and I bear sole responsibility for the arguments and portrayal of events illustrated in this book.

Abbreviations

AETF	Agricultural Economics Task Force
CCOF	California Certified Organic Farmers
CDM	Clean Development Mechanism
CFC	Chlorofluorocarbon
CMM	Cutaneous malignant melanoma
CRP	Conference Room Paper
CUE	Critical Use Exemption
DDT	Dichlorodiphenyltrichloroethane
DEA	U.S. Drug Enforcement Agency
DPR	California Department of Pesticide Regulation
DU	Dobson Units
E.C.	European Community
EIA	Environmental Investigation Agency
EPA	U.S. Environmental Protection Agency
E.U.	European Union
ExMOP	Extraordinary Meeting of the Parties to the Montreal Protocol
GATT	General Agreement on Tariffs and Trade
GEF	Global Environment Facility
GRULAC	Grupo Geopolítico de América Latina y del Caribe (Group of Latin America and the Caribbean countries)

GWP	Global Warming Potential
HCFC	Hydrochlorofluorocarbon
HFC	Hydrofluorocarbon
ICI	Imperial Chemical Industries
IENGO	International Environmental Nongovernmental Organization
IIED	International Institute for Environment and Development
IMF	International Monetary Fund
IPCC	Intergovernmental Panel on Climate Change
LDC	Less-developed country
MBTOC	Methyl Bromide Technical Options Committee
MDI	Metered dose inhaler
MeBr	Methyl bromide
MITC	Methyl isothiocyanate
MLF	Multilateral Fund
MOP	Meeting of the Parties to the Montreal Protocol
NAFTA	North American Free Trade Agreement
NASA	U.S. National Aeronautics and Space Administration
NGO	Nongovernmental organization
NOAA	National Oceanic and Atmospheric Administration
NRDC	Natural Resources Defense Council
ODP	Ozone-depleting potential
ODS	Ozone-depleting substance
OECD	Organization for Economic Cooperation and Development
OEWG	Open-Ended Working Group of the Parties to the Montreal Protocol
QPS	Quarantine and preshipment
TEAP	Technology and Economic Assessment Panel

TOC   Technical Options Committee
UNCHE   United Nations Conference on the Human
         Environment
UNCTAD   United Nations Conference on Trade and
         Development
UNDP   United Nations Development Programme
UNEP   United Nations Environmental Programme
UNFCCC   United Nations Framework Convention on
         Climate Change
UNIDO   United Nations International Development
         Organization
USDA   U.S. Department of Agriculture
UV   Ultraviolet
WMO   World Meteorological Organization
WTO   World Trade Organization

1

Introduction

When Agriculture Meets the Ozone Layer

The U.S. has striven to be fair in working to devise Protocol processes that put aside politics in favor of scientific and technological approaches. We do not rely on private agendas or backroom deals. We seek nonpolitical solutions to nonpolitical problems that are open and transparent. . . . A process that would single out the United States, willfully ignores our national needs, and rejects the work of the Protocol's technical and scientific bodies is clearly not one that we should adopt. . . . My fellow delegates, if our exemption request is not approved, the Protocol's record of fairness and the very foundation upon which this treaty is based will be undermined. Such an outcome could shatter the fragile coalition within the United States that enables us to make progress in international bodies. I urge delegates to avoid such an outcome.

—Claudia McMurray, U.S. Delegation, 15th Meeting
of the Parties to the Montreal Protocol

We should learn about the knowledge production process itself, in situ, questioning why it is treated as truth and expertise and asking what larger project such faith in global knowledge serves.

—*Michael Goldman*, Imperial Nature

I n the late 1980s scientists began naming and measuring a new threat to the environment: the depletion of the ozone layer. In rapid succession, chlorofluorocarbons, or CFCs, were identified as a major source of ozone depletion, and science, journalism, public opinion, and civil society (including environmental) groups, and even corporations and governments converged in supporting the Montreal Protocol, an international treaty designed to phase out the use of CFCs and other ozone-depleting chemicals. Since then, the Montreal Protocol and the conditions that allowed it to be created and implemented have become the gold standard for global environmentalists hoping to replicate its success in the Kyoto Protocol (the global climate-change agreement) and other instruments for global environmental remediation.

Nevertheless, the rosy picture of the Montreal Protocol with regard to eliminating CFCs is misleading in several significant ways. The Protocol was passed before the scientific evidence that supports it was firmly established. Thus, the process of passing it was always more deeply political, contingent, and indeterminate than the "just-the-facts-ma'am" brand of science some environmental groups would have us believe. While an agreement to eliminate CFCs without scientific certainty is in itself promising, it also shows that science is political. Luckily, the political milieu of the time was open to precautionary measures that compelled groups to take action despite a lack of scientific certainty, a situation that, again, was extremely promising for environmentalists wishing to eliminate potentially disastrous global environmental threats.

That political milieu, however, has changed over the years to focus on profit, not precaution. I refer to this change as the "neoliberal turn," which is meant to emphasize the gradual (and sometimes abrupt) increase in free market logic in political, economic, and other areas of social life. Under neoliberal ideology, individuals, corporations, and social groups should seek to improve their condition in a marketplace unhindered by the government, and global governing bodies should reinforce this action. Of course, the ideology does not manifest perfectly in real life—there is no truly "free" market, just as there is no such thing as a "free lunch." This emphasis on the free market, however, has a way of changing the ways that actors engage, debate, and interpret knowledge— including the Montreal Protocol. Since the neoliberal turn, the Montreal Protocol itself has been challenged and threatened with failure as it has sought to extend its work beyond CFCs to the regulation of other highly toxic ozone-depleting substances, or ODSs. Much of this book focuses on the near failure of the Montreal Protocol to deal effectively with methyl bromide (MeBr), used predominantly by the U.S. strawberry industry, or to minimize the number of exemptions from phaseout that the U.S. government could demand.

In this book, I will explore how science, governments (national and supranational), industry, and civil society co-create solutions, some strong and effective, some much less so, to global environmental challenges. In this work, historical time, the epoch in which international protocols are negotiated or sabotaged, also plays an important role. In an era when the precautionary principle was strong, the Montreal Protocol was ratified, even over initial industry objections, and signed by a conservative U.S. president (Ronald Reagan). In contrast, even a liberal president, like Barack Obama, has proven to be less effective on the global stage in a strongly neoliberal climate that emphasizes individual freedom and profit at the expense of the precautionary principle applied to global environmental (and human) health.

The single most important global environmental agreement in human history is the Montreal Protocol on Substances That Deplete the Ozone Layer. The ozone layer is, in a nutshell, the earth's sunscreen. It absorbs up to 99 percent of the sun's ultraviolet (UV) radiation. Without this layer, life on earth would be impossible; the UV radiation simply would be too destructive to most forms of life, including humans. Unlike tropospheric (or low-level) ozone, which occurs at the lowest levels of the earth's atmosphere and is created mainly by vehicle and industrial emissions reacting with sunlight, causing air pollution (i.e., smog), the stratospheric ozone layer is a natural filter. The Montreal Protocol was created to eliminate the human-made ODSs that destroy the ozone layer. ODSs destroy molecules in the ozone layer, thus letting in more UV radiation, which increases rates of skin cancer and skin diseases, eye cataracts, damage to the immune system, and sunburn in humans and other animals.

Even as ODSs are being phased out through the Montreal Protocol, the ozone layer has thinned, in some cases leaving "holes" in the atmosphere. Even under the most optimistic scenarios it will not be completely rebuilt until near the end of this century and at different rates worldwide.[1] The most famous and largest ozone holes occur in the Antarctic. The year 2006 marked the largest Antarctic hole in terms of thinness and breadth. The U.S. National Aeronautics and Space Administration (NASA) stated that in September 2006 the Antarctic ozone hole reached a record area of 29.5 million square kilometers, making it larger than all of North America; in October a new record was set for the thinnest levels of ozone ever recorded. "Nearly all of the ozone in the layer between eight and 13 miles [33.7 kilometers] above the earth's surface had been destroyed," noted Rob Gutro; instruments measured Dobson Unit (DU) levels as low as 1.2 in this region. David Hofmann, director of the Global Monitoring Division at the National Oceanic and Atmospheric Administration (NOAA) Earth System Research Laboratory stated that "these numbers mean the ozone is virtually gone in this layer of the atmosphere."[2] While most of the land under the Antarctic ozone hole is uninhabited, parts of the hole reach into some populated areas. Moreover, the hole is quite capable of moving and has been observed over South America and the Falkland Islands.[3]

And there are other ozone holes, just as significant but perhaps less known to the general population than the famous Antarctic hole. There is an Arctic hole, for example, and it has an impact on humans just like the Antarctic hole, especially now that ozone depletion has become so intense in this region. The 2011 Arctic ozone hole moved from the pole into Scandinavia and Greenland, covering both countries. Inhabitants were strongly urged by the World Meteorological Organization (WMO) to take daily precautions to protect their health in the presence of much stronger UV rays. Parts of Canada and Russia have also been affected.[4] Furthermore, there is the possibility that "ozone-depleted air" will continue to move south with the Arctic polar vortex. Thus, a constantly moving ozone-deficient mass is "often pushed southward to 40 or 45 degrees latitude by natural atmospheric disturbances," which means it has the potential of reaching northern Italy, New York, and San Francisco, where "the surface intensity of UV radiation could lead to sunburn within minutes for sensitive persons, even in April."[5] Even the Mediterranean is on watch to see if the ozone-deficient area will make its way farther south.[6]

In June 2005, unexpected ozone thinning was detected above the Czech Republic and spawned government health warnings all the way to Germany. UV levels reached an all-time record high and were especially dangerous for the fair-skinned population living in the region. During this same period, the European Space Agency forecasted the UV index (an international standard measurement of the strength of UV radiation from the sun, whereby health organizations recommend the use of skin protection when measures of 3 or higher are recorded) over Berlin, Frankfurt, and Vienna to top 8.2 through June 30, 2005. This shocking and dangerous ozone thinning is ascribed to shifting wind patterns over the Mediterranean Sea and North Africa. Karel Vanicek, chief of the Czech Solar and Ozone Observatory, "does not think the change was caused by ozone-depleting chemicals," but "[he did] not rule out a possible link to global climate change."[7] A 2009 study in Spain looked at the impact of "ozone mini-holes" over the country and the UV impact of ozone thinning—specifically increased human exposure to UV radiation. The study noted that "ozone mean levels have been declining about 10 DU per decade from 1979 to 2006."[8] During the study, 119 holes were found in Spain, and increases in the number of holes per year have been observed since the 1990s.

Ozone depletion is not the only cause of global increases in skin cancer. In some countries people may simply be spending more time in the sun now than they did in previous generations. Nevertheless, some scholars argue that "an increase in the amount of solar ultraviolet light that reaches the earth is considered to be responsible for the worldwide increase in skin cancer."[9] Certainly it would also be foolish to ignore entirely the links between the state of the ozone layer and increases in cancer rates worldwide. The U.S. Environmental Protection Agency (EPA) has made estimates on the long-term effects of increased UV exposure, such as one that noted the "potential damage at 150 million cases of skin cancer and three million deaths during the course of the twenty-first century at an economic cost of $6 trillion."[10] Moreover, although the Montreal Protocol has done much to alleviate such numbers, the EPA states that even so, "200,000 Americans have died or will die from skin cancers associated with excess ultraviolet radiation brought about by CFC-caused ozone destruction."[11] Beyond skin cancer, reduced ozone has also been shown to "increase rates of malaria and other infectious diseases."[12]

According to the American Cancer Society, in 2010 in the United States alone more than 1 million new cases of skin cancer were expected, 68,000 of which would be melanoma (the leading cause of death from skin disease), resulting in close to 12,000 deaths. The odds of contracting melanoma increased from 1 per 250 to 1 per 84 over the last quarter-century, and eye cataracts are expected to increase 0.5 percent for every 1 percent of ozone-layer loss. By the age of seventy, two-thirds of Australians will be diagnosed with skin cancer, accounting for 80 percent of all new cancers diagnosed each year in Australia and resulting in over 1,800 annual deaths. More than 1,000 people in Australia are treated for skin cancer daily, 430,000 annually, creating an annual cost of $300 million to the Australian health system—more than any other cancer.[13] In southern Chile, where ozone-layer thinning is also extreme, skin cancer rates have escalated 66 percent since 1994. The results of a 2009 study concentrating on the rising UV levels in Arica, Chile, and the subsequent rising levels of malignant skin tumors found that "the incidence of skin cancer significantly increased" between 2000 and 2006, "most probably due to the high levels of ultraviolet light to which individuals are exposed throughout the year."[14]

UV radiation also contributes to genetic disorders— especially in small aquatic species and amphibians. While plants require solar energy to photosynthesize, too much UV radiation stunts plant growth and can lead to a decrease in yields for important crops. The general rule of thumb is for every 1 percent increase in UV exposure, crop yield will decrease by 1 percent. Additionally, more UV radiation creates other economic costs by accelerating the degradation of materials such as plastics, paints, and rubber.[15]

ODSs such as CFCs were first used in the late nineteenth century, when they became chief ingredients for fire extinguishers. By the early 1970s, two hundred thousand metric tons of CFCs were used in aerosols each year in the United States alone. Soon after, it became increasingly evident that CFCs had a major side effect: they depleted the ozone layer. Many people today likely remember when CFCs were used widely as refrigerants in air conditioners and refrigerators under the trade name Freon, produced by the American chemical giant DuPont. CFCs were also used as propellants in aerosols and asthma inhalers. These uses are being eliminated through the Montreal Protocol because CFCs and other ODSs threaten life on earth. Today, every single country on the planet has ratified the Montreal Protocol.

In 1974, chemists Mario Molina and F. Sherwood Rowland published an article in *Nature* predicting that CFCs would deplete the ozone layer. Molina and Rowland discovered that CFCs would persist long enough in the atmosphere to reach the stratosphere, where they could then be broken down by UV radiation that would release chlorine from the CFC molecule. These chlorine atoms could then potentially break down large quantities of ozone. Molina and Rowland were awarded the Nobel Prize in Chemistry for their groundbreaking work on ozone-layer depletion.

Early scientific research on the effect of CFCs on the ozone layer was hotly contested by the chemical industry. However, after Molina and Rowland testified before the U.S. House of Representatives in 1974, considerable funding was provided to tackle the problem. In 1976, the U.S. National Academy of Sciences confirmed the link between CFCs and ozone-layer loss, leading to a flood of research on modeling the exact effect of CFCs on the ozone layer. Based on this and other scientific evidence, in 1985—the same year that the first ozone hole was discovered in Antarctica—the Vienna Convention for the Protection of the Ozone Layer was established to initiate international cooperation in research on the potential of ozone-layer loss resulting from human activity. Although not a legally binding agreement, the Vienna Convention set the stage for creating a framework for an international approach to ozone-layer protection. As late as 1987, the chemical industry still denied the validity of the scientific findings on CFCs, evidenced by the Alliance for Responsible CFC Policy's testimony before the U.S. Congress. Nevertheless, in 1987, the Montreal Protocol was ratified by twenty-nine countries and the European Community (E.C.), representing over 80 percent of world CFC consumption.

Since the ratification of the Montreal Protocol, levels of CFCs in the atmosphere have either leveled off or declined. Ninety-five percent of CFCs have been taken out of production processes. Concentrations of halon (another ODS) are still increasing but at a slower rate than previously. Scientific research predicts that without the Montreal Protocol, by 2050 even the middle latitudes of the Northern Hemisphere would have lost half of their ozone layer, and the Southern Hemisphere would have lost 70 percent. Today, on average it takes fifteen minutes for a fair-skinned person to get a sunburn in the summer in New York or Shanghai (i.e., in the northern mid-latitude region), but without the Montreal Protocol it would have taken less than five minutes.[16] As Jonathan Shanklin of the British Antarctic Survey (and one of the three scientists who discovered the Antarctic ozone hole in 1985) put it, "[the Montreal Protocol] is working. We can quite clearly see that the amount of ozone-destroying substances in the atmosphere is declining."[17]

Due to its successes, the Montreal Protocol has been often acclaimed an example of exceptional global cooperation. Newspaper columnists describe it as "the most successful global environmental agreement ever negotiated."[18] Former U.N. secretary general Kofi Annan went further, hailing the Protocol as "perhaps the single most successful international agreement to date."[19] In his keynote address to the 19th Meeting of the Parties to the Montreal Protocol (19th MOP) in 2007, held in Montreal, the Canadian prime minister, Brian Mulroney, was more assertive, proclaiming it "*the single* most successful international agreement to date." At the 20th Anniversary Seminar of the Montreal Protocol, acclaimed ozone politician and scholar Richard Benedick declared that "the ozone process provides the key to success in international negotiations." At the same celebratory gathering, Drusilla Hufford of the U.S. EPA stated that "clear policy goals, smart NGOs, transformative industry leadership, and gold-standard science" were the main reasons for the successful implementation of the Montreal Protocol.[20] In their mainstay environmental law text, *International Environmental Law and Policy*, David Hunter, James Salzman, and Durwood Zaelke note that never before had global society worked together to address an environmental threat so successfully.[21] In 1990, the Intergovernmental Panel on Climate Change (IPCC) even recommended (successfully, in fact) that the Vienna Convention, the predecessor to the Montreal Protocol, be used as the model for framing the United Nations Climate Change Convention in order to garner global participation on reducing greenhouse gases.[22]

Many scholars working in global environmental governance have rightly welcomed the apparently unparalleled successes of the Montreal Protocol. Many share Benedick's position that the Protocol contains all the ingredients necessary for any successful global environmental regime: scientific consensus and good networking among the participating scientists; cooperative nation-states willing to put global health ahead of national concerns; and cooperative and well-informed global civil society/nongovernmental organizations (NGOs).[23] We are told that the successes of the Montreal Protocol may shed light on additional global treaties such as the Kyoto Protocol, in which attempts at real action to thwart climate change remain stalled. Recognizing that the Montreal Protocol arose out of specific circumstances, many ozone scholars maintain nevertheless that it is possible that those circumstances could be replicated in other global environmental treaties.

Reading such statements, one might conclude that there must have been clear scientific consensus regarding ozone depletion and that there must be less consensus regarding other more contentious global environmental problems, such as global climate change. Yet the Montreal Protocol was ratified *before* any scientific consensus was reached on the actual effect of CFCs on the ozone layer.[24] This is similar to the "shadow of a doubt" (with more than 90 percent probability) regarding the human effect on global climate change witnessed since the second half of the twentieth century. Today, evidence of the anthropogenic effects of global climate change is arguably as conclusive as, and perhaps even stronger than, our knowledge of the human effects on ozone depletion in the early years of the ozone debates.[25] Thus, such early ratification reveals that the Montreal Protocol was created at a moment when a precautionary ethic was strong. Government, industry, civil society groups, scientists, and journalists all participated in global governance, but they did so against a background of a strong precautionary standard. On the whole, these same actors now focus on climate-change issues, but they do so in a strongly neoliberal context in which the precautionary stance is less powerful and concern for individual (and corporate) freedom is stronger. Thus, making the case for concern for humans and the environment in climate-change discussions faces a tougher political battle.

Younger scholars might conclude that the United States' lack of commitment to environmental agreements like the Kyoto Protocol is linked to the George W. Bush administration, that the Montreal Protocol was signed under a different, more environmentally conscious administration. While the

Bush administration was indeed notorious for its skepticism regarding global climate change, for delinking itself from all manner of international agreements, and for its unilateral foreign policy agenda in general, such a conclusion would be far too simplistic. The Obama administration, despite the hopes of many environmentalists who felt Obama would become a leader in global climate change due to his campaign promise to "re-engage with the U.N. Framework Convention on Climate Change (UNFCCC)," has been reluctant to take a precautionary stance on climate change.[26] Rather, and ironically perhaps, the Montreal Protocol was signed in 1987 under the Reagan administration, not recognized as the most environment-friendly of U.S. administrations.[27] Scholars, therefore, need to recognize the distinct and separate historically contingent political and scientific processes that together will determine the outcomes of environmental governance.

For example, some link the success of the Montreal Protocol to strong support for its ratification from civil society groups in the United States. U.S. civil society was indeed involved in the CFC phaseout, a movement that eventually put pressure on the U.S. government to reduce ODSs. Moreover, especially since the release of Al Gore's film *An Inconvenient Truth* and the release of a report in 2007 by the IPCC on climate change, there has existed growing concern among the U.S. public regarding global climate change. For instance, Lydia Saad found that 60 percent of those polled in the United States in 2009 worried "a great deal" or "a fair amount" about global warming, and 38 percent believed it was going to be a serious threat in their lifetimes.[28]

Clearly, things must have been different on many levels when the Montreal Protocol was signed in order for it to have stayed so successful for so long. If we look at the Protocol today, we can see that it has suffered recently from major setbacks that more closely resemble climate-change politics than ozone politics in the early days. Comparisons could even be made between the Climate Gate scandal that erupted in late 2009, where climatologists were accused by climate skeptics of "acting political" by manipulating climate data, and the Montreal Protocol, where ozone scientists were also accused of "acting political" and manipulating MeBr data by the U.S. government.

Urgency regarding global environmental challenges has only grown over the years. If anything, the rhetoric of imminent environmental disaster proclaimed by some environmental advocates has found increasing support in the scientific community. Such support even applies to the ozone situation today. In 2011 the BBC reported that "ozone depletion is often viewed as an environmental problem that has been solved," but much uncertainty remains with regard to ozone-layer recovery, especially since climate-change science is so complicated and interconnected with the ozone layer.[29] "The ozone layer remains vulnerable to large depletions because total stratospheric chlorine levels are still high, in spite of the regulation of ozone-depleting substances by the Montreal Protocol. Chlorine levels are declining slowly because ozone-depleting substances have an extremely long lifetime," warns Paul Newman, an atmospheric scientist and ozone expert at NASA's Goddard Space Flight Center.[30] In the winter of 2011, the ozone layer over the Antarctic reached new levels of damage due to unusually cold weather in the upper atmosphere. By the end of March, an unprecedented 40 percent of the ozone in the stratosphere had been destroyed, against a previous record of 30 percent. Additionally, as noted above, "severe ozone depletion has been seen over Scandinavia, Greenland, and parts of Canada and Russia" in the Arctic region.[31] Scientists admit that they do not understand why Arctic winters are getting colder, and they are as uncertain about the effects the colder climate will have on the ozone layer. "For the next few decades, the [Arctic ozone-depletion] story is driven by temperatures, and we don't understand what's driving this [downward] trend," admitted Markus Rex from the Alfred Wegener Institute for Polar and Marine Research in Germany. "It's a big challenge to understand it and how it will drive ozone loss over the coming decade."[32] In the middle latitudes, the situation is possibly worse; a full recovery of ozone in the tropical and mid-latitudes is not expected to occur until after the year 2100.[33]

The issue of illegal trade in CFCs is also troublesome with regard to threats to ozone-layer recovery. Illegal CFC use has been a problem ever since the early 1990s. According to the Environmental Investigation Agency (EIA), mid-1990s numbers of illegal CFC trade in Freon and other refrigerants were around twenty thousand tons annually through "sophisticated smuggling networks" representing 20 percent of the global legitimate market.[34] Between 1994 and 1996, the port of Miami was flooded with so many illegal CFCs that they had the second-highest-selling street value, trailing only cocaine. In 2000, there was no sign that the illegal trading was slowing down, internationally or in the United States. Recently, illegal CFC trade routes have been seen paralleling narcotics trade routes, such as on the Pakistan-Afghanistan border, where it has been noted that "at least 20–25 Pakistani businesses were dealing in CFCs smuggled in as part of the heroin trade."[35] This Asian heroin trade route, stretching between the Middle East, China, and India, seems to be one of the most popular for transporting canisters of CFCs destined for refrigeration equipment and aerosols that are supposed to be ODS-free. Additionally, a 2005 investigation by the U.S. EPA and the U.S. Drug Enforcement Agency (DEA) led to the discovery of illegal CFC-113, which is used in the process of making methamphetamine.[36]

More and more, the claims of environmental doomsayers are being given sobering recognition by the scientific community. Today, interest groups attempting to hold back global and regional environmental governance appear to be up against a growing wall of scientific evidence that humans are having serious negative effects on the global environment. Ironically, at such a moment of heightened environmental awareness, the Montreal Protocol entered a moment of uncertainty. In fact, it is not an exaggeration to say that from 2003 to 2008 the Montreal Protocol experienced a bona fide legitimation crisis.

Methyl Bromide
HOW STRAWBERRIES NEARLY FRACTURED
THE MONTREAL PROTOCOL

Famous for the phaseout of most CFCs in the industrialized world, more recently the Montreal Protocol almost completely stalled in its efforts to phase out methyl bromide. MeBr is extremely toxic, comparable to arsenic and dichlorodiphenyltrichloroethane (DDT); it is readily absorbed through the lungs, damages the central nervous system, causes birth defects, can kill in relatively small doses, and depletes the ozone layer. The U.S. EPA classifies MeBr as a "Category I acute toxin," the most lethal category of chemical substances. Most cases of toxic exposure to MeBr have occurred among pesticide applicators, but incidents of pesticide drift to nearby communities have also been reported.[37] As early as 1997, the

San Diego–based Environmental Health Coalition (EHC) legally fought the San Diego Port District to end the use of MeBr to fumigate imported produce because of the health risks to nearby communities. The EHC would become the "only local environmental group to participate with national and international NGOs in 1997 . . . during [the initial MeBr] discussions on the Montreal Protocol."[38]

In the years 2003–2008, MeBr, an ODS with high ozone-destruction capability that had arguably marginal importance for society, became the center of a great controversy in the Protocol. This neurotoxin is used primarily as a pre-plant fumigant in strawberry and tomato production and for quarantine and pre-shipment. MeBr is injected into the soils under plastic tarps that cover entire fields, and there it kills everything it touches—insects, bacteria, fungi, mold, every-thing. According to the watchdog organization Environmental Working Group, a 1997 report released by the California Department of Pesticide Regulation (DPR) revealed that millions of pounds of MeBr were being used near schools and day-care centers and that MeBr drift levels from fields to such public spaces, as well as to suburban neighborhoods, greatly exceeded the DPR's safety standards.[39] MeBr became the sub-ject of heated controversy that threatened the potency of the most successful global environmental treaty in history. As the introductory epigraph highlights, in 2003 the United States threatened that it would withdraw from the Montreal Protocol if it were not allowed to use MeBr in its strawberry production beyond the phaseout year of 2005. This threat was staggering for Protocol advocates; before it, the Protocol had experienced relative smooth sailing. This threat marked a new chapter for the Protocol and indeed for global environmental governance in general.

Contrary to standard interpretation, the Montreal Protocol, the treaty that above all others is looked to for guidance on dealing with other environmental problems like global climate change, provides a cautionary tale about what can go wrong with even the most successful of environmental agreements. The story of a respected and successful treaty coming near to failure is deeply important, as it serves as a harbinger of the difficulty of implementing successful global environmental agreements in a neoliberal world. Indeed, with policymakers and commentators proposing to transfer success—and even link regulations—between the Montreal Protocol and global climate-change agreements such as the Kyoto Protocol, understanding how the MeBr controversy forged a chapter of near-failure for the Montreal Protocol is crucial for both ozone and climate global governance.

The Protocol recently experienced a significant deceleration in the phaseout of ODSs through the application of Critical Use Exemptions (CUEs) to the phaseout of MeBr. Since 2003, MeBr has generated a great deal of controversy and debate among powerful nations, less-developed countries (LDCs), the agro-chemical industry, ozone scientific experts, and other actors. The phaseout controversy has marked a serious challenge for the Montreal Protocol that has slowed, at times stalled, and even briefly reversed efforts to phase out ODSs.

Since the turn of the century, opposition from U.S. and international civil society groups regarding the U.S. CUEs from the scheduled phaseout of MeBr has been largely ignored by the U.S. government. U.S.-based environmental watchdogs such as the Natural Resources Defense Council (NRDC), which has over five hundred thousand members in the United States; the EIA; and Greenpeace all have voiced strong disapproval of the continued use of MeBr with little visible impact on deliberations at Montreal Protocol meetings. Instead, the U.S. government chose to side with what Daniel Faber describes as the "polluter-industrial complex": the agro-chemical companies that produce and disseminate toxic substances—in this case MeBr—and the conventional straw-berry industry that relies on MeBr to maximize profits.[40] Additionally, points made by global scientific experts on MeBr and the efficacy of MeBr alternatives have been subject to much condemnation by the United States and allied delegations and by corporate and other interest groups during plenary discus-sions and small-group sessions at Protocol meetings. Instead, the United States has reduced MeBr use on its own terms—slowly—replacing this ODS with other chemicals that have their own, albeit locally contained, serious problems.[41]

These issues played out in Montreal Protocol delibera-tions on MeBr and its alternatives in the years 2003–2008, leading to the stalling of its phaseout and likely delaying recovery of the ozone layer. In fact, if MeBr levels were to stay at their 2009 amounts, "a small ozone hole . . . would continue to form for decades beyond 2065, according to work done by [a] Princeton lab," meaning that by the end of the century, ozone recovery would still not be complete. For 2005–2011, the United States was granted 70 percent of all MeBr CUEs (almost 40,000 out of roughly 56,800 metric tons), every sin-gle year requesting and receiving greater exemptions than all other developed countries combined. For 2011, the U.S. exemptions made up almost 90 percent of all exemptions.[42]

The reasons for such failure to phase out MeBr effectively are far from simple. One is that the United States is steadfast in holding onto MeBr in order to protect its strawberry industry from foreign competition, even though the majority of the

world believes that the bulk of U.S. MeBr exemption requests
are unjustified. As the epigraph above indicates, the United
States claims that it has "put aside politics" and "backroom
deals" regarding the MeBr issue, and its relation to strawberry
production in particular, and seeks "nonpolitical solutions to
nonpolitical problems" regarding strawberry production.
Moreover, the United States claims that this nonpolitical
approach includes relying on the science/knowledge of the
Montreal Protocol's scientific experts, the members of the
Protocol's Technology and Economic Assessment Panel (TEAP),
and its sub-bodies for guidance on how to handle the MeBr
phaseout. Here it is clear that the United States is claiming,
rhetorically at least, that Protocol science/knowledge is politics-
free. It is claiming that other constituents are "acting political"
while it is not. Yet the United States played a major role in
helping shape the scientific knowledge of the Protocol to its
advantage.

　　The United States was a main advocate for the initial ratification of the Montreal Protocol, so why would it jeopardize
past progress in phasing out ODSs on a commodity as trivial as
strawberries, going as far as to suggest that it would leave the
treaty if its demands were not met? After all, the CFC industry
was much larger, much more important economically to the
United States and globally. Clearly, science/knowledge, politics,
economics, and NGO involvement coproduce one another in
unique ways, depending upon the specific circumstances at
hand. To discover exactly how, we must take seriously Michael
Goldman's recommendation (in the epigraph above) to
investigate what larger project is served by legitimating
particular forms of science/knowledge over others.

　　Such an understanding forces us to take seriously the
barriers facing all environmental agreements today. Many

observers of environmental agreements attribute the inability
to enforce a viable climate-change agreement to the lack of
clear evidence or to the lack of an economically feasible option
for global powers, like the United States. With climate change,
as ozone-hole discoverer Shanklin argues, we are often told
that "the political changes that are necessary to change our
lifestyles so we consume less are much harder to achieve" than
eliminating ODSs.[43] But the MeBr controversy illustrates that
the reasons are much more complex than simply consuming
less, and it exemplifies the political challenges facing global
environment governance that have only intensified since the
late 1980s. While the MeBr controversy culminated during the
George W. Bush years—a situation that certainly contributed
to tensions among nations, industry, NGOs, and scientists
working on the MeBr issue—the increasingly skeptical attitude toward global scientific knowledge, global governance,
and precautionary action so celebrated in the post-1972 U.N.
Conference on the Human Environment era had been on the
rise for over a decade prior. The early success of the CFC
phaseout in the Montreal Protocol reflects faith in and application of the "Stockholm principles," whereas the MeBr phaseout reflects a neoliberal turn in ozone governance that does
not mesh with these erstwhile principles.[44]

The MeBr controversy involves much more than just
economics per se (although it certainly does involve economics!); it also involves protecting the legitimacy of U.S. science
in a neoliberal era of globalization. While the global community pushes for acknowledgment of global scientific knowledge on the alternatives to MeBr, U.S. actors stress the primacy
of U.S. scientific knowledge based on data provided by the
private sector. Therefore, while the United States is indeed
interested in protecting its economic interests, the MeBr case

shows that it is perhaps just as keen on protecting the legitimacy of U.S.-based scientific knowledge as the spokesperson for global science/knowledge on MeBr and its alternatives. Ironically, perhaps, changes in the rules and political attitudes of the Montreal Protocol from precaution (the CFC case) to ones based on neoliberal principles have made the MeBr controversy possible. This book, then, will investigate the intricate connections between—or the coproduction of—science and political economy in a newly neoliberalized ozone governance world. It is an environmental governance world that has gradually shifted away from precaution-first toward profit-first tenets, from social concerns to individual concerns, from public knowledge to private-sector science.

Theoretical Approach

To date, the Montreal Protocol has generated rather scant discussion in sociology, with Penelope Canan and Nancy Reichman's intensive investigation being a noteworthy exception.[45] Sociology, however, has a long history of analyzing the global political economy, the "world polity," and the impact of capital and power on social (and socio-ecological) relations, going as far back as Karl Marx.[46] My theoretical approach contributes a critical component to the important "social capital" assessment of the Montreal Protocol presented by Canan and Reichman. Drawing from critiques of recent theorizations of social capital, I will show how social networks are often formed to benefit those with power at the expense of others.

The achievement of social networks embodies a social construction that is attached to class differences and other forms of exploitation. The MeBr phaseout clearly benefits the powerful more than less-powerful actors in the social networks of the Protocol and beyond. The Protocol, as well as global environmental governance in general, is situated within the global economy, and the impact of its various actors is consequential to uneven access to power found in social relations. Here social capital is more than social networking; it is the establishment of social relations that create systems of power that are exclusionary, self-supporting, and based on uneven social conditions.[47]

In *Ozone Discourses,* Karen Litfin provides a sociological assessment of the formation of the Protocol, introducing the "knowledge broker" perspective. Drawing from Michel Foucault, Litfin looks at discourse as "sets of linguistic practices and rhetorical strategies embedded in a network of social relations." Litfin argues that scientific groups and low-level officials held significant power in formulating ozone politics because they were able to disseminate their interpretation of ozone science to higher-ranking officials and thus influence policy making.[48] My approach also considers discourse, at Protocol deliberations, but my analysis sides more closely with Foucauldian approaches to discourse that stress the deep connections among the state, capital, and the discourse used by all participants in governance deliberations, including facets of civil society.[49] Like Litfin's assessment of the implementation of the CFC phaseout, I notice with the MeBr phaseout the coproduction of science and politics, and discourse at Protocol meetings reveals this coproduction. My fieldwork, however, suggests that struggles over conditions of capitalist production, global competition, and global hegemony play dominant roles in shaping how that interpretation happens.

Struggles over MeBr use are the consequence of struggles over unevenly distributed production conditions at national and sub- or supranational scales. Political discourses surrounding

MeBr debates, or any environmental debate, employed at the global scale are articulations of those struggles, intricately linking capital, politics, and global governance. Hence, discourse in global environmental governance is linked to struggles taking place at other scales of political and social life, as critical geographers and political ecologists have well illustrated.[50] In the MeBr case, global discourse is intricately tied to the sociopolitical and ecological conditions of the California strawberry production complex and those of its competitors. In other words, the processes taking place at the national and regional levels of MeBr governance affect global decision making.

ANALYZING NEOLIBERALISM

Powerful actors (states, multinational corporations, global governing institutions, etc.) facilitate global environmental governance in an uneven, geographically contingent way. Neoliberal policies represent an effort by industrialized nation-states in the North to generate and enforce global markets and re-regulate national markets in ways that unevenly benefit the North. Along these lines, economic globalization represents an effort to force market competition on the global South while continuing to protect key industries in the North, at times at the expense of environmental protection/conditions. Globalization in this light is perhaps best understood as the continuation of political-economic domination by the industrialized North furthered by the manufacture and disciplining of markets in the South via market mechanisms organized and managed by the former. Current neoliberal policies can be seen as the instantiation of the New Right's economic standards for global policies, which were implemented as a response to fiscal crises of the state in the late

1970s and early 1980s and deepened as the Cold War came to a close in the 1980s and as globalization became widespread in the 1990s.[51]

It is very important to remember that neoliberalism never exists in some ideal type but always in specific articulations that make "absolute" neoliberal policy and/or discourse impossible to realize. Neoliberalism "in action" is far removed from the "monetarist" rhetoric of its architects.[52] To capture this distinction, "actually existing neoliberalism" is a term often used by environmental sociologists and geographers to explain how neoliberal ideology becomes a part of policy and social decision making in distinct ways. In other words, neoliberalism in action is never the wholesale adoption of free market logic but rather is understood as being located in real situations with real pressures from nation-states, civil society groups, and other actors that play roles in determining its makeup.[53] In this book, neoliberalism is used in the sense of (1) economic (particularly corporate) interests taking priority over other interests; (2) the usage of market-based, competitive principles to resolve environmental problems; (3) a concern for individual actors to have unfettered access to economic gains via competition, unhindered by state regulation; and (4) the replacement of global, public scientific knowledge with private knowledge justified by the specific needs of specific interest groups, or what I describe as "locally based knowledge."

We will see how the stalled MeBr phaseout via the Montreal Protocol involves protection of the California strawberry industry amid neoliberal concerns for free trade and individual rights. Neoliberalism often creates such contradictions (protection in a "free market"), the outcomes of which are rooted in the situatedness of particular policies and particular conditions of production.[54] Nation-states, corporations, landowners, etc., protect their profit-making interests as they always have, and the degree to which they are able to do so is linked to their power vis-à-vis other sectors of capital, the state, civil society, and environmental and other geographically contingent conditions.[55]

As market activity tends to degrade social and ecological conditions, historically the nation-state has acted as a primary mediator of the circuits of capital and facilitated the expansion and reproduction of capital and its impacts on ecological, personal, and communal conditions.[56] Neoliberalism, the process of freeing the state of its social and environmental responsibilities, varies due to social, cultural, economic, political, and ecological differences across spaces and production processes. How the Montreal Protocol has taken a "neoliberal turn," a shift toward market-based logic and reliance on private, site-specific (sometimes individualistic) scientific knowledge in its policy making, is reflective of shifts noted in other major sites of global environmental governance, such as the World Bank and the World Trade Organization (WTO; formerly GATT).[57] The neoliberal turn in MeBr policy making will have long-reaching effects on societies and their surrounding environments for generations.

POWERFUL STATES AND CONDITIONS OF PRODUCTION

The nation-state is, necessarily, the primary focus of any analysis of global environmental governance. Global environmental governance is clearly facilitated by powerful nation-states, which often promote economic expansion first and environmental protection only secondarily.[58] Additionally, environmental governance tends to ignore society-ecology relations, attempting to treat "the environment" or some aspect thereof as separate from its multi-scalar and interdependent components. Access to water, for example, is treated as separate from public health, tropical forest conservation as separate from indigenous survival needs, and ozone protection as separate from climate change and geopolitics. Global environmental governance has sometimes exacerbated such effects, re-inscribing with market-based solutions the treatment of specific environmental conditions separate from the broader socio-ecological relations that created the problems being addressed.[59] At times, nation-states have "rolled back" state-led environmental protection in favor of letting the market handle environmental issues and "rolled out" a broad array of legal reforms and institutional arrangements in order to facilitate neoliberal environmental governance.[60] Consequently, environmental social movements have risen up to defend what is now much less defended by nation-states, what James O'Connor defines as capitalist "conditions of production."[61]

Understanding conditions of production is important for analyzing recent failures in the Montreal Protocol because the reasons for failure are intricately tied to the socio-ecological conditions in particular places. Conditions of production perhaps are most easily thought of as the natural, human, and social capitals necessary to produce goods and services.[62] O'Connor argues that the process of producing goods degrades the very base upon which the system operates (i.e., conditions of production), and this degradation may engender social movements to rise in protection of the natural environment. The state has historically mediated capital's relation to these conditions of production, as well as the public's relation to its conditions of life.[63] Since the rise of the liberal/social democratic welfare state, successful social movement demands that

capital's depletion and degradation of the conditions of production be remediated can be seen in the state's ever-increasing
budgets for wilderness preservation, resource conservation,
pollution reduction, scientific research, technological development, medical innovations, educational reforms, cultural
programs, and infrastructural development.[64]

Although O'Connor did not disaggregate the conditions
of capitalist production from the conditions of production
necessary for specific sectors and/or firms, we can take that
step here with regard to agriculture. Capital at the abstract
level requires natural resources, labor power, and a social
infrastructure in which to work, and "it" treats these conditions as commodities, as the economic historian Karl Polanyi
famously explained.[65] More specifically, the agro-industrial
sector requires these conditions to produce agricultural commodities, but it is bound strongly to the socio-ecological
conditions of particular spaces. In fact, some agro-industrial
complexes, such as California's strawberry production, are
built around particular historico-geographically constituted
production conditions that are very difficult to change. With
powerful actors influencing Montreal Protocol MeBr deliberations, California strawberry production relies on certain
technological innovations (e.g., strawberry varieties dependent on certain chemicals to combat plant pathogens), certain
ecological conditions (e.g., climatic, soil, and hillside conditions that make water-soluble chemicals dangerous to apply,
leading to township caps on their usage), and a consistent,
accommodating labor supply (i.e., seasonal Mexican and
Mexican American laborers). Without these specific production conditions, the system would likely fail to prosper. Thus,
California agro-industrial strawberry production demonstrates how conditions of production are socio-ecologically

determined in a way that provides natural conditions with an active role. In this case soil pathogens play an agential role in shaping the conditions of production as much as do labor supplies, strawberry growers, policymakers, and technological innovations.[66]

We are reminded here of how local, national, and international scales are established in relation to one another. The socio-ecological conditions existing in and around California agro-industry extend from the local to the global scale, and the process by which powerful actors shape those arrangements changes as they move across scales. In this way, the dynamic institutionalization of global environmental issues is "embedded within networked or territorial *scalar configurations that extend from the local milieu to global relations.*"[67]

It is important to note that the protection of the conditions of production does not happen in all instances. In fact, the United States has let go of certain agricultural complexes much more easily than the strawberry case suggests. In the MeBr case, however, protectionism is intricately connected to the defense of the scientific knowledge base situated in the United States. The MeBr case potentially threatens to delegitimize the U.S. hold on certain facets of scientific knowledge in global environmental governance, and such a threat instigates the need for the United States to hold fast to its strawberry industry. The U.S. strawberry production complex originated with reliance on MeBr, its strawberry varieties coproduced with the chemical. The discrepant views held by U.S. policymakers and U.S.-based MeBr experts vis-à-vis the global community are likely tied to the U.S. need to defend its scientific knowledge. In other words, the MeBr story is not only about defending U.S. strawberries per se; it is also about defending the knowledge base upon which it is founded.

CONDITIONS OF SUBJECTS: GOVERNMENTALITY

The MeBr case also supports the conceptualization that citizens, states, NGOs, scientific knowledge, and institutions are all shaped in part by the political-economic milieu in which they are embedded—which is currently neoliberal. In the Montreal Protocol, the impact of neoliberal norms and discourse on actor involvement is most obvious with the interventions of NGOs and scientific experts. While it will likely surprise no one that powerful nation-states make use of free market rhetoric and policy language to obtain protection of their industries, it might be surprising to witness how these influences change the interpretation of scientific "facts"—even among scientists themselves—and how NGOs reformulate their own interventions in Protocol debates based on these neoliberal ideals. This "self-management" amid a neoliberal milieu is understood here through the work of Michel Foucault on governmentality. Governmentality refers to the ways that subjects are produced to help stabilize and rationalize systems of power. People acting in politics take on a rationale that serves the interests of the powerful in a way that simple coercive theories of power cannot explain. In this understanding, the ways that NGOs choose to intervene, the manner with which scientists disseminate their findings, the rhetoric utilized by delegations (among other factors) are as indispensable to the "general functioning of the wheels of power" as are money, might, and political influence; they become "vehicles of power" that powerful states utilize. States and institutions enter into agreements with their counterparts and other facets of society in ways that solidify how certain activities will be conducted by all actors.[68]

Yet production processes are still important, a fact of which Foucault was well aware. Once production choices are put into action, the flexibility of decision making wanes, leaving the state with limited flexibility on how to negotiate across scales. Such limitation is certainly true with regard to strawberry production. With strawberries, however, the entire production complex is under pressure from global environmental governance. In its efforts to maximize yields, the U.S. landgrant system created a highly productive and profitable strawberry complex second to none. Since 1997, however, the United States has been pressured to shift its production practices.

As the following chapters will show, the United States created a virtually MeBr-dependent strawberry production system. Without MeBr, the United States was likely to lose market share to foreign competitors unless it could find a substitute as lethal and effective. That search was seemingly coming near the end with the recent registration of methyl iodide, a very toxic carcinogen that has generated heated debate among NGOs, communities, Nobel Laureate chemists, and the U.S. EPA, but the problems created will be long term. Due to the "endurance" of the MeBr-dependent production complex, the United States has struggled with the global community to maintain the conditions of production that allow it to persist, when it might better have spent its time and resources searching more fervently for viable, ecologically sustainable strawberry production practices. Of course, the United States would not have had the luxury of holding on to problematic agro-industrial production complexes if it were an LDC under pressure from global environmental governance to shift production methods.

Organization of this Book

Chapter 2 provides a brief history of global environmental governance. Environmental governance began with a

strong footing in precautionary measures, with broad support
from the public and policy makers for command-and-control
government regulation and with faith in the global scientific
community. Gradually that faith has waned, replaced with
neoliberal concerns for free markets, business-led environmentalism, cost-effective approaches, and government
deregulation. Public global science is constantly questioned by
the private sector. As the chapter shows, this history of
environmental governance follows the path trod by environmental economists over time.

Chapter 3 provides a critical review of the CFC phaseout
versus the MeBr phaseout in the Montreal Protocol. Such a critique suggests that the Protocol's earlier successes are deeply
entrenched in the economic opportunities that were made
available to phase out CFCs. The Montreal Protocol, in other
words, was a "best-case scenario" for CFC producers. This condition may be problematic for policymakers, ecological modernization theorists, and other scholars who look to the
Montreal Protocol for guidance in phasing out other global
environmentally harmful substances and practices that are not
as economically efficient. The CFC phaseout will be contrasted
with the lack of profitability available with MeBr alternatives
by the same firms that produce MeBr and the threat to the
legitimacy of U.S. science/knowledge explored in subsequent
chapters. Changes in what constitutes a viable exemption to the
phaseout of CFCs versus MeBr mark a shift away from concern
for the general functioning/welfare of society and toward
neoliberal concerns for the market performance of specific
individuals. This shift runs parallel to a lack of economic
incentives to phase out MeBr in the United States. This
historical reference will provide the background necessary to
understand the disputes among nations and their impact on

scientific knowledge, NGOs, and the MeBr phaseout process in general in subsequent chapters.

Chapter 4 provides an overview of the framework of the Montreal Protocol as a social institution. While much scholarship has been devoted to the Montreal Protocol, relatively little discussion has materialized from within the discipline of sociology, especially around the controversies surrounding the MeBr phaseout. The chapter contributes to the predominant "social capital" assessment presented in existing sociological research on the Protocol by drawing from theoretical contributions in critical sociology, human geography, and political science perspectives on uneven power relations. A critical sociological perspective sheds light on the reasons for the recent shift to failure in phasing out remaining ODSs in the Montreal Protocol, specifically MeBr. A case study on the delegitimization and dissolution of the Agricultural Economics Task Force (AETF) illustrates how powerful actors can vertically penetrate the horizontal "social capital" relationships, a process that is often overlooked in social capital analyses.

Chapter 5 demonstrates how the MeBr phaseout debate has heightened tensions among nation-states and competing economic blocs. Tensions between the United States and Western Europe on alternatives to CFCs for essential uses were very high, and their political differences sometimes led to the seemingly deliberate stalling of other contested issues, such as the MeBr phaseout, where political differences were even greater. This chapter illustrates these tensions as they transpired during 2003–2006. These and similar tensions exist among global powers as they jockey for position in the global economy (primarily the United States, the European Union, and China). This chapter will highlight the significant differences (and similarities) among the three largest strawberry production complexes, centered in the United States, the European Union, and China and explain how these areas are attempting to outdo competitor regions. Such tensions have an inadvertent effect on the developing world, which expressed great concern in Protocol meetings over the number of exemptions granted to the industrialized world and the effect these will have on their own terms of trade. The chapter shows how many countries consider CUEs a new form of economic domination over the global South and forecast future phaseout delays in their own countries. Tensions between less-developed and industrialized countries are clearly exacerbated by MeBr debates, reflecting the fracturing of global cooperation on ODS reductions and the threat of the globalization of strawberry production to the well-established hub of U.S. strawberry production. A major message here is that the neoliberalized Montreal Protocol is more tightly tied to competition in the global economy and the protection of science/knowledge claims than to environmentalism, and this shift is deeply impacting progress.

Chapter 6 highlights several interviews conducted with prominent members of the Methyl Bromide Technical Options Committee (MBTOC) of the Montreal Protocol. A rift developed between pro-MeBr MBTOC members, who expressed support for private economic interests, and anti-MeBr MBTOC members, who supported the global scientific community and expressed concerns for public health and the global environment. Some pro-MeBr MBTOC members accused others of supporting irrelevant knowledge claims about MeBr alternatives based either on political interests or on scientific knowledge that is not transferable to specific locales. The interviews suggest that while scientists often comprise a part of civil society, there are evident differences in scientific understanding about the efficacy of MeBr alternatives that are reflective of geopolitical competition and U.S. attempts to maintain a hold on scientific knowledge claims. Here the United States is particularly responsive to the interests of the strawberry industry, and certain experts appear to lack even the rudiments of relative autonomy. The chapter also will reveal how the protection of the U.S. strawberry industry illustrates how U.S. science is used to defend U.S. interests and how the protection of U.S. strawberries is really about defending U.S. science. A major message of this chapter is that political-economic debates influence the interpretation of science, with significant effects on how scientists interpret and govern themselves.

Chapter 7 focuses on the roles that NGOs play in the Montreal Protocol, specifically with the MeBr phaseout. In this chapter, it will prove useful to draw upon Foucault and other scholars that use governmentality to understand the neoliberalization of global environmental governance. The MeBr case shows that we must be cautious about touting NGO influence in the current neoliberal moment of global environmental governance. Indeed, if the MeBr case is reflective of a broader pattern in neoliberal globalization today, then the role of NGOs at the global scale must be reassessed. In the MeBr case, NGOs that attempt to address the environmental implications of a stalled MeBr phaseout are ignored in Protocol deliberations. However, NGOs that adopt the neoliberal rhetoric of the treaty have gained some notice and even provided information for nation-states to use in the deliberations to attempt to minimize MeBr use in the industrialized North. I argue that this shift in discourse, increasingly taken by NGOs, reveals how they are learning to manage themselves in a neoliberal way that helps to reinforce the regulatory structure in place rather than helping nations take a more environment-friendly stance. Here we will see how NGO activity is affected by political and economic conditions in ways similar to the scientific experts.

In conclusion, I will suggest some possible ways forward. A major issue relevant to contemporary environmental problems worldwide is that the Montreal Protocol is still touted as a model for future environmental agreements, especially for resolving problems with global climate change and the Kyoto Protocol in particular. I will show the links between global climate-change negotiations and ozone politics. The problems with the MeBr phaseout suggest that the neoliberalization of ozone governance and the increasingly globalized economy will present serious problems to an environmental governing process incapable of handling global competition. If the MeBr debate is any gauge, global powers will protect their economies, science will be coopted, NGOs will remain rather ineffective, and the environment will degrade. It may be possible to configure an environmental governance strategy in which public scientists and global civil society have more influence in decision making. Achieving such an outcome will no doubt be extremely difficult, likely requiring activity by global civil society outside the confines of treaty negotiations, increased action by citizens of the powerful countries, and proactive, empowered scientists.

I

Transitioning from Precaution to Profit in Global Environmental Governance

2

From Public to Private Global Environmental Governance

A Brief History

I n order to understand the significance of the neoliberal
turn that has occurred in the Montreal Protocol, it is
important to understand that it is really a broader trend
in microcosm. Then the recent controversies over the
MeBr phaseout can be appreciated as the product of a larger
political and economic transformation that has made global
environmental governance difficult to successfully implement
in many areas of ecological import.

Economic sociologists have identified what I call here
the "neoliberal turn" in economic globalization, albeit with
distinct formulations accounted for by divergent political,
social, economic, and institutional conditions. Briefly, since
the mid-1970s, nation-states have adopted policies that are
decidedly more "market oriented" than were policies of the
previous period, which some scholars call the "Golden Age" of
capitalism for having achieved sustained economic growth
and high employment rates and which occurred roughly in

the period 1945–1970.[1] This period is often associated with the macroeconomic approach of John Maynard Keynes, who argued for government intervention in the economy—especially in economically hard times—in order to improve dangerously low levels of employment,[2] and the establishment of the Bretton Woods institutions (such as the International Monetary Fund [IMF] and what is now called the World Bank), which, among other things, were designed to help regulate and stabilize the world economy so as to prevent another world war. Perhaps most popularly associated with the economic theories of Friedrich August von Hayek and Milton Friedman and the Chicago school of economics more generally, neoliberalism in theory postulates the opposite of Keynesian economics—that is, that deregulation and non-intervention by government in the economy will yield the best long-lasting results. This school of thought rejects the Keynesian macroeconomic policies of government intervention to stabilize business cycles during times of recession. Politically, U.S. president Ronald Reagan and U.K. Prime Minister Margaret Thatcher are often recognized as the chief spokespeople for reducing the role of government over individuals and market forces, both domestically and globally via international trade restructuring. During the Reagan/Thatcher era, "liberalization" and "deregulation" became catchwords. Today, some scholars note that the neoliberal norms of economic globalization pressure actors (e.g., nation-states) to participate in the liberalization process to such an extent that its promotion as *the* economic ideology has become "inevitable."[3]

Worldwide, various state-owned sectors of the economy have been pressured to take on a market orientation by adopting any of the following: the privatization of state-owned industry; the separation of regulatory oversight from the executive branch; the depoliticization of the regulatory authority; and an opening of markets to the private sector.[4] Of course, states have taken on neoliberal policies to varying degrees, yet the global governing structure has served as a legitimating force that places such economic policies and practices above all others. Growth in international trade, public employment cutbacks, and intense political debates over reducing the size of governments are all dominant themes in the neoliberalized discourse articulated by intergovernmental economic organizations. In world polity parlance, intergovernmental organizations have established a "world culture" in which neoliberal ideology is the dominant (albeit often contested) discourse.[5]

Theoretically, neoliberalism argues that the freedoms of the individual are of the utmost importance, especially economic and political freedoms. Economically-free people will undoubtedly find political freedom, which will lead to liberated, prosperous societies. Critics, however, point out that there are contradictions between theory and practice. While individualism is prized, neoliberalism is opposed to individuals forming unions to bargain collectively; while political freedom is valued, society should not support parties of state intervention; while democracy is held sacred, it is undergirded by strong global "undemocratic and unaccountable" institutions, such as the U.S. Federal Reserve and the IMF. David Harvey argues that when the IMF was given full authority to negotiate debt relief in 1982, the contradiction between the responsibility of individuals (especially in banks) to act rationally in the free market and the actions of an undemocratic authority that could reduce limits to risk (i.e., protect bankers from default) was fully realized.[6]

Pierre Bourdieu described neoliberalism as "a programme for destroying collective structures which may
impede the pure market logic." It has successfully branded
itself as "the scientific description of reality," which instills in
all individuals the "freedom" to better themselves in an ostensibly free and competitive world. This individualism pressures
actors toward self-control and self-responsibility for success
or failure. An overly competitive world leads to "precarious
arrangements" that produce insecurity in society. Important
for environmental protections, neoliberal ideology moves
responsibility for environmentalism away from the nation-
state toward the individual, where social groups must represent their cases before government. Bourdieu laments that
only "those connected to capital rise to the top."[7] I would add
that their expertise channels are also often the most legitimate,
especially when they use knowledge in a way that comple-
ments the tenets of neoliberalism.

One of the most noticeable ways to witness the intersec-
tion of the economic and political dimensions of neoliberal
globalization with its environmental dimension is by focusing
on the political discourses surrounding the major global environmental conferences of the past four decades: the 1972
Stockholm Conference; the 1992 Rio Earth Summit; the
2002 Johannesburg Earth Summit; and the 2009 Copenhagen
Summit. These meetings represent the establishment of particular norms in global environmentalism about how global
environmental problems should be tackled at the global scale.
Surrounding these meetings we find political rhetoric and
economic theorization that roughly match the environmental
rhetoric of the time. Over the years, policy prescriptions and
possible solutions to environmental problems proposed by
environmental economists have become normative standards

upon which some of the major environmental discussions are based.

The history of global environmental governance involves the gradual move from precautionary, "command-and-control" state regulatory solutions to private, market-based solutions. The United Nations Conference on the Human Environment (UNCHE), held in Stockholm in 1972, took place during an era when public environmental awareness was extremely high, as was public faith in government intervention to regulate industrial pollution, despite strong industry opposition.[8] These were the formative years of the environmental dimension of the world polity, when pro-environment legislation became a central political concern, primarily among the industrialized countries. Occurring near the apex of the Civil Rights Movement of the 1960s, the green movement writ large demanded both democratic decision making and unequal resource distribution. While environmental agendas changed over this period—pollution control in the 1970s and pollution prevention in the 1980s—the general theme was that government regulation would help resolve global ecosystem degradation. It was during this period that the United Nations Environmental Programme (UNEP), the most important of the intergovernmental environmental organizations, was established, and it is in this period that the major success stories of global environmental treaty making, lauded by global governance scholars and environmental sociologists, are situated.[9]

The Ecologist, a leading magazine in ecological thought founded in 1970, put forth a special issue ahead of the Stockholm Conference in order to support the establishment of the global environmental vision that was needed. In it, contributors (including the famous ecologist Edward Goldsmith) provided a set of guidelines that included "controls" in the transition to a sustainable society. They acknowledged that such controls would pose a "heavy burden on our moral courage" and would require self-restraint. Additionally, "legislation and the operations of police forces and the courts [would] be necessary to reinforce this restraint," but "full public participation in decision-making" and a sympathetic government were also essential to success.[10] The apparent contradiction among providing holistic solutions, egalitarianism, and top-down control was not limited to ecologists or political radicals. As Robyn Eckersley notes, many social groups in the industrialized world linked global ecological degradation to the "destructive logic of capital accumulation." Statements from the Stockholm meeting reflected confidence in and reliance on global scientific expertise/knowledge and optimism about multilateral governance, describing "the international expression of the huge surge of environmental concern then occurring at the national level, especially in key industries," with participants calling upon "states to cooperate in developing international environmental law."[11]

Such regulations were not seen as being necessarily at odds with democracy or political freedoms. The popular environmentalist and political theorist William Ophuls exemplified this sentiment when, in 1974, he described the times as "the politics of scarcity" and argued the need for a powerful state to curb environmental crises. "Man is a passionate being," Ophuls stated, and therefore there must be "checks on will and appetite; if these checks are not self-imposed, they must be applied externally as fetters by a sovereign power."[12] Ophuls also wrote of the choice between an environmentally friendly Leviathan versus complete ecological destruction:

"How can we avoid reaching the conclusion that Leviathan is inevitable? Hobbes shows why a spaceship earth must have a captain. Otherwise, the collective selfishness and irresponsibility produced by the tragedy of the commons will destroy the spaceship, and any sacrifice of freedom by the crew members is clearly the lesser of two evils."[13] Centralized leadership and the surrender of individual freedoms were necessary to avoid a "tragedy of the commons" or, on a more systemic level, what Barry Commoner described as a choice between a "rational, social organization of the use and distribution of the earth's resources, or a new barbarism."[14]

This environmental approach typified the public political culture of the welfare state, which "sought to 'decommodify' certain aspects of economic and social life, both through the provision of resources and entitlements to certain categories of people and the formulation of 'command-and-control regulations' that imposed limits on externality-producing practices by capital."[15] Bolstered by a growing scientific knowledge base about pollution and its effects, civil society groups and public scientists pressured governments to place limits on industry, sometimes with significant levels of success.[16]

The Stockholm meeting resulted in a surge of international and global environmental treaties, along with the creation of the UNEP. The U.N. General Assembly proclaimed that UNEP's main purpose (adopted unanimously by the 113 attending countries) would be to "provide guidelines for . . . action by governments and international organizations designed to protect and improve the human environment . . . by means of international co-operation."[17] The "Stockholm Declaration" placed the burden of socioeconomic change on nation-states and local governments, but it also emphasized the need for resources to help less-developed countries meet their goals, global cooperation among nation-states, and the establishment of international law and intergovernmental organizations to help with these efforts. This building of an international environmental management infrastructure indicated a rise in conviction that strong state intervention, combined with new multilateral environmental agreements and international governance law, could resolve international environmental issues.[18]

After the Stockholm Conference, international panels of scientists published all manner of reports on global environmental concerns, strengthening legitimization of the global public science community. Due to now famous scientific research reports, such as Frank Rowland and Mario Molina's study and the National Academy of Sciences' Charney Report,[19] ozone depletion and climate change gained increasing attention. In addition to initiating discussion of global climate and ozone regimes, the reports compelled governments to adopt precautionary policies for public protection against other uncertain environmental effects and strong policies to control pollution at the local and global levels.

In 1987, Montreal Protocol signatories were successful in adopting this kind of strong regulatory approach in the CFC phaseout even before the science on CFC ozone depletion was fully conclusive. While industry and the White House originally opposed any regulation on the grounds of scientific uncertainty, public pressure combined with EPA support and NGO promotion of a precautionary approach prevailed. Consistent with strong state sovereignty attitudes about environmental regulation, the CFC phaseout utilized command-and-control measures that motivated industry to rapidly seek ways to incorporate CFC substitutes.[20] In a report celebrating twenty years of the Montreal Protocol, Danielle Fest Grabiel noted delegates' sentiments regarding the Protocol's past and future: "Participants. .. pointed out that the [Montreal] Protocol's straightforward, command-and-control style of regulation . . . proved that a 'back to basics' approach to regulation can be the most cost-effective and expeditious way to achieve environmental protection."[21] For two decades, the impetus to create stronger global governance, begun in Stockholm, continued to strengthen. Optimism for new international relationships that typified the early 1990s, after the fall of the Berlin Wall, led some to call for "planetary democracy." Vaclav Havel characterized the era as "part of an endeavor to find a new and genuinely universal articulation of that global human experience [in which we all may] engage in a common quest for the general good."[22]

Concurrently, scholars in international environmental law called for the centralization of global environmental governance and for global governing bodies to have increased power over states, just as states had conceded power to the WTO on issues of international trade. Global environmental problems required a global environmental institution to which nations would limit their sovereignty, thus giving authoritative power to global governance bodies that would "create a proper international environmental agency within the United Nations system that has real power and authority."[23]

The 1992 U.N. Conference on Environment and Development in Rio de Janeiro, commonly called the Rio Earth Summit, has often been acclaimed as the high point of public global environmental governance. With the promotion of the Brundtland Report at Rio, "sustainable development" discourse gained prominence, linking environmental degradation to poverty.[24] In fact, the agreements that emerged from the Rio meeting predominantly reflected the gradual shift from public to private, neoliberal forms of environmental governance. For example, Principle 15 of the "Rio Declaration" stresses "the use of the precautionary approach where there are threats of serious or irreversible environmental damage."[25] Yet unlike the usage of the precautionary principle at the Montreal Protocol, where the risk of chlorine loading to the ozone layer led to a regulated phaseout of CFCs, its usage was more market oriented. The precautionary principle decided upon at Rio emphasized that *cost-effective* measures should be applied where scientific uncertainty remained and thus emphasized the role of the market and private industry. The UNFCCC agreement initiated at Rio also made use of cost-effective precautionary measures due to uncertainty over the consequences of climate change.[26]

The environmental management strategy at Rio clearly favored market mechanisms over command-and-control regulation and questioned "limits to growth" arguments popularized at the 1972 Stockholm meeting. An influential message coming from business, represented through the Business Council for Sustainable Development, was that governments concerned with long-term sustainability must not limit business growth as long as natural resource consumption could be sustained. At the same time, however, it had become widely accepted that NGOs should play a role in shaping global environmental objectives, generating optimism that sustainable development could be orchestrated to meet the needs of the common people.[27]

At the Rio Summit, the transition in global political and economic norms toward the "decline of social democracy" with the rise in neoliberal economic globalization was becoming embedded in significant ways into global environmentalism.[28] Nevertheless, government and global environmental governance was still seen as the primary process through which sustainability should be orchestrated. The Montreal Protocol had proven that global environmental governance could successfully alter production in a way sustainable to both industry profits and the global environment. Here, global environmental governance was deemed necessary in order to push governments to comply with environmentally friendly goals. The authoritative role of states in global governance at Rio is perhaps best brought home in the influential report *Our Common Future,* where most of the twenty-three principles for environmental protection begin with the same phrase: "states shall."[29]

The United States played a very different role at Rio than it had at Stockholm or even in the formulation of the Montreal Protocol five years prior. The financial crisis of the late 1980s; the rise of Reaganism and Thatcherism, which prompted a "Third Way" response in opposition; and the emergence of the post-Soviet era had begun to infiltrate the U.S. position on global environmental politics just as they had infiltrated economic policy. U.S. environmental policy increasingly reflected the structural adjustment approaches of international financial institutions such as the World Bank's "global managerial state of mind," emphasizing "the neoliberal question of the *freedom and sovereignty of capital.*"[30] Under this new neoliberal political regime, the United States promoted the privatization of state-run institutions, providing markets for phenomena previously protected from market forces through the elimination of command-and-control public regulatory instruments, and promoting private stakeholder politics over society-based measures.[31]

Suffering from economic problems of its own, the industrialized world promised scant funds at Rio to help the global

South with sustainable development assistance and refused to commit to a specific date to provide them. As the neorealists would point out, the position of the global hegemon has a way of directing the institutionalization of global norms. The U.S. position was clearly to strengthen the involvement of the World Bank in global environmentalism by supporting the intergovernmental financial organization the Global Environment Facility (GEF) as the primary distributor of environmental moneys and thus to pursue environmentalism through market avenues. The United States declined to sign the Biodiversity Convention (as it had promised) unless the convention included the GEF as its financial mechanism.[32] Observers such as Lester Brown of the Worldwatch Institute disparaged this neoliberal political turn, arguing that "the U.S. is no longer capable of leading."[33] In fact, the United States *was* playing a leadership role but one of different design. It was applying to environmental issues the same strategies it was applying to global economic issues—ones that emphasized free marketeering and decentralized governance instead of governmental control. This new "Washington Consensus" was "increasingly negative on multilateralism, environmental regulation, the United Nations, foreign aid, and treaties and similar agreements, and, indeed, *government itself*."[34]

Moreover, the "neoliberal turn" was more than just a change in politics; it was a change in which knowledge counted as legitimate in formulating solutions to public problems. The influential reader *Economics of the Environment* provides an excellent representation of the transition from public to private knowledge in environmental policy. First published in 1972, the year of the Stockholm Conference, and most recently in 2005, this reader has been a major mainstay in environmental economics courses, covering "classic" readings on the subject. The first two editions exemplify the era of public environmental knowledge and command-and-control government policies. Co-editor Robert Dorfman provides a substantial introduction focused on the problem of "common resources" and the limits of the "invisible hand" in managing resources efficiently because common goods are "non-excludable" public goods. Environmental problems, from this perspective, are public problems concerning the protection of public goods—such as the ozone layer—that require joint action through state intervention, public services, and strong controls over use.[35]

The third edition of *Economics of the Environment* represents a transition between public and private/neoliberal governance and accompanying forms of knowledge. Published a year after the Rio Summit, the volume provides no introduction with an overview of the field. Although Dorfman is still co-editor, his earlier introduction is now an article representing a single view, that of welfare economics. In this edition, an alternative view, that of "economic incentives," appears that includes the privatization of common property resources, especially the market trading of pollution permits. According to market-based incentive theories, total pollution control expenditures are less costly under a private trading regime because the cost of controls varies from one emission source to the next. The market enables more cheaply controlled sources to control their emissions and sell the rights to those whose controls are more costly.[36] Nevertheless, Rio-based multilateralism remains very much in evidence in the volume, as reflected in articles showing the benefits of global participation in environmental agreements.[37]

In the latest two editions of *Economics of the Environment*, the new editor is Robert Stavins, one of the major proponents of market-based environmental policies.[38] Stavins, a Harvard economist, headed Project 88: Harnessing Market Forces to Protect Our Environment, a bipartisan initiative supported by the Environmental Defense Fund; the project provided much momentum for the 1990 U.S. Clean Air Act's permit system for sulfur dioxide emissions.[39] In these latest editions, welfare economic approaches are significantly underplayed, replaced almost entirely with an economics of private interests. In contrast to the previous volumes' positive take on the mutual benefits of multilateral agreements, the articles in these editions emphasize the negative tradeoffs of global environmental governance. One article states unequivocally that "any action combating global warming will be, intended or not, a foreign aid program" between industrialized and less-developed countries.[40] Instead of global environmental governance, individual economic development is the "sound advice" for environmental improvement in less-developed countries because development "reduc[es] their reliance on agriculture and other such outdoor livelihoods."[41] In fact, the economic analysis showing that individual countries can benefit from global cooperation no longer appears in the most recent additions of this influential textbook.

       Throughout the 1990s, evidence of economic considerations overriding environmental ones continued, most visibly seen in the famous *Tuna/Dolphin Case* of the United States vs. Mexico in 1991 (GATT Case DS21), where international trade in tuna caught with techniques dangerous to dolphins was upheld by a panel of the General Agreement on Tariffs and Trade (GATT) because restriction of such trade was perceived as protectionist. Soon, however, negotiations on the North American Free Trade Agreement (NAFTA) impelled both governments to remain silent on the controversy.[42] The UNEP soon disseminated the economics-over-environment logic as well, and it would have institutional and legal effects on its global environmental message and its treaty facilitation. The influential *Global Environment Outlook*, published in 1997, argued that command-and-control methods were more effective when it came to "simple" (i.e., low-cost, low-risk, easily quantifiable) environment problems. "Complex" (i.e., global, high-risk, virtually unquantifiable) problems, however, would require "a combination of policy instruments to achieve environmental goals without constraining economic growth, development, and human well-being."[43] The neoliberal turn is clearly witnessed here, but the successes of erstwhile regulatory standards are not easily dismantled from institutional structure, especially in proposals that affected the less-developed world, where markets were deemed less "rational" than Western ones.[44]

By 2002, the UNEP began to express more vividly the effects of neoliberalism in its various publications and presentations. For example, a 2002 brief on economics, trade, and sustainable development drew from Stavins's assessment of environmental policy and economics to explain that the economics of environmental protection consisted of "policy approaches that encourage behavior through their impact on market signals rather than through ... control levels."[45] In 2004, Klaus Töpfer, the executive director of the UNEP, stated to the United Nations Conference on Trade and Development (UNCTAD) that the "environment should be seen as an opportunity for trade promotion and market access and not as a constraint for trade liberalization."[46] While it is still instilled in the UNEP to use regulatory practices in the interim and to "identify the role, nature and pace of liberalization suited to achieving each country's sustainable development objectives," in the long term, the goal is a global free market.[47]

The 2002 World Summit on Sustainable Development in Johannesburg exemplifies the disappearance of faith in governmental regulation and "the public" from environmental policy, leading business groups in attendance to hail "the call for [business-government] partnerships ... *and a serious doubt about whether a multilateral system is able to effectively address our sustainable development challenges.*"[48] The summit contained no set of principles as there had been at Stockholm and Rio, and it is unlikely to have any impact on global environmental governance. The "Johannesburg Declaration" recognized that there were many global environmental problems, but it simply restated that the goals of Rio needed further commitment from nation-states.

The increased interconnectedness among nation-states via global environmental governance has led to an increase in the number of environmental treaties facilitated by the UNEP and other intergovernmental organizations. From 1992 through 2009, at least ten significant global environmental treaties had entered into force, including the Kyoto Protocol, the Biosafety Protocol, the Climate Change Convention, and the Stockholm Convention on Persistent Organic Pollutants. However, the same period has also "witnessed a marked decline in virtually every important global environmental indicator."[49] Global civil society groups disparaged Johannesburg's clear shift to neoliberal governance. Meena Raman of Friends of the Earth argued that "there were no reasons to be optimistic" [about the Johannesburg Summit] and emphasized that NGOs were extremely frustrated. She added that "nothing [has] happened since Rio in 1992 because governments embraced a neo-liberal agenda, which represents the interest of big powers."[50]

The 2009 Copenhagen Summit exhibited a similar reve-
lation. This was a time in which many environmentalists
hoped for significant progress on committing big-polluting
countries to resolutions to reduce carbon emissions. After all,
U.S. president Barack Obama had recently been awarded the
2009 Nobel Peace Prize "for his extraordinary efforts to
strengthen international diplomacy and cooperation between
peoples," and during his presidential campaign he had promised to "re-engage with the U.N. Framework Convention
on Climate Change (UNFCCC)."[51] However, outcomes of the
Copenhagen Summit further suggested that global environmental governance was experiencing a devolution moment
as markets and market-based principles were employed to
defend environmental (in)action. Since first refusing to sign
the Kyoto Protocol in 1998, the United States has argued that
a global trading scheme would be unfair to industrialized
countries because the global South was exempt from any
immediate carbon reductions, although the United States had
led in the adoption of the Montreal Protocol, which also did
not bind peripheral countries to immediate cuts. Here, the
"Copenhagen Accord," which was "taken note of" but not
adopted, was drafted by the United States, China, India, Brazil,
and South Africa behind closed doors. Although the Yale Project on Climate Change Communication—a group based in
Yale University that conducts research and outreach projects
on climate change science and public understanding of such
science—found in a 2009 national survey that a vast majority
of Americans—regardless of political affiliation—supported
the passage of federal climate and energy policies, including
over 70 percent supporting the regulation of carbon dioxide
(CO_2) as a pollutant, U.S. leadership at the global scale
remained tenuous.[52] Some critics blamed Copenhagen failures

on the U.S. Senate and President Obama. They argued that the "Copenhagen Accord," negotiated with only a select group of nations, excluded most U.N. member states. Others observed that the British and American governments both blamed China for the failure of the talks, but others still noted that Obama had placed China in an impossible position by demanding concessions while offering none.

These arguments are all valid, yet it is important to also remember that current environmental crises require a historically unprecedented conversion in frame of mind for citizens in the core countries. As George Monbiot laments, "It is a campaign not for abundance but for austerity . . . not for more freedom but for less . . . not just against other people, but against ourselves."[53] But Monbiot's sentiments echo arguments made by Ophuls and others in the 1970s, and they appear grossly outdated when considering the neoliberal turn in global environmental affairs. Rather than putting restrictions on carbon emissions (and society), solutions posed by the neoliberalized governance structure are more aptly described as encouraging the efficient emission of carbon. Rather than establishing a "world authority" and providing support via multilateral funding, as The Hague Conference suggested in 1989 in a markedly Stockholmesque proposal, the predominant solutions posed by the global powers are in "a range of convoluted market and economic mechanisms involving especially emission trading schemes and joint implementation." The U.S. has led in criticisms of command-and-control mechanisms and direct transfers to resolve climate change, arguing that "flexible market mechanisms were more efficient as they allow action to be taken without compromising economic growth," and these market-based mechanisms "continue to form the thrust of policies for actions against climate change by the international community to date."[54] Any policy prescriptions reminiscent of command-and-control regulation, such as "cap-and-trade" schemes, are now designed to be as price-like as possible.[55]

To be sure, there are exceptions to this general characterization of the historical trajectory of global environmental issues from public to private. Even at Johannesburg, environmentalists, the United Nations, and several delegations hoped for commitments to projects that would give governments a leading role in sustainable development and the implementation of the Rio Summit's Agenda 21, the proposed plan of action "blueprint" for governments, intergovernmental organizations, and other stakeholders to undertake in order to achieve sustainable development. Yet the principal outcome of Johannesburg reflects a shift in dominant ideology to neoliberal environmental governance.[56]

This gradual transition from public to neoliberal environmental policy/knowledge has provided the epistemological basis for the neoliberal turn in environmental economic analysis. It is most obvious in the wholesale adoption of market-trading instruments as the main policy option under the Kyoto Protocol, which committed countries to a "cap-and-trade" scheme in which private parties bought the rights to emit CO_2 from those that had reduced their emissions. Economists support this scheme because according to neoliberal economic theory, it is deemed the most cost-effective option.[57] While the goal of cap-and-trade schemes is laudable—the cheaper control of emissions—the wholesale embrace of market-based solutions over public authority made private interests tantamount over any form of public decision making. In the end, both the United States and Australia refused to participate in the Kyoto negotiations,

mostly because of the "cap"—public intervention—aspect
of the cap-and-trade policies in the treaty. In the latest plan
(described in Stavins's volume), economists propose a trading
scheme that proceeds entirely through private economic
instruments, abandoning any notion that the public has any
sovereignty over private business via government regulation.[58]

Recent changes within the Montreal Protocol parallel the
move away from welfare economics analyses of environmental
policies that emphasize the benefits of governmental management of public goods and global environmental governance in
favor of economic analyses that emphasize market-based and
private/neoliberal governance solutions.

The Neoliberalization of the Montreal Protocol

Problems we see today in the Kyoto Protocol were also
evident in the early days of the Montreal Protocol. Industry
initially refused to become fully invested, making attempts to
question the viability of ozone research and stressing the high
costs of investing in alternative technologies. Additionally,
CFC producers argued that alternatives would need to be protected, not transferred to competitors. Unlike in the Kyoto
negotiations, however, leadership from first the United States
and the European Union, pushed by their respective environment ministries and civil society groups, and subsequently
from corporate and military groups, eventually led to an
agreement on the conditions for the transfer of CFC alternative technologies. Effective multilateral funding of ODS-
reducing investments in the less-developed countries from the
protocol's Multilateral Fund (MLF) and the GEF, combined
with a cohesive, highly respected scientific advisory group
that provided technical support on ODSs and alternative

technologies, orchestrated (with the UNEP) a successful phaseout of most CFCs and other ODSs in the industrialized world.[59]

In contrast, the MeBr phaseout, scheduled for completion in 2005 in the industrialized world, proceeded agonizingly slowly. MeBr was added to the Montreal Protocol's list of controlled substances in the Copenhagen Amendment to the Protocol in 1992. Subsequently, MeBr use remained at high levels several years beyond the phaseout date of 2005.[60]

While the Copenhagen Amendment of 1992 (so called because the annual meeting of the Protocol took place that year in Copenhagen) mandated the MeBr phaseout in the industrialized world in the year 2005, an amendment decision accompanying Article 2H at the 1997 meeting held in Montreal allowed for a new category of exempted use, called "critical use exemptions," or CUEs, which significantly slowed the phaseout (as well as extending the phaseout to the year 2015 for less-developed countries). Meanwhile, in 2000, the ozone hole over Antarctica had reached almost 28.5 million square kilometers. Also in 2000, ozone-layer recovery was predicted to extend twenty years longer into the future than originally expected, to 2070. Nevertheless, in 2003, parties agreed to allow for significant CUEs to the MeBr phaseout, mainly for strawberry and tomato production in several industrialized countries. Since then, the majority of CUEs continued to go to California strawberry growers. By 2005, the U.S. request for CUEs had expanded to over half the exemptions worldwide, almost ten thousand metric tons. By the time of the 2009 exemption requests, the United States was awarded 92 percent of total exemptions.[61] While total use has declined to less than half of the 2005 request, the U.S. share of 2009 exemptions shows that the United States has maintained the majority share of exemptions and fought bitterly to maintain them while awaiting the registration of viable alternate chemicals.

The vast quantities of CUEs are connected to the changes in the political language of what constitutes an exemption to the ODS phaseout; these changes reflect growing reliance on neoliberal ideology and shrinking reliance on concerns for the general public and the global environment. While the details of these changes and their negative effects on state, civil society, and science relations and interactions will be documented in subsequent chapters, the shift deserves a brief introduction here.

To illustrate these changes in political language, let us review the difference between exemptions to the CFC phaseout and the MeBr phaseout. Indeed, the CFC phaseout also contained a clause for exemptions. However, the definition of exemptions under the CFC phaseout was significantly more restrictive and "administered sparingly and with discrimination."[62] Despite pressure from U.S. industry lobbyists to push the scientific community to accept broad-based exemptions for air-conditioning refrigeration and other uses, "the [scientific] panel was unafraid to say no to the U.S. and others" that wanted to maximize exemptions in that case.[63] Instead, the CFC "essential use exemption" clause included only three minimal uses deemed "necessary for the health, safety or [that are] critical for the functioning of society."[64] In contrast, determinations of exemptions to the MeBr phaseout, found in Decision IX/6—and drafted in accordance with Article 2 H—rely on market criteria as interpreted by particular interest groups, including "the lack of availability of MeBr for that use [which] would result in a significant market disruption" and in which there are "no technically and economically feasible alternatives."[65] For MeBr phaseout exemptions the parties focused on the economic impact of the MeBr phaseout on specific interest groups, even on *individual users* of MeBr, not on the protection of public health or social welfare.

The private cost criteria for MeBr CUEs have deflected demands from civil society groups and certain nations to meet the terms of the phaseout, as they do not reflect market-based concerns written in Decision IX/6. The scientific and technical experts advising parties on the MeBr issue, the MBTOC, and other technical committees that have worked on the CUE issue, such as the Economics Options Committee and the AETF, were equally delegitimized in favor of information provided by private lobby groups on costs of compliance. In particular, the United States has protected its own economic interests by drawing attention to the unique local conditions of domestic strawberry production, as presented by strawberry industry experts, while delegitimizing the claims made by the MBTOC. The contention between pro-MeBr and anti-MeBr MBTOC members reflects the rift that exists among other groups, including nation-states, due to their view of the role of the public, the state, and scientific expertise. The U.S. delegation and pro-MeBr CUE MBTOC members have responded with skepticism to much of the general scientific expertise presented on behalf of significantly reduced CUEs, instead offering arguments in favor of "local conditions" and private costs. The E.U. delegation, anti-MeBr CUE MBTOC members, and NGOs note the importance of precaution, command-and-control regulations, and public scientific knowledge. Much of this conflict has occurred in and around MBTOC discussions at Montreal Protocol meetings.

MeBr Controversy a Harbinger of Future
Problems in Global Environmental Governance?

MeBr controversies in the Montreal Protocol mark a growing problem with global environmental governance in general that will likely get worse before it gets better. That is, powerful national governments such as the United States appear to be touting neoliberal rhetoric in more areas of global environmental governance, protective of national economic interests and scientific knowledge. For example, the WTO appears not to have progressed beyond many problems with protection of national science and technology as identified over a decade ago. Even today, WTO signatories are far from disbanding protectionist measures, especially in agriculture.[66]

Considering the MeBr controversy, the Montreal Protocol is similarly becoming subject to incidents of national protectionism of economic interests and scientific knowledge amid rhetoric of free markets, market fairness, and stakeholder involvement. This book explores the links among science, technology, and political and economic interests in order to reveal the interconnectedness of these areas because state delegates and policymakers seldom grasp its full importance. This failure is likely a reason why global environmental governance is unsuccessful in many instances: "States and firms, for their part, appear to be operating with a vastly oversimplified understanding of the interconnected and culturally contextualized nature of [science and technology]. For researchers in science and technology studies, this means that the globalization of [science and technology] offers much room for investigation and theoretical clarification."[67]

Recent controversies in the Montreal Protocol also should give pause to those promoting it as an ideal model for other instances of global environmental governance in a neoliberal world. It is important to note that since 2005 MeBr has been used in significant quantities in the United States via CUEs to the phaseout, and the phaseout will likely encounter delays when the less-developed country deadline approaches, in 2015. The use of MeBr by the heavily protected U.S. agro-industry reveals "how science and politics co-evolve dynamically" at multiple scales.[68]

The Montreal Protocol has not completed its mission to rid the world of ODSs, nor has it been entirely successful, as the stalled MeBr phaseout demonstrates. Ozone scientific experts are divided on their interpretations of alternatives to MeBr, nation-states have appeared to retreat to their realist stances of protecting national economic interests, and civil society groups (including scientists) have been ineffective in convincing parties to work together to phase out MeBr in a systematic manner. The MeBr case indicates that much that has been taken for granted regarding the Montreal Protocol and the use of environmental governance to alleviate society-nature relations needs to be questioned anew. Indeed, if the MeBr case is the direction for the future—a neoliberal future—then the current formation of global environmental governance desperately needs our attention. Science and technology, civil society, and political economy, including the protection of national interests, appear to intersect in complex ways that may reflect new problems with neoliberal global environmental governance.

U.S. MeBr CUEs have caused considerable internecine polemic among Protocol actors. Both the industrialized and less-developed countries have expressed concern with the disproportionate size of U.S. CUEs vis-à-vis other CUEs. Less-developed countries have refused to discuss their own phaseout schedules for MeBr until U.S. CUEs are eliminated. Political conflict between the European Union and the United States regarding MeBr has likewise decelerated cooperation on ozone-related policies, all of which stipulate the need to investigate how science, knowledge, and global politics are intimately linked to national-level political economy.[69]

3

A Critical Review of the Successful CFC Phaseout versus the Delayed MeBr Phaseout in the Montreal Protocol

The Montreal Protocol doesn't work anymore.

—*Lobbyist attending the 16th MOP (2004)*

There are many histories of the Montreal Protocol that paint a coherent picture.[1] These accounts often highlight how corporations and nation-states— pressured by civil society—and the scientific community were able to put politics and economics aside vis-à-vis compelling scientific knowledge in order to achieve a global good: ozone-layer protection. While there is indeed truth to this image, we must critically examine the reasons for success in phasing out CFCs and the reasons for failure subsequently in expediting the phaseout of MeBr. It is useful to revisit the years leading up to the adoption of the Montreal Protocol, showing how CFC reductions were only possible with strong civil society pressure, and even then only in cost-effective areas of production. Industry contested scientific findings until such data and the political climate made rather clear the imminence of a global CFC ban. The Montreal Protocol was likely the best-case scenario for key actors: CFC producers, the United States, and the United Kingdom. While CFC alternatives were not immediately available, history shows that the largest CFC producers benefited the most from the "substitutes game." The Protocol's scientific community played a significant role in helping make CFC alternatives feasible for the biggest players. Finally, such favorable conditions changed dramatically with the phaseout for MeBr, a case embedded in neoliberal global environmental (as well as political and economic) governance. MeBr producers and U.S. agro-industry strongly opposed a MeBr ban for economic reasons, the scientific community disagreed on the feasibility of MeBr alternatives due to its connection with the MeBr industry, and the United States pushed for exemptions to the ban to protect its market share. The language of what constitutes an acceptable exemption to the MeBr phaseout in the Protocol's CUE clause is critical. Unlike the CFC "essential use exemption" clause, which requires that an exempted use be necessary for the general functioning of society, CUEs emphasize the market conditions for individual MeBr users. This shift and the concomitant delay in the MeBr phaseout may be a harbinger for global agreements that look to the Montreal Protocol for guidance to eliminate other environmentally harmful substances.

A critical review of the history of the Montreal Protocol reveals the strong role that the chemical industry and its atmospheric scientists (working in conjunction with NASA atmospheric scientists) played in facilitating the phaseout of CFCs. It also reveals the strong connection among science, industry, and powerful nation-states. As we revisit this history, it seems clear that the CFC phaseout would have experienced significant setbacks had alternatives to CFCs been considerably more expensive or if scientific knowledge regarding alternatives to CFCs had not been close to the implementation stage. True, civil society pressure in the United States played a significant role in pushing the U.S. government to phase out CFCs, regardless of whether the international community would do so. But civil society's role at that time influenced the phaseout of CFCs only in the most economically efficient production area: aerosols.

According to the London School of Economics Center for Civil Society, "civil society" is situated somewhere between the market and the nation-state. It "commonly embraces a diversity of spaces, actors and institutional forms, varying in their degree of formality, autonomy and power," and is comprised of a variety of organizations, including charities, environmental NGOs, trade unions, social movements, business coalitions, and advocacy groups. While theoretically civil society is considered distinct from state and market institutions, "in practice, the boundaries between state, civil society . . . and markets are often complex, blurred and negotiated."[2] However, it is important to remember that civil society groups operate in *processes of governance,* especially when negotiating on behalf of their constituents in environment treaty discussions, and those processes are part and parcel of the global political and economic logic that surrounds them.

In the case of the Montreal Protocol, we must consider the chemical industry's push to ensure that the inevitable regulation of CFCs was in their favor as an effort from an influential facet of civil society. Here, business coalitions played an important role in shaping Protocol rules and procedures more so than did environmental NGOs. While NGOs, specifically from the United States, encouraged the aerosol ban and would certainly contribute to revisions and enhancements to the Protocol, it is clear that the quasi-coalitions formed among environmental NGOs, the chemical industry and its atmospheric scientists, and the U.S. government (often through collaboration with NASA and interpretation of scientific findings by the EPA) served to quell NGO demands for "stronger global regulation of ozone-depleting substances (ODSs) under the Montreal Protocol in the second half of the 1980s."[3]

The dynamic relationship between business/industry coalitions and environmental NGOs in the arena of civil society and governments contributes significantly to the outcomes of environmental treaty negotiations. As groups focused on changing state/civil society relations, environmental NGOs in particular "put states and international organizations under political pressure to strengthen their efforts for the international management of environmental problems; and ... [provide] expertise that states and international organizations can make use of when managing environmental problems at the international and domestic levels."[4] In the case of the Montreal Protocol, however, expertise is historically found primarily in the realm of the chemical industry, and pressures were applied from it and "knowledge brokers" in policy-making positions and from government scientists/ experts.[5]

Debates throughout the history of the Protocol involving scientific expertise; political, economic, and civil society pressures; and government deliberations provide opportunities to assess how scientific knowledge and politics are coproduced, sometimes in ways that lead scholars to criticize science for pursuing the state's aims.[6] Yet disputes among experts over scientific assessments are often said to reveal the limitations of the scientific establishment in the hands of the state.[7] The outcome of such disputes, ecological modernization theorists anticipate, will be the democratization of scientific knowledge and the adoption of ecologically friendly production.[8] In the Montreal Protocol, however, what appears to fill the gap in scientific indecision almost exclusively is industry. Industry, after all, provided almost all of the funding for the initiation of the search for alternatives to CFCs, it played a major role in shaping policy for powerful states like the United States and the United Kingdom, and it made up the majority of members on the CFC scientific expert panels operating within the Protocol.

Of course, private interest groups can be considered, as noted above, a fraction of civil society. Here, ecological modernization theorists would contend that green movements (another faction of civil society) push state and economic institutions toward ecological sustainability, prompting market innovations and the implementation of more efficient technologies. Additionally, ecological modernization theorists have traditionally expected the role of the state to remain limited to "steering" economic activity in a sustainable direction, resulting in environmental governance becoming "decentralized."[9] A critical review of the Protocol demonstrates that environmental civil society groups can often play a relatively minor role in terms of influence and pressure on the decision-making process in times of scientific and economic uncertainty, especially in a neoliberal environment, as evidenced in the MeBr controversy. Such patterns of influence within the Protocol fit with certain critiques of ecological modernization because rather than providing an opportunistic moment whence a deliberative democratic approach could emerge, the gap in scientific evidence appears to be captured by private interest groups, the polluter-industrial complex, and powerful states that benefit from such capture.[10]

The history of the Protocol suggests that some ecological modernization assumptions require reassessment, such as that the role of the state will remain limited to that of providing environmental regulation and that environmental civil society groups will, in a participative manner, provide pressure on corporations to engage in green production.[11] True, the urgent calls for precaution from science and demand for action from U.S.-based environmental NGOs in the CFC phaseout seem to represent a "greening of modernity" by the achievement of a win-win situation in terms of sustaining production and environmental protection.[12] However, the chemical industry did not accept the Protocol until it was relatively clear that it had profitable alternatives in the pipeline and its own scientists were convinced of the impact of CFCs on the environment. When scientific knowledge and economic growth are uncertain, alternative strategies proposed by environmental civil society groups that place environmental protection above economic costs are not considered viable.

Unlike the CFC case, the phaseout of MeBr, as noted, has been subject to significant delays and problems, with the United States even making threats to withdraw from the Protocol entirely in 2003. The MeBr phaseout provides an excellent opportunity to compare with that of CFCs because the relative conditions were the same: both CFCs and MeBr are substances regulated through the Montreal Protocol, and both chemicals are intricate parts of production processes important to the United States—a dominant player in geopolitics. The different outcomes of the CFC and MeBr cases are strongly linked to the economic viability of alternatives to maintaining production within the United States in both cases, the economic opportunity for chemical producers, and changes in global attitudes toward environmentalism. We see how the United States—under much less pressure from civil society (including the chemical industry) to phase out MeBr than it had faced with CFCs and much more pressure from agro-industry to keep MeBr—successfully stalled its elimination well beyond the scheduled phaseout date of 2005.

There are other differences as well. Unlike the inclusion of CFC experts into the Montreal Protocol scientific community, the inclusion of MeBr chemical industry interests has led to discord and dispute over the viability of alternatives and delay in ODS phaseout. Most important, the rules regarding the exemption of MeBr are very different from those regarding CFCs, in many ways reflective of neoliberal economic reasoning, being much more reliant on particular interpretations of scientific knowledge by private interest groups and concerned for individuals in the marketplace than for the conditions of the global environment. For CFCs, essential uses were created to ensure the safety and general welfare of human beings and global economic stability. For MeBr, the economic impact of MeBr alternatives on individual producers is a primary concern used to award exemptions and to ensure the continuance of the status quo in the production of relatively unimportant commodities in terms of global market stability (i.e., strawberries and tomatoes). This concern signifies the "neoliberal turn" in Protocol decision making.

The Phaseout of (Most) CFCs via the Montreal Protocol

In *Governing Water,* Ken Conca argues that global regimes are more suited to resolving global environmental issues than local problems with global effects. Issues such as water abundance and quality are resolved most effectively by multilateral cooperation that involves state, civil society, and scientific collaboration. On the other hand, global issues such as stratospheric ozone-layer depletion or global climate change fit more snugly into the global regulatory approach. But even here "conventional regimes may or may not respond effectively to the problem of pollution beyond borders."[13] Even global problems such as stratospheric ozone-layer depletion are not always handled well by established international environmental agreements if the conditions are not right. Indeed, Conca's thesis might apply well to the Montreal Protocol in the neoliberal environment in which it is situated. Here, an international environmental agreement that experienced success for a long period has recently experienced significant setbacks due to the fact that an issue of local concern—MeBr use in U.S. strawberry and tomato production—has global implications—the depletion of the ozone layer.

The point here is certainly not to overlook the clear successes of this treaty. The Montreal Protocol is exemplary in many ways, enticing global cooperation on all manner of environmental issues to phase out the bulk of ODSs over a fairly short period. Its model of state, science, corporate, and civil society involvement provided hope that subsequent global environmental challenges, such as global climate change, could be overcome. Although scholars rightfully question the transferability of its framework to other issues, its notable success in eliminating most ODSs is still predominantly attributed to the soundness of its framework in generating cooperation.[14]

The history of the Montreal Protocol and its almost complete phaseout of CFCs is well documented by scholars both inside and outside the Protocol's decision-making process. Many accounts remark that its success in phasing out 95 percent of ODSs can be transferred to other efforts to alleviate global environmental harms. As Edward Parson notes in the preface to *Protecting the Ozone Layer*, "The ozone story offers important new insights into regime formation, negotiation strategy, and how scientific knowledge can help shape policy outcomes. . . . Its specific lessons . . . may apply to other issues where conditions are sufficiently similar."[15]

The CFC phaseout included in no small manner political and economic opportunism on the part of the chemical industry and powerful nation-states. And immense problems still remain in phasing out MeBr, caused by disagreements over scientific knowledge and the economic impact that the MeBr phaseout could potentially have on global powers, especially the United States. Here, arguments by ecological modernization proponents that prosperity and growth can be made ecologically sustainable via state, science, and corporate cooperation requires a nuanced understanding of the negative effect that scientific uncertainty regarding technical and economic feasibility, as well as neoliberalized treaty discourse, can have on nation-state environmental decision making.[16] Language on what constitutes a CUE to the MeBr phaseout has served to delegitimize certain interpretations of feasibility, a result that might be interpreted as a weakening of democratization. The MeBr case shows that without scientific certainty and a clear account of the economic gains for the future phaseout in the United States successes will be unlikely at the worst and sluggish at best.

THE EMERGENCE OF REGULATION OF ODSS

Stratospheric ozone-layer concentrations are rather small, making up only 8–10 parts per million (ppm) at an altitude around 20–35 kilometers. This small concentration of ozone buffers atmospheric radiation and regulates—in part— earth's temperature and air circulation. When put into contact with UV radiation in the stratosphere, CFCs break down into chlorine molecules, which destroy ozone by depriving the ozone molecule (O_3) of one of its oxygen atoms and giving it to another. Once stratospheric chlorine reaches equilibrium, ozone begins to decline. The long-range implications of these findings: "Even if CFC emissions were to cease immediately, ozone loss would roughly double over one or two decades before beginning a 50-to-100-year recovery."[17] CFC compounds were used in many forms for many applications (e.g., CFC-12 for early home refrigeration and wartime insecticide sprays; CFC-13 for commercial cooling and refrigeration; CFC-11 for domestic toiletries and cleaning products in aerosols); by the early 1970s two hundred thousand metric tons were being used in aerosols each year in the United States alone.[18]

Concern with public opinion in the United States gave rise to action by corporations and governments prior to any scientific consensus on how to deal with the ozone problem. Likely linked to public awareness of other environmental problems occurring in the United States, states within the United States enacted bans (either upheld by legislation or voluntarily enforced) on CFC aerosols, passed a labeling law for CFC-containing products, and "bills to restrict CFC aerosols [were] introduced in twelve other states and the U.S. congress.[19] By 1975, CFC aerosol sales plummeted in the United States. By 1978, all CFC aerosols were banned in the United States, with medical essential uses (such as CFCs for metered dose inhalers) remaining exempt.

It should be noted that the 1978 CFC aerosol ban covered only half of the CFC uses in the United States, and this was in the most cost-effective market. Additionally, without global participation in CFC reductions, overall CFC levels worldwide would have surpassed their then-current levels by 1985. Moreover, the CFC ban on aerosols led to increased CFC use in other areas unrestricted by U.S. legislation, and foreign competitors that used a higher quantity of CFC aerosols than the United States refused to make any high-cost transition. For these and other reasons, no legally binding international agreement was put into effect until 1987. Yet after the 1977 UNEP Governing Council meeting, countries in the European Community began placing bans similar to those enacted in the United States on CFC aerosols. The United Kingdom (along with Italy and France) was the exception, being a staunch rejecter of any attempt to regulate the CFC industry, likely due to the neoliberal position of Margaret Thatcher's government and the fact that Imperial Chemical Industries (ICI), the largest CFC producer in the country, was its largest industrial firm. In short, a CFC aerosol ban would have negatively affected the European firms more than U.S. firms, and consumer rejection of CFC products was less extreme in the United Kingdom than in the United States. Likewise in the United States, "with the inauguration of the Reagan administration and the appointment of Anne Gorsuch as EPA administrator, the issue fell into neglect." In short, global ozone politics prior to 1986 was almost a complete failure, largely because enforcement of a CFC production ban would have disturbed the status quo of economic activity. It was not until the Reagan administration had formulated an economic argument that the benefits of regulation outweighed the costs for the adoption of the Montreal Protocol that the United States took a leadership role.[20]

Even when the United States changed its position and called for an international ban on non-essential CFC aerosols in 1983, the global community maintained the position that any convention barring the production of CFCs should be voluntary (the Soviet Union opposed even the voluntary ban). Industry worldwide opposed such regulation, arguing that the science was dubious on what effect CFCs had on the ozone layer. In 1981, two major CFC producers, DuPont and ICI, stopped research on alternatives due to the increased costs associated with them, and some scientific research showed ozone depletion levels to be lower than expected.[21] Therefore, the 1985 Vienna Convention, albeit useful in empowering the UNEP as secretariat of ozone negotiations and in establishing intergovernmental cooperation in monitoring ozone depletion, research, and CFC production, was nonbinding and ineffective in slowing CFC growth. It should likewise be noted that not a single environmental NGO attended the Vienna Convention when it was adopted.[22]

Parson makes the observation that the common explanation for industry support of an international CFC ban likely had little to do with the discovery of CFC alternatives per se. Even by the early 1990s industry would still complain that some CFC alternatives were not perfect substitutes, so substitutions meant higher costs and less satisfaction from users of the industry's products. However, the potential benefits of a CFC phaseout to big producers were significant. Big CFC producers—DuPont, Allied, and Pennwalt being the largest in the United States and ICI in Europe—were at a competitive advantage to increase market share in the chemical industry as a whole as CFCs transitioned to alternatives. The increased cost could be absorbed and reduced more easily by the large producers than by the smaller producers; as a result, business would be consolidated in the hands of a few large chemical companies.[23]

In other words, the chemical industry was well aware that scientific data and public opinion were moving closer toward certainty regarding the environmental consequences of CFCs, and it was in the interests of the large corporations to attain a regulatory mechanism that would be to their benefit. As Litfin puts it, "The issue of substitute availability, which appears to be a straightforward matter of fact, actually hinged on perceptions about market trends, and this in turn hinged on the political question of regulatory policy." DuPont's policy toward CFCs, for example, changed only when it felt future regulation of CFCs was imminent. Yet without feasible substitutes, regulation would have been extremely difficult to ratify.[24]

It follows, then, that although the Montreal Protocol was not a consequence of CFC alternatives ready to replace CFCs at no cost, its inception still was largely driven by corporate interests to minimize the impact of their regulation, and the applicability of alternatives drove Protocol decision making: "The relative availability of substitutes for various uses of ODSs often helped to explain industry's positions toward the

[Protocol] negotiations. As substitutes became available in industrialized countries, for example, their support for stronger controls on the specific ODS would increase."[25]

For a decade after the Molina and Rowland study came out, industry and the scientific community debated the legitimacy of their respective claims, the latter improving scientific models to measure ozone depletion, the former working on profitable CFC alternatives. In 1985, under much public pressure and with coordination by the UNEP, several industrialized countries adopted the Vienna Convention for the Protection of the Ozone Layer.

RATIFICATION OF THE MONTREAL PROTOCOL

In Montreal on September 16, 1987, the Montreal Protocol on Substances That Deplete the Ozone Layer was adopted. The adoption led to legally binding agreements to phase out most CFCs from production and consumption. More than twenty years later, the Montreal Protocol now touts 197 signatories.[26]

The initial provisions included five CFCs and two halons that would be controlled, with production reduced on an incremental basis. CFC production and consumption would be frozen at 1986 levels, with 20 percent reductions occurring in 1993 and 30 percent reductions in 1998. Halons would undergo a production freeze in 1992. What became one of the most notable and successful provisions of the Protocol was the phaseout schedule for developing countries; phaseout was to be delayed by ten years "as long as their CFC consumption remained below .3 kg per capita," a principle commonly known in international environmental law as "common but differentiated responsibility." The Protocol was designed to encourage ratification by placing trade restrictions on non-party countries: "Parties were forbidden to import controlled substances from nonparties after one year, and products containing controlled substances after about four years."[27]

In order to avoid trade discrimination suits under GATT, any country that abided by Protocol provisions but had not signed the treaty would be considered a signatory in terms of trade. Such restrictions on trade are thought to be the real teeth of the Montreal Protocol, discouraging free rider behavior. Another innovation of the Protocol was that it would become active with only eleven countries (holding two-thirds of CFC global production) as signatories. This provision was likewise designed to encourage expedited membership by all countries. At least every four years, scientific information on ozone depletion is reevaluated, and the Protocol's controls can be altered to reflect up-to-date knowledge, with a two-thirds majority representing half of global CFC consumption.[28]

The Montreal Protocol, while not being the consequence of consensual science on ozone-layer destruction, nor of the discovery of seamless CFC alternatives, was likely the best-case scenario for U.S. industry and for large CFC producers as a whole. It allowed the United States to establish international regulations that would meet the growing political demands for a CFC phaseout domestically and that simultaneously would push out small domestic competitors while appeasing domestic civil society groups. It also allowed for global competitors to avoid possible unilateral legislation by the United States to block trade in CFC products, were the United States forced to adopt such legislation due to no international agreement. And it provided developing countries with a ten-year lag in order to implement CFC alternatives while still importing them from the industrialized world. In line with an ecological modernization scenario, initiating ozone-layer protection involved meeting the needs of the chemical industry as much as it did convincing chemical industry scientists of the need for a precautionary approach.[29]

While the giant CFC producers might have had the most to gain from a CFC ban because they were furthest along in the substitutes game, they were major players in the Alliance for Responsible CFC Policy. DuPont and other CFC producers would likely not have come on board the Montreal Protocol so easily were their chief scientists not persuaded by discoveries in ozone science. Clearly, the discovery of the ozone hole over Antarctica played a leading role in moving all actors toward precautionary action as well.[30] The discovery served to reframe the issue to one of reducing chlorine concentrations in the atmosphere "even though delegates agreed not to consider the evidence or its cause." Here it is clear that "it was not science, but bargaining that determined the decisions adopted in Montreal."[31]

What seemed to be a primary concern with Protocol formation were matters of trade: "E.C. producers, who dominated export markets and had more effective excess capacity than North American producers because so much of their output was still going to aerosols, wanted the terms of the Protocol to help them maintain their export markets. North American producers wanted to weaken the E.C.'s dominance of exports, or at least not have the Protocol strengthen their position."[32] Parson, who argues that DuPont did not necessarily consent to the Protocol because it would improve its profits, nonetheless notes that the CFC phaseout through the adoption of hydrochlorofluorocarbons (HCFCs) provided a commercial and potential patent opportunity for big, monopoly-like CFC producers such as DuPont: "Consequently, while alternatives markets posed many risks, it was also plausible that barriers to entry could make them more favorable than CFC markets for the largest and most technically sophisticated producers."[33]

It is difficult to see big industry's compliance not as a profit-making maneuver, especially when considering that DuPont proposed publicly in 1988 to phase out the remaining 50 percent of its CFC production by the year 2000, *thirteen years* after the Protocol's ratification—ample time to develop viable CFC alternatives that were already showing promising results in key areas. U.S. president George H. W. Bush would later echo DuPont's proposal in preparation for the London meeting of the Protocol in 1990.[34]

Although in 1987 alternatives to CFCs had still yet to reach the substitutability stage, the future would reveal the advantages to DuPont in leading the transition to CFC alternatives. For example, as early as 1988 DuPont patented a process to produce HCFC-141b and HCFC-142b as replacements for CFC-11. When this technology proved to deplete ozone at higher levels than anticipated (by law, DuPont would still have thirty years to eliminate the process from production), it patented HCFC-123. Soon after, both ICI and DuPont became primary producers of HCFC-134a, a replacement technology for CFC-12. Other renditions of HCFCs soon hit the market, all promoted and produced by ICI, DuPont, Allied, and other large CFC-producing firms, generating returns up to ten times those of CFCs. By 1990, only three years after industry had stated that alternatives were "far from available" in economically competitive forms, the largest CFC producers began closing their CFC production capacity and taking advantage of their near-monopoly over efficient HCFC production. Consequently, the three smallest U.S. producers, including Pennwalt, were all sold by 1989.[35]

The proposed alternatives (mostly HCFCs) themselves depleted ozone but at lower levels (at 2–10 percent that of CFCs). Therefore, the early years of the Protocol can be described as successful in that it balanced industry and social demands for the services provided by ODSs. In other words, the outcome was not an immediate ban on ODSs but involved rather a protracted transition to ozone-free production and hopes for a complete ozone-layer recovery over the long term. The 1990 London Amendment to the Protocol resulted in a nonbinding agreement that HCFCs would not require a phaseout until 2040. The 1992 Copenhagen Amendment would see that time span reduced to 2030. And by 1992, it had become clear that growth levels of CFCs were beginning to slow down but not to decrease.[36]

THE ROLE OF TEAP AND ITS TOCS

Perhaps the most important achievement of the Montreal Protocol was the establishment of a requirement for parties to "periodically support assessments of relevant developments in science, impacts, technology, and economics, and then review the controls in force to consider whether these developments suggested changing them."[37] Such a policy was important due to the uncertainty over how strict controls on CFCs needed to be in order to protect the ozone layer. Ostensibly, it also allowed the expert assessment panels to make recommendations relatively delinked from political and industrial interests. For one thing, no CFC producers were allowed to be on the overseeing Technology and Economic Assessment Panel (TEAP) of the Protocol. But they were allowed to be on the various subsidiary technical options committees (TOCs), to make presentations to the TEAP, the

Technology and Economic Options Committee, TEAP task forces, and party delegates on their findings and to provide the latest information on CFCs and their alternatives. Initially, the two most influential panels, those for atmospheric science and technology, reported results on recent findings in ozone-layer attributes, especially developments in assessments of the ozone hole found over Antarctica and the availability and efficacy of alternatives to ODSs. Each panel's TOC, made up of leading technical and scientific experts, was in charge of assessing the feasibility of phasing out particular chemicals. The technology panels did not consider the costs of alternatives but only assessed their efficacy in not "substantially affecting properties, performance or reliability of goods and services from a technical and environmental point of view."[38]

It is no secret that the TOCs are made up of representatives of the affected industries. These, after all, are often the most knowledgeable experts on the substances considered for phaseout. Most Protocol scholars do not find such representation a problem, perhaps because the results were near-consensus on a complete CFC phaseout in almost all areas. Rather, the TOCs are seen as a primary force behind the CFC phaseout by providing technical solutions to problems with alternatives. Yet the initial discussion in the halons TOC provides a different picture. The halons TOC could not agree on a full phaseout due to the imperfect substitutability of alternatives and opted instead for a 60 percent cut in production, achieved by merely promoting the efficient uses of these chemicals and by freezing, but not reducing, halon production.[39] The halon case provides evidence that if CFCs had only substitutes that substantially affected goods and services, the Protocol likely would have been delayed and required more substantial government regulation of the chemical industry.

At the same time, halons were phased out of production
prior to any other CFC (by 1993) due to "reducing unnecessary
discharge and better managing of existing stocks" and the
fact that "the large existing stock, and the small fraction of
consumption actually used when it mattered, allowed production to be eliminated long before chemical alternatives were
fully commercialized."[40] It seems clear here that efficiency
in production was the driving force behind the success of the
halons phaseout, not science per se, nor concern for the fact
that bromine (a component of the compound) destroys ozone
at a rate forty times greater than chlorine.[41]

A Change in Ozone Political Economy
DELAYS THROUGH THE MEBR PHASEOUT

In April 1991, the EPA reported new data suggesting that
the rate of ozone loss was likely double the estimates made by
the Montreal Protocol assessment panels. For the United
States alone, this meant that skin cancer deaths would increase
by two hundred thousand or more over fifty years.[42] Ozone
holes continued to appear each year with increased size and
for increased periods from 1989 through 1992, with a hole
estimated to develop in the Arctic over the next few years.
Record-breaking ozone hole extent and severity would extend
into 1995, with 1994 ozone percentages up to 25 percent below
average and 18 percent losses over the United States. In 1992,
ozone levels over northern Europe and Canada reached their
lowest levels in recorded history. Research summarized by the
UNEP showed that the quantity and productivity of phyto-
plankton had diminished in the vicinity of the Antarctic
ozone hole. Then U.S. senator Al Gore warned of an ozone
hole imminent over the New England region, and the Senate

call for an ODS phaseout "as fast as possible" passed unanimously.[43] It was in this mood that MeBr gained prominence as an ODS.

Historically the United States has been the largest producer and consumer of MeBr. In 1991, it used approximately twenty-five thousand metric tons, almost 40 percent of total MeBr used globally. In 1991, about 50 percent of MeBr used by the United States went to two crops in two states: California strawberries, where 90 percent of U.S. strawberries are grown, and Florida tomatoes. In 1992, pre-plant soil sterilization represented 75 percent of total MeBr use in the United States.[44] In 2005, the year initial exemptions would be allowed to the MeBr phaseout, the ozone hole over Antarctica neared the record set in 2003.

As the last of the bromine-containing substances included in the provisions of the Montreal Protocol, MeBr had the potential to contribute significantly to the reparation of the ozone layer. Out of all the possible amendments that could have been written into the Protocol, the MeBr phaseout was considered both the most cost-effective and the most ozone-saving option available. Here was an opportunity to put the "greening of modernization" to the test in global environmental governance.[45] The production and distribution of MeBr, however, would involve a complex arrangement of government, industry, consumers, and other civil society actors amid a neoliberal environment that made the CFC case look rather simplistic.

INITIATING THE MEBR CONTROVERSY

MeBr became a primary topic of discussion because its reduction would advance total ozone loss considerably:

"Controlling MeBr was a high-payoff opportunity to reduce ozone loss: under certain conditions, each 10 percent reduction in MeBr emissions would achieve as much as a three-year advance in the CFC phaseout."[46] However, the inclusion of MeBr into Protocol provisions created a new set of controversies for science, nation-state cooperation, and industrial and other civil society involvement. Most significant, it meant that a new set of chemical producers—agro-chemical producers— from the polluter-industrial complex would become involved in informing the TOCs of their technical, scientific, and economic situation vis-à-vis MeBr alternatives. Initially, these firms included Great Lakes Chemical and Ethyl Corporation from the United States, Rhône-Poulenc and Atochem from France, and Dead Sea Bromine from Israel.[47] MeBr's ozone-depleting potential (ODP) was estimated at .7 of CFC-11 and up to seven times that of CFC-11 over a period of ten years in the stratosphere.[48]

Due to the Clean Air Act Amendments of 1990, MeBr unquestionably required an immediate phaseout in the United States, having an ODP greater than .2 (the threshold set by the Clean Air Act), and initially it was slated for complete phaseout under legislation by 2000. The international community did not bend to U.S. pressure during Protocol deliberations to globally phase out MeBr by 2000. France and Israel, both home to large MeBr producers, opposed any international restrictions on its use. Domestically, U.S. agricultural producers and the Department of Agriculture were also strongly opposed to the MeBr phaseout mandated by the Clean Air Act but were unsuccessful at the time in changing the government's position. In 1992 at the Copenhagen meeting, the United States recommended a phaseout of MeBr by 2000 for industrialized countries and 2010 for developing countries, while other countries recommended incremental phaseouts over a longer period or, as in Israel's case, delaying any discussion of phaseout until 1995. The adopted outcome was a freeze in MeBr production and consumption at 1995 levels. Consequently, the George H. W. Bush administration put off any control of MeBr under the Clean Air Act, and it was not until December 1993 under the Clinton administration—under extreme pressure from MeBr producers and users—that a domestic MeBr phaseout was enacted in unison with the Copenhagen agreement. However, the domestic legislation went beyond the Copenhagen agreement in one way, scheduling a complete MeBr phaseout in the United States by 2001.

After the 1992 meeting, ozone scientists reported that ozone-layer losses were occurring at record levels. If all amendments to the Protocol authorized at the Copenhagen and London meetings were followed, by 2045 there would still be two parts per billion of chlorine in the stratosphere, with losses peaking at 12–13 percent in 2000. These losses, it was estimated, would be much larger if there were a volcanic explosion (evidenced from the Mount Pinatubo explosion) or if the Arctic winter were colder than usual. That was not all. Further findings by Montreal Protocol science and technology panels suggested that ozone-layer losses would have effects on the human immune system that would increase infectious diseases like malaria and herpes and would alter the recycling of nutrients in terrestrial ecosystems. Such evidence was considered serious enough by the global community for it to try to tighten controls of ODSs further. As noted, of all possibilities, MeBr provided the most "bang for the buck." Eliminating MeBr by 2001 would reduce "integrated excess chlorine" in the atmosphere by 13 percent, producing a far greater effect than the elimination of any other substance, including halon banks, HCFCs, and CFC banks.[49]

However, it was during this same period that the ozone regime experienced the beginning of what Parson calls a "revisionist backlash" from the United States. The United States began denouncing scientific findings that, in its view, unduly stressed the risks associated with ozone loss in the Northern Hemisphere: "Through 1993 the movement gained support from several conservative political figures and a few scientists with no prior expertise in the issue. . . . The backlash appealed to some members of the 104th Congress, who sponsored hearings to debunk supposedly alarmist science supporting unsound policy decisions, and introduced bills to weaken or abolish controls on ODSs."[50] At the 1994 meeting in Nairobi, the parties agreed on "essential use exemptions" for MeBr in quarantine pre-shipment uses. Also in 1994, the sixty-five-member MBTOC released a report on the substitutability of MeBr with other substances. By 1996, most of the backlash had declined among conservatives, but it did not alter some U.S. resolve to avoid the MeBr phaseout via exemptions or to make sure that it would not have adverse effects on the agrarian economy. At the international level, debates between the European Union and the United States regarding the tightening of controls of a MeBr phaseout continued.

There were several key differences between the MBTOC and the initial CFC assessment panels. For one, the MBTOC included agro-chemical producers who "had no plans to market alternatives to their current product. Predictably, this was a highly contentious group: manufacturers and many users fought to have the report conclude that there were no alternatives to MeBr, charges of bad faith were widespread, and manufacturers and many users attacked the report on its release."[51] Consequently, the final report was relatively vague, mentioning that alternatives existed for a number of uses but that there were no viable alternatives ready for "less than 10 percent of 1991 MeBr use."[52] A subsequent 1995 report showed that the majority of MBTOC members felt that 50 percent reductions in MeBr production were feasible by 2001, while a minority felt that either all MeBr or only a few percent could be reduced by 2001. Prior to the 1995 MOP held in Vienna, the MBTOC reported that it had decided a 25 percent cut in 2005 and a complete phaseout by 2011 would be possible but that such an effort would cost over $300 million. This debate occurred while the largest ozone hole in recorded history was discovered in Antarctica, and record ozone losses were found again in the Northern Hemisphere.

The 1995 Vienna meeting created an incremental phaseout of MeBr, with a 25 percent cut in production and consumption in 2001 from 1991 levels, a 50 percent cut in 2005, and a complete phaseout in 2015 in the industrialized world. Developing countries agreed to a 2002 freeze in production and consumption of MeBr, based on their average levels over the 1995–1998 period. Regarding agriculture, a provisional exemption for "critical agricultural uses" also was passed (a response to U.S. opposition to MeBr controls from its agroindustry), with extreme reluctance and accusations of bad faith by the European Community. One of the MBTOC's most important roles for the next meeting would be to assess the viability and effect of such exemptions. The TEAP also recommended that MBTOC membership be reduced and that MBTOC experts be evaluated based on whether they represented companies that marketed MeBr alternatives. The idea here was to moderate the obvious biases that existed within the MBTOC. For years to come, the apparent illegitimacy of the MBTOC would be used as a political tool by both sides of the debate.[53]

At the 1997 annual Protocol meeting in Montreal, the MBTOC presented new scientific evidence on MeBr's ODP, reducing it from .7 to .4. Despite the reduction in its ODP, MeBr was still given the highest priority at the meeting; its elimination still had the potential to swiftly reduce ozone-layer destruction, and its ODP was still double the Clean Air Act ceiling of .2. This time, the MBTOC reported that 75 percent reductions were possible in both the industrialized and less-developed countries. But "industry countered that the estimate was too optimistic and simply reflected political pressure from the U.S." Nevertheless, the MBTOC responded in the plenary "that the [chemical] industry was obstructing progress by working to preserve the status quo rather than attempting to develop and implement alternatives."[54]

The MeBr phaseout changed in 1997 but not as much as the United States would have liked, pushing up the complete phaseout to 2005, with incremental reductions in 1999 (25 percent), 2001 (50 percent), and 2003 (70 percent). Parties agreed on an incremental phaseout for the less-developed countries, with 20 percent reductions in 2005 and a complete phaseout in 2015.[55]

MEBR CRITICAL USE EXEMPTIONS: A SHIFT
FROM PRECAUTION AND SOCIAL WELFARE
TO NEOLIBERAL CONCERNS

Criteria for CUEs for MeBr differ greatly from the criteria for essential use exemptions for CFCs. In many ways, the criteria are much more lenient than those specified in the CFC exemption clause and much more based on concerns for individuals' economic security than the conditions of the global environment. Problems caused by the move away from precaution toward market disruption (described below) suggest that the reliance of some ecological modernization scholars on "neoliberal-style market instruments" needs to be cautious. Here, any "significant market disruption" potentially caused by MeBr alternatives is enough for an exemption to be granted to the MeBr phaseout. As the EPA puts it, "Under the Essential Use provisions [for CFCs], in order to even be considered for an exemption, it was necessary for each proposed use to be 'critical for health, safety or the functioning of society.'" This high threshold differs significantly from the criteria established for MeBr CUEs. Indeed, for MeBr, the parties left it solely to the nominating governments to determine whether the absence of MeBr (as reported by MeBr users, such as strawberry growers) would create a significant "market disruption."[56] The European Union struggled for stricter language regarding exemptions but ultimately failed.

The MBTOC announced at the tenth MOP, held in Cairo in 1998, that it had assessed that there were alternatives for 95 percent of MeBr uses and that not a single agricultural crop needed the chemical. In 1999, the European Union resolved to ban all MeBr consumption in 2005. Parties to the Protocol requested that the MBTOC report again on alternatives to MeBr in 2003. After this meeting, the EPA again revised the domestic phaseout of MeBr to match that of the Protocol. However, the United States would continue to seek CUEs for agricultural uses of MeBr, especially in strawberry production.[57]

The main U.S. argument for CUEs has revolved primarily around the phrase "market disruption." Yet it is unlikely that any disruption in the strawberry market will be linked to MeBr per se, but rather to other factors of production, such as labor and land costs.[58] The growing fear among some U.S. agro-industry advocates has been a loss of market share to foreign competitors.

While fresh strawberries are notoriously quick to spoil, the frozen strawberry market is indeed global. In 2003, China replaced the United States as the largest exporter of frozen strawberries to the lucrative Japanese market. U.S. strawberry growers are eager to reverse this new trend. For example, in 2008 California governor Arnold Schwarzenegger commented that California strawberries would be shipped to China during the 2008 Olympic Games (in August and September, when the Chinese strawberry harvest is minimal), the first time China has allowed California strawberries across its borders. Rapidly increasing exports now make China one of the major frozen strawberry suppliers in the world; as a result, the United States and the European Union have instigated acts of protectionism.[59] By 2005 over 25 million pounds (11.3 million kilograms) of fresh strawberries were produced annually in China, with only very limited usage of MeBr. California growers have been fighting a losing battle to enter both Europe's and China's growing markets while China has boosted its exports to both the United States and Europe. China's strawberry fields are already six times greater than California's, although they are not as productive. Still, China is now the leading strawberry producer in the world, with more than 1 million metric tons of product in 2003.[60]

In 2003, parties reluctantly agreed to allow for almost ten thousand metric tons of MeBr for U.S. strawberry and tomato production for 2005. While the MBTOC reported in 2003 that alternatives to MeBr were both economically and technically viable for all uses in strawberry and tomato production, the changes to the exemption clause allowed the United States to draw from particular studies based on research conducted in particular sites to override the MBTOC's report. The decisions for granting the U.S. MeBr exemptions were based on a "market disruption" valuation performed by agricultural economists and scientists at the University of California at Davis—with financial support from the California Strawberry Commission.[61] While studies supported by the MBTOC showed that the phaseout of MeBr in strawberry and tomato production was efficient from a general welfare viewpoint, the market disruption approach showed that a reduction of MeBr would have a negative economic impact on some U.S. strawberry growers and would allow competing regions to gain market share over them.[62] By sidestepping the general welfare viewpoint, the Protocol had circumvented a key concern of ecological modernization: improving overall social and environmental welfare.[63]

The key differences between the optimistic and pessimistic views of adaptation to a change in the regulatory environment for strawberry growers were the definition of "market disruption," the price change and demand elasticity estimates used, the estimated change in consumption over time, and the use of data on costs and yields from the nominations themselves versus experimental plots used to justify exemption nominations in the United States.

To demonstrate the contrast between the U.S. claims of the impact on strawberry growers and optimistic estimations, witness: "*Even under conservative assumptions,* final cost burdens incident on growers are *a fraction* of up-front cost estimates provided in the Critical Use Nomination for this sector."[64] Here, it is clear that market disruption is determined to be minimal, making other factors, such as growing competition from China, likely much more important than this agricultural input. Concurrently, the case demonstrates how certain expert discourses regarding the MeBr phaseout have become delegitimized, a sort of "de-democratization" that ecological modernization proponents would denounce.

Reminiscent of the global economic shift away from government regulatory controls and toward neoliberal freedoms, the change in evaluation of what constitutes a CFC essential use exemption and what constitutes a MeBr CUE has shifted focus from the general functioning and health of society to the economic interests of individuals in the marketplace. As a result, the United States has successfully protected its own economic interests by drawing attention to the unique local conditions of strawberry and tomato production in the United States while delegitimizing the claims made by the global knowledge of the MBTOC. By 2007, U.S. MeBr "critical uses" would still remain sizable, totaling over five thousand metric tons. The second largest exemptions for 2007 went to the European Union, at only seven hundred metric tons. Presently, California strawberries represent the largest MeBr exemption in the world, and they have always comprised either the largest or second-largest exemption worldwide. Whereas in 2005 U.S. MeBr exemptions accounted for almost half of all exemptions worldwide, by 2009 the U.S. share of exemptions would reach over 90 percent of the total. Among all industrialized countries still requesting CUEs (the United States, Japan, Australia, and Canada), the U.S. rate of usage is decreasing the slowest. The United States has put forward CUE requests until 2014, and there still is no national plan for a complete phaseout.[65]

The European Union and China contain competitive strawberry production platforms that—were MeBr to be phased out—might have gained even more of a significant market share in the global strawberry economy. In the 1990s, the United States was under a great deal of domestic pressure to abide by the mandates of its Clean Air Act and thus was pressured to phase out MeBr domestically. An earlier U.S. phaseout would allow the E.U. strawberry industry, for example, to gain an advantage and use MeBr at least until 2005. This is likely the reason why the United States revised its 2001 domestic phaseout to match the 2005 phaseout of the Protocol. As it turns out, even the 2005 phaseout was virtually eliminated due to the large number of CUEs. The MBTOC is very much divided on whether these CUEs were, or still are, legitimate given the mandates of the Montreal Protocol.

From its inception, the MBTOC faced great difficulties in deciding how to assess MeBr. In fact, to this day it is still divided on how to assess MeBr and its alternatives: some members feel alternatives exist in virtually all areas; some say none exist for strawberries. This divisiveness has occurred while the MBTOC was formed under virtually the same conditions as the CFC and halon TOCs, with one difference: from the beginning it involved MeBr producers as experts, and they had no economic gain in promoting MeBr alternatives. As Jonathan Banks, the then MBTOC co-chair, commented, this was "the first time the agricultural sector [and agribusiness] came under the scrutiny of the Montreal Protocol, [and] unlike other industrial sectors affected by the Montreal Protocol, the MeBr industry produces no alternatives and therefore has no business interest in alternatives."[66]

Regarding the indecisive and contested science among the global MeBr experts and its alternatives, Parson writes, "leaders of the process reported that they experienced here the kind of obstruction they had expected from CFC producers in 1989 (and for this reason excluded them), but had never experienced from them once they were included."[67] This insight makes clear the deeply political and economic reasons for CFC phaseout success. For CFCs, "the stakes were high, because many of the goods and services provided using CFCs, most notably refrigeration and electronics, were essential. . . . As industry argued with some justification, CFCs were intermediate goods that were incorporated into other products of substantially higher value that depended on them."[68] For MeBr, no such claims could be made, especially for strawberry and tomato production, which presently relies on a chemical virtually eliminated from similar production platforms in other parts of the world. The overall welfare of the global economy and products that depend on components that require CFCs changed with MeBr to concerns for a few growers who contributed comparatively little to the global economy. Unlike Montreal Protocol CFC amendments, since 2003 MeBr amendments have at times *increased* MeBr use, not always tightening restrictions on use.[69]

The potential for the United States to lose market share in strawberry and tomato production to competitors is no small point. The shift to the impact of market conditions on individuals has been promoted to a large extent by the United States since the 1980s. Here, in microcosm, was the convergence of neoliberal economic ideals and environmental protection, a position that the United States pushed in earnest.[70] In fact, as noted, the potential loss of market share was important enough for the United States to threaten to withdraw from the Montreal Protocol entirely. Witness the U.S. closing statement at the 2003 MOP in Nairobi, after parties refused to grant CUEs to the United States: "My fellow delegates, if our exemption request is not approved the Protocol's record of fairness and the very foundation upon which this treaty is based will be undermined. Such an outcome could shatter the fragile coalition within the United States that enables us to make progress in international bodies. I urge delegates to avoid such an outcome."[71] The strength of the U.S. agro-industry, the selectivity of scientific knowledge to justify its claims, and the delegitimization of alternative scientific claims, combined with state support, have led to significant delays in the MeBr phaseout. Here, the rift among scientific claims on the efficacy of MeBr alternatives has been filled by protectionist civil society groups concerned about the long-term economic viability of a non-MeBr agricultural production regime, not by environmental advocacy groups (including scientists and other experts). Collaboration at the global scale of MeBr ozone diplomacy, then, has excluded certain scientific knowledge and civil society actors in ways that scholars working to promote reflexive strategies for greening modernization need to consider.[72]

The Montreal Protocol is indeed a shining star in a relatively bleak history of global environmental governance. Due to the CFC phaseout, its framework, levels of nation-state cooperation, and relative autonomy of scientific experts are portrayed as components possible to emulate in other international environmental agreements. Yet the history of the agreement shows that its success has a lot to do with the interests of industry and powerful nation-states and their ability to organize an agreement that would maintain economic viability in the midst of change to less harmful production practices.

The success of the Montreal Protocol was as much due to politics as to economics. Parson relates, "Direct scientific claims had highly limited effects on policy debates and none on policy outcomes. *The only use of direct scientific claims was the selective adoption by policy actors of results that favored their position.*[73] This situation changed in 1985–1987 with the discovery of the Antarctic ozone hole.[74] Here, increasingly solidified scientific evidence, coupled with pressure from U.S. environmental civil society groups, persuaded the chemical industry to adopt alternatives prior to any definitive proof that they would work and be profitable.

When we recall the 1992–2002 MeBr history of the Protocol, it is hard not to envisage the contested timelines between the United States' proposed 2001 phaseout and the European Union's proposed 2005 phaseout as an issue of competitive advantage in MeBr-related production. An early U.S. phaseout would have allowed the European Union to gain an advantage by using MeBr for an extended period, researching alternatives, and possibly increasing market share. When the United States aligned its phaseout to match the Protocol's 2005 deadline, U.S. agro-industry fought hard to maintain MeBr use indefinitely. Debates about the economic impact of MeBr alternatives on individual users led to heated plenary debates among nation-state delegations and between delegations and factions of the MBTOC in small-group sessions, as well as internecine polemic in the MBTOC. Indeed, allowance in the CUE process for the consideration of economic impact on individual users of MeBr has instigated discord and dispute among Protocol actors from the beginning. Instead of considering the general functioning of society (the CFC exemption criteria), consideration had shifted to that of individual market conditions, with powerful countries left to determine what those conditions may be.

This change in affairs in the Montreal Protocol demonstrates how changes in treaty language to suit the (neoliberal)

market conditions of particular actors can forestall the elimination of globally harmful substances. These changes deserve
our attention and our scrutiny, most especially at a time when
the Montreal Protocol is increasingly looked to for guidance
with regard to other global environmental issues. Furthermore, the history illustrated here suggests that environmentally conscious facets of global civil society engaging with
global environmental governance might require new strategies, likely ones divergent from some of the analytical radars
of many ecological modernization theorists and like-minded
civil society advocates.

In the following chapter, I will show how a critical sociological approach sheds light on the MeBr controversy and
helps us understand that this is a problem deeply rooted in the
social fabric of neoliberal environmental governance. To date,
the Protocol has been studied from various approaches
situated in various disciplines, but sociology has made only a
limited contribution. I will contribute to the predominant
social capital sociological assessment of the MeBr phaseout
a critical assessment that focuses on the powerful, vertically
integrated social forces that have made the MeBr phaseout
so difficult.

II
The Methyl Bromide Controversy

4

Social Capital and the Vertical Integration of Power

We are quite shocked by the TEAP's interpretation of [its] own language. It is not a reasonable interpretation of plain English!

—*U.S. Delegation, 15th MOP plenary*

M ost accounts on the Montreal Protocol come from the political/legal sciences or international relations, which often debate the reasons for the Protocol's high level of success in phasing out CFCs.[1] A number of contributions stemming from international economics/business aim to assess the reasons for implementing the Protocol given the estimated economic benefits, changes in production behavior, and other economic reasons for cooperation.[2] Accounts from former and current members of institutions affiliated with the Protocol also abound, usually explaining the important role of the United

Nations in facilitating cooperation between nation-states and industry and the importance of working with developing nations to comply with the Protocol via trade incentives.[3] Reports from the natural sciences, such as the atmospheric and geophysical sciences, shed light on the efficacy of the Protocol by monitoring levels of ozone and harmful chemicals in the atmosphere, stratosphere, troposphere, etc., since its inception and the concomitant effects on the earth's biota.[4] In the United States, environmental NGOs and local stakeholders give locally specific accounts of the effects of the Protocol on certain industries, most recently the effect of a MeBr phaseout on agro-industry, often clashing over the feasibility of alternatives to ODSs.[5]

As noted, little discussion of the Montreal Protocol has materialized in the discipline of sociology specifically, with a few notable exceptions.[6] Recognizing Canan and Reichman's work as the most comprehensive assessment of the Montreal Protocol from within sociology proper, I will draw here upon their "social capital" assessment of the Protocol, concentrating on their analysis of the early years of the MeBr issue. Although Canan and Reichman's analysis predates the MeBr controversies of 2003–2006, they and others were prescient in recognizing that problems would arise due to the penetration of a change-resistant faction of the agro-industrial complex into the scientific networks of the Protocol.[7]

The MeBr controversy represents a moment of temporary failure in the otherwise successful history of ozone diplomacy. While a social capital framework helps us understand successes in global environmental governance due to social networking, in cases of networking failure it is important to be critical of the social forces that impact that networking. Using the MeBr case as a reference point, I will contribute a critical sociological assessment of the social organization of the Montreal Protocol, its institutional structure, and the impact of its various actors vis-à-vis social relations of power. A critical sociological approach contributes to a social capital conceptualization of the MeBr controversy by focusing on the uneven power relations embedded within the network of social actors involved. This extension of the social capital framework, when combined with perspectives of discourse in policy making and "knowledge broker" influence provided by Litfin in her seminal examination of the formation of the Montreal Protocol, offers a rich understanding of the sociopolitical barriers to effective global environmental governance.[8]

A reassessment of the MeBr controversy and the Protocol in general from a critical sociological perspective is useful on several fronts. Leading literatures draw strongly from a social capital conceptualization of the science and technology networks operating at the Protocol in order to explain the reasons for success with phasing out CFCs and for the early controversies surrounding MeBr. Such assessments contain valuable insights into the social networks created by the Protocol and the problems related to the unique way in which the MBTOC was formed relative to the Protocol's other scientific committees. However, the critical sociological conceptualization of power used here extends our understanding of the reasons for failure in the MeBr phaseout by concentrating—theoretically and empirically—on the broader social forces that penetrate the Protocol at multiple scales. Typical studies of global environmental treaties do not incorporate scale into their assessments. Yet as we know from the critical geography literature discussed in chapter 1, social relations in particular sites, with particular sets of power relations and specific ways of producing goods (such as strawberries) and supported by decidedly powerful actors (such as the U.S. government and the U.S. polluter-industrial complex), have a way of extending their influence from local geographies to the global stage. In "neoliberal environments" those extending influences include the dissemination of political and economic practices designed to maximize profits in markets made increasingly enticing to powerful interest groups.[9]

In addition to scale, we must consider that not all social linkages are positive or productive. Critiques of the social capital conceptualization argue that social networks include uneven power relations, the outcomes of which are not always as productive as is commonly portrayed in social capital scholarship.[10] Because social capital frameworks look at relationships horizontally (as equal and mutually beneficial), they can construct false equalities that are not extant in situations where power penetrates vertically. The MeBr controversy involves such a vertical penetration of power from powerful nation-states and corporate interests linked to these powerful states into the scientific networks of the Montreal Protocol.

As discussed, MeBr has been protected from complete phaseout through the application of CUEs, exemptions granted largely to U.S. agro-industry. Controversies surrounding the CUEs reveal that powerful actors are able to dominate Protocol deliberations and the interpretation of scientific knowledge in global environmental governance. Additionally, the MeBr controversy reveals that the efficacy of the Protocol's scientific networks and the interpretation of their findings are now deeply affected by the market-based (neoliberal) provisions, as is the ability of governments to interpret those provisions on an independent basis. We will explore the reasons why the United States is the major opponent to the

phaseout of MeBr while it was a strong supporter of the phaseout of earlier ODSs. I will illustrate how U.S. opposition to
the MeBr phaseout has been influential in slowing progress
toward eliminating MeBr through its ability to shape the
interpretation of the findings of the global MeBr science and
technology experts.

Ultimately, an interdisciplinary approach is necessary
for understanding the organization of global environmental
governance amid neoliberal globalization: global environmental problems cut across disciplinary boundaries in ways
that make it difficult to analyze international regimes from a
single discipline. The immediate objective here is to contribute a critical sociological account on a case that has put into
question the efficacy of what is arguably the most successful
global environmental treaty in history so as to help discover
the reasons for its failure.

A Brief Overview of Montreal Protocol
Rules and Procedures

After twenty years of ratification, the Montreal Protocol
now touts 197 signatories, a large increase from the original
46 participating countries. The treaty commits the signatories
to schedules for eliminating ODSs in order "to protect human
health and the environment against adverse effects likely
to result from human activities which modify or are likely to
modify the ozone layer."[11] It was signed at the Montreal meeting in 1987 and went into effect in 1989, "committing those
nations to reduce production of CFCs by 50% of the 1986
baseline values by 1996."[12] Since ratification, additional parties
are encouraged to sign the treaty via restrictions on trade with
nonsignatories (i.e., free riders).

Over the years, the Protocol has been adjusted to accelerate the phaseout schedules of some ODSs. It has also been amended to introduce different control measures and to insert new substances to the list of those controlled. National governments are not legally bound until they ratify both the Protocol and the four amendments (London [1990], Copenhagen [1992], Montreal [1997], and Beijing [1999]).[13] MeBr was added to the list of controlled substances in the Copenhagen Amendment in 1992. The MLF was also permanently established at the Copenhagen meeting.

The Protocol is considered innovative for having included a lag time for phaseouts of ODSs in less-developed countries of 10–15 years, depending on the chemical. LDCs are noted in Article 5, and developed countries are often described as "non–Article 5" countries. Another innovation is the MLF, a financial mechanism created with the recognition that developed countries should be responsible for helping LDCs eliminate ODSs. It has an independent secretariat and an executive committee "composed of equal representation of developed and developing countries."[14] U.N. agencies—such as the World Bank, the United Nations Development Programme (UNDP), and the United Nations Industrial Development Organization (UNIDO)—were put in charge of implementing projects for LDCs funded by the MLF. To date, the MLF has funded over five thousand projects in over 140 countries. In addition, the UNEP established National Ozone Units in LDCs; these are MLF-funded capacity-building government offices/programs (sometimes only a single staff person) designed "to extend U.N. support [into LDCs to eliminate ODSs] and to organize networks of regional action and exchange of technology and information."[15]

All parties to the Protocol are required to report annually to the Ozone Secretariat of the UNEP on their production, import, and export of each chemical they have agreed to phase out. An implementation committee assesses the parties' progress annually and makes suggestions to the parties on how to handle any noncompliance issues. Another innovation is that the Protocol includes an amendment provision that allows new chemicals and institutions for monitoring them to be added without the need for any tedious national ratification process. This is also considered very adaptive: Article 6 requires that parties reassess the control measures "on the basis of available scientific, environmental, technical and economic information" at least every four years.[16] One year prior to each assessment to the Ozone Secretariat, scientific experts report updated information so that parties can amend the Protocol to fit new findings. Essentially, with Article 6 the signatories created the TEAP and the five original TOCs. Article 6 is seen as essential for allowing the TEAP (the Protocol's scientific body that provides assessments of ODSs and their alternatives) and its TOCs to make adjustments to their suggestions to parties based on current science and technology. Periodically, the TEAP and its TOCs provide updates on their research, including (among many other matters) estimates of the impact of the Protocol on ozone-layer recovery, estimates of the ozone-depleting potential of certain ODSs, and advice for acceptance or rejection of nominations for exemptions to phaseouts. It is widely cited that the Protocol's four amendments were possible due to the advice of the TEAP and TOCs: "A major reason that new substances could be added and earlier target deadlines could be established was the tremendous technological developments that have been achieved over the decade, many of them the direct contributions of experts on the TEAP."[17]

There is an official annual Meeting of the Parties (MOP), which is preceded by annual Open-Ended Working Groups

(OEWGs) designed to prepare parties for the MOPs.[18] MOPs take place "at the seat of the Secretariat"; the Ozone Secretariat facilitates the plenary meetings, helping the president-elect and vice presidents keep the meetings flowing, providing translations of documents in U.N. languages, drafting the agenda, providing guidance on procedures, and performing other housekeeping activities. "Extraordinary meetings" are allowed under Rule 4.3 but were not needed until 2004 amid the MeBr controversy. Nonsignatories to the Protocol, NGOs, and other nongovernmental groups may attend MOPs and OEWGs (as long as no party objects to their attendance), but they have no voting power. Each signatory holds one vote, with a two-thirds majority prevailing for the adoption of adjustments and amendments to the Protocol. For other matters, decision is by consensus. All participants have the opportunity to speak in plenary in the order that they request the floor. However, nonsignatories and observers are typically allowed to speak only once the floor is clear and then only if time permits. Committees and ad hoc working groups designed to discuss particular issues can be established during the meetings if the parties decide they are needed. For example, a Methyl Bromide Ad Hoc Working Group was established during the Geneva OEWG in 2004 in order to discuss the upcoming U.S. proposal for "multi-year critical use exemptions" for the MeBr phaseout.[19]

A review such as this one of how the Protocol is organized, however, cannot identify the social forces operating within and external to the Protocol. For example, TEAP assessments are not necessarily value-neutral, as science would ostensibly suggest. The MLF is not simply a helpful funding agency; it is also a leverage tool for the industrialized countries. The scientific and technical advice of the TOCs is treated as legitimate not simply due to their "global authority" in science and technology, but also because of the leverage provided to certain knowledges by powerful actors. As international relations studies inform us, national governments strongly influence the outcomes of global environmental governance.[20] But the MeBr controversy reveals that the Montreal Protocol has experienced drastic changes in the levels of influence of powerful actors, in its regulatory structure, and in how science and technology are interpreted. In the next section, I will describe how the MeBr phaseout process and exemptions to it were designed differently from the CFCs phaseout process from the start. These differences mark a new moment in the Protocol in which market conditions supersede environmental concerns. They have shifted the dynamics of the treaty, allowing corporate and nation-state interests to penetrate the Protocol's rules and procedures more drastically than previously recorded.

From CFCs to the MeBr Phaseout
FROM SUCCESS TO FAILURE

The successful phaseout of CFCs under the treaty by the specified 1996 date prompted analysts to declare the Montreal Protocol to be the most successful global environmental regulatory treaty in existence. However, the phaseout of MeBr has been greatly delayed, prompting criticism by environmental advocates and portions of the scientific community. While the issues surrounding MeBr and its impact on ozone depletion are more complicated than those of the CFC case, advocates of MeBr use extensions have emphasized the differences to the point of not admitting any MeBr impact on ozone depletion. However, the most important factor in the maintenance of

MeBr use has been the difference in the policies that allow for exemptions to the ban. Because a few publicly important uses of CFCs were not readily replaceable by alternatives, the treaty provided for exemptions for these particular uses. At the 1992 meeting in Copenhagen, the Montreal Protocol created the category of "essential uses" of CFCs. A use was deemed essential if it met four criteria: "1. It is necessary for the health, safety or is critical for the functioning of society (encompassing cultural and intellectual aspects); 2. There are no available technical and economically feasible alternatives or substitutes that are acceptable from the standpoint of environment and health; 3. Steps have been taken to minimize emissions; and 4. ODSs of sufficient quantity and quality are not available from existing stocks."[21]

Based on these criteria, three essential uses were exempted from the CFC ban: (1) CFCs used as propellants in metered dose inhalers (MDIs) for treatment of asthma and some pulmonary diseases; (2) methyl chloroform for certain applications on the U.S. space shuttle; and (3) CFCs "essential [for] laboratory and analytical uses."[22] Analysts justified these exemptions by showing that the social welfare and public benefits of the particular uses of these substances outweighed their environmental costs to society.

In 1992, the parties to the Montreal Protocol added MeBr to the list of ODSs and set a schedule for its phaseout (part of the Copenhagen Amendment). In 2003, however, as the ban on MeBr was about to go into effect, the United States strongly advocated the heavy use of Decision IX/6, worked out during the 1997 MOP in Montreal. This decision was an exemption clause that enabled states to change the criteria for exemptions as they applied to MeBr from "essential" to "critical" use, a significant change in definition. The decision stated "That a use of MeBr should qualify as 'critical' only if the nominating Party determines that: (i) The specific use is critical because the lack of availability of MeBr for that use would result in a significant market disruption; and (ii) There are no technically and economically feasible alternatives or substitutes available to the user that are acceptable from the standpoint of environment and health and are suitable to the crops and circumstances of the nomination."[23] In effect, the parties eliminated the general weighing of costs and benefits to society in favor of exemptions based on the impact of market disruptions on specific interest groups, even on individual users of the chemical.

This shift from "essential" to "critical" use occurred in the context of a large-scale neoliberal turn toward stakeholder participation in regulatory governance processes. For example, *Environment and Urbanization Brief,* a publication of the International Institute for Environment and Development (IIED), put out a special issue on participatory governance in 2004, with a justification that stated, "Much has been made possible by more democratic and decentralized government structures, and by bottom-up pressures and coherent alternative development approaches from citizens and civil society organizations."[24] Following in the steps of the United Nations' economic consortia, the UNEP has moved toward participatory governance and market competitiveness to achieve results, involving greater participation by nongovernmental experts and civil society groups.[25] Additionally, in the United States, the regulation of MeBr was facing strong pressure from the Department of Agriculture (USDA) and agricultural producers. The move away from general welfare to particular economic impacts opened the door to using the Protocol as a form of industry protection. As a result, most of the MeBr CUEs that have been granted simply maintain the economic stability of a relatively small number of users in a relatively minor agricultural industry—namely, 600–800 strawberry and tomato producers in a few small U.S. growing regions in California and Florida.[26]

Environmental NGOs such as Greenpeace, citing statistics concerning the significant global health impacts of ozone-layer depletion, (including sunburn, skin cancer, snow blindness, and eye cataracts), as well as environmental impacts (such as stunted plant growth and deformation and mortality of aquatic organisms) and economic impacts (including degradation of wood materials, plastics, rubber, and paint), condemned the extensions at Protocol meetings: "The ozone layer is now in its most vulnerable phase, and we know from our scientists that we may well be in for some more nasty surprises, such as the ozone hole over central Europe this past week. . . . We urge the parties to be mindful of the fact that the 13,466 metric tons recommended for CUEs for 2006 represent over 130,000 tons of more ODP tons being produced in the world."[27] Yet such interventions did not visibly shape MeBr policy, as the arguments concerning market disruptions for strawberry and tomato farmers were emphasized over the loss of universal health and environmental security.

This turn of events does not mean that other countries have remained silent on the issue. Indeed, the position taken by the United States on CUEs has triggered international questions about the phaseout process. At the 2004 First Extraordinary Meeting of the Parties to the Montreal Protocol (1st ExMOP) the Japanese delegation noted the mixed message that the U.S. exemptions sent to other farmers in the industrialized world: "CUEs must be kept to an absolute minimum. Japanese farmers . . . under the guidance of the government, have lower nominations [for MeBr use]. We still believe [the U.S. request for higher use of MeBr] is misleading to our farmers."[28]

The LDCs also expressed serious concerns. As noted, the Montreal Protocol provided these countries with a longer time period for compliance with the ban. However, the amounts these countries are allowed to use are based on their 1995–1998 averages of consumption and production. Since many of these countries were still in the process of establishing an industrial agriculture base in the 1990s, their historical use ceilings hampered their ability to compete in high-value agricultural crops dependent on MeBr, such as strawberries and tomatoes. Comments from the less developed countries, including China, have reflected anxiety that the CUEs are a form of agricultural trade protectionism for industrialized countries, particularly the United States. The Dominican Republic expressed concern that CUEs represented an attempt to extend the "period of domination" of agriculture by the industrialized countries.[29] The Chinese delegation stated that many LDCs had "already started the process of phaseout of MeBr. Some of them [were] even completed. [Industrialized] countries consume a lot [of MeBr] in CUEs, [and this might] give rise to some unfair . . . terms of trade."[30] As a result, the LDCs began to hold back on their commitment to the MeBr phaseout. For example, the European Union has put forth "conference room papers" to aid developing countries in systematically preparing for their upcoming phaseout of MeBr in 2015, with incremental reductions in use leading up to the final phaseout. Due to the U.S. exemptions, developing countries have refused to consider such proposals in deliberations.[31]

The MeBr CUE case illustrates that under the market-based rules created for exemptions to the phaseout, a small number of growers and fewer than five agro-chemical companies can represent their interests in the international neoliberal regulatory arena to the point of threatening the continued existence of an international environmental treaty that was designed to protect the world from the significant and global health impacts of ozone depletion. This is vastly different from the CFC case, where industry, nation-states, and civil society groups all saw advantages to upholding the phaseout of ODSs. This difference marks a significant shift in Protocol procedures that places more power in the hands of the powerful.

To date, most assessments of the Montreal Protocol have chosen to focus on cooperation, cohesive networking within the institutional structure, and individualistic accounts of the pursuit of "social capital" rather than on the uneven—and geographically contingent—power dynamics at work. Such a framework is somewhat unprepared to explain the reasons for failure in phasing out MeBr because the MeBr case involves social forces that routinely penetrate the horizontal networks that are the subjects of social capital analysis.

Social Capital in the Montreal Protocol

In *Ozone Connections,* Canan and Reichman provide a detailed account of how MeBr came to enter the Protocol and how it was treated differently from previously introduced ODSs. The authors utilize a social capital framework in order to illustrate the intricate networking among scientists, chemical engineers, and other important actors that allowed for successful phaseouts of CFCs and other ODSs. They find that there was less cohesiveness among MeBr actors, a consequence of the penetration of pro-MeBr interest groups that (among other things) led to mistrust among the networked actors.

Canan and Reichman's *Ozone Connections*, which has been appropriately described as offering "an unprecedented view of politics and science at work in a global space," centers on the role that scientific experts played in forging the successes of the Montreal Protocol.[32] Following Benedick and Peter Haas, these sociologists assign a causal role to a "particular combination of technical, interpersonal and political skills" that made implementation of the Protocol possible. The capability of specific social actors in science to work cohesively, autonomously, and independently from politicians within the institutional structure of the Protocol led to its success because of "the social practices enabled by the treaty."[33]

Canan and Reichman argue that scientific experts (mainly chemical engineers) were able to network and build relations from within the institutional confines of the Protocol using "social capital." This, in the authors' assessment, "is the real stuff of global regulation, the stuff that goes beyond, or goes underneath, theories and proclamations in order to find out how implementation works . . . through social connections." Here, "human, social and cultural capital are more important than shared beliefs and common policy interests" as explanations for the successes of the Protocol.[34]

Of course, it is well known that the Montreal Protocol relies on the scientific knowledge and the technical expertise of the TEAP and TOCs in order to inform policy making. The high level of trust and partnership among TEAP and TOC members enabled these scientific groups to "act creatively and collectively" and as a cohesive unit to influence Protocol policy. Here, "can-do attitude," the fact that "kinship felt real," and "career advancement" opportunities among networked members are seen as important reasons for the TEAP's success in shaping a successful treaty. The social capital of the TEAP was so strong as to ensure that its voice "would come to *dominate* the ozone-layer policy process."[35] It seems clear that the TEAP and original TOCs were able to provide sound scientific/technical advice that was received by parties in a way that accepted their knowledge as legitimate.

The TEAP was established in 1989 by Mostafa Tolba, former executive director of the UNEP. Members of the five original TOCs—those for aerosols, foams, halons, refrigeration, and solvents—were selected by the original TEAP co-chairs, Stephen O. Andersen of the United States and Steve Lee-Bapty of the United Kingdom, members of the UNEP, national delegates, and "a few governments' agency officials." Canan and Reichman highlight the independent nature of membership on the original TOCs, despite the members' employment in industry, and the lack of a later-formed TOC for methyl bromide (MBTOC): "Panelists were recruited for their expertise and for their leadership positions in important networks, primarily located within industry. But when they served on the panels, they were required to abandon their employers' interests and pursue consensus based on the best interests of the planet. The charge for independence was successfully carried out by all TOCs except one that was formed in 1994 [the MBTOC]. This committee grew out of two hastily assembled meetings convened in preparation for the 1992 Meeting of the Parties, an industry-wide conference, rather than being carefully constructed by institutional entrepreneurs such as [Stephen O.] Andersen."[36]

A major difference between the MBTOC and previous TOCs was that the former included agro-chemical manufacturers and suppliers. Its first co-chairperson, Jonathan Banks, also notes that this was "the first time the agricultural sector came under the scrutiny of the Montreal Protocol. The industrial sector—agri-business—was not accustomed to the process. Furthermore, agricultural users of MeBr are a risk-averse and conservative user group. An additional problem is that, unlike other industrial sectors affected by the Montreal Protocol, the methyl bromide industry produces no alternatives and therefore has no business interest in alternatives. As a result, the producing industry has no stake in advancing alternative chemicals or technology and is very much on the defensive."[37]

Indeed, the MeBr case soon became a thorn in the side of the Protocol due to the inability of the MBTOC to form a consensus on the efficacy of alternatives to MeBr and the growing uncertainty regarding the legitimacy of the MBTOC's scientific advice due to private interest politics: "It has become increasingly difficult to reach consensus within MBTOC and much of the debate is now taking place outside the committee meetings and is being taken to the farming community and government legislators through a well-financed private-sector lobbying and publicity campaign. This carefully orchestrated criticism of MBTOC activities taking place outside the Protocol makes it increasingly challenging for the committee to provide the parties with objective policy-relevant information. This situation is destabilizing the MBTOC and represents a threat to the total Montreal Protocol process."[38] This criticism of the MBTOC is still alive today, especially in the controversies surrounding the CUEs granted to powerful countries—mainly the United States—for MeBr use in strawberry production.

The ability to work independent of political and economic interests, cohesiveness among scientists, and trust are indeed important factors in the success of the phaseout of most ODSs. It is likely that a lack of these traits contributed to the controversies surrounding the MeBr phaseout. As Canan and Reichman state, the cohesiveness of the scientific networks "help(s) to explain the success of the TEAP as an important governing institution."[39] Using social capital as the conceptual frame with which to understand these scenarios, however, limits how we look at the networks of actors.

While the social capital conceptualization helps explain the lack of cohesion in the MeBr network, it misses the element that these social networks are sites of interaction among parties of unequal power and uneven ties to powerful social groups and/or geographic locales of influence that extend across spaces. The social capital framework, rather, focuses on the *horizontal relationships* among actors. In a network of relative equals, such a focus is not a problem. The MeBr issue, however, involves a network of the powerful and the not-so-powerful, so the network is more *vertical* in terms of power relations. This is not to say that other ODS issues do not involve weak and powerful actors. Rather, the MeBr case involves the vertical penetration of powerful actors into the scientific networks in a more pronounced way that compromises the legitimacy of the scientific community on MeBr issues. In other words, the MeBr case truly reveals the limitations to a social capital conceptualization of the successes experienced in the Montreal Protocol. This is not to say that camaraderie and other forms of cohesion are not important for TOC success but that there are considerable patterns of inequality built into the TOC network from other actors that a horizontal analysis fails to notice. Although the MBTOC was assembled and structured differently from other TOCs, the social capital conceptualization does not capture how those differences involve the penetration of power operating at different scales—the nation-state and agro-industry. These actors form part of the network of scientists and other actors working on the MBTOC in a way that reflects uneven power dynamics more than horizontal cooperation.

Next, I will highlight some of the reservations scholars have raised about this take on social capital. Recent work in the social sciences has noted the limitations of such economic, or individualist, models used in sociology.[40] A critical socio-logical approach supplements the social capital explanation of failure in phasing out MeBr by focusing on the powerful social forces that operate in the Protocol.

CRITIQUE OF SOCIAL CAPITAL

The usage of social capital as a causal explanation stems from a long line of scholarship that has gained prominence in American sociology. Briefly, this take on social capital posits that group membership has positive, productive impacts on both individuals and their networks.[41] Drawing from Robert Putnam's explication of the importance of social capital for democratization, Canan and Reichman state that "careful investment in relationships produces positive returns to individuals in terms of careers, job earnings, promotions and the like, and at the same time, facilitates the resolution of problems for collective action." Thus, "capital" is gained as individuals become more cohesively linked in networks, and the outcome benefits both the individuals and the group as a whole; it reduces transaction costs, increasing sharing, cooperation, and efficiency in problem solving. For the TEAP, the intellectual capital (a part of social capital) gained from networking "can be told as a story of investment in social capital—the mobilization of expertise and connections to facilitate the transformation of technical knowledge into the workable implementation of the Montreal Protocol."[42]

In the social sciences, some scholars have expressed concern about this conceptualization of social capital, arguing that it implicitly ignores power in the sociological sense.[43] Social capital as its progenitor, Pierre Bourdieu, understood it, was not meant to be a primary analysis but was designed rather to "help isolate attributes of social advantage which individuals in concrete contexts enjoy."[44] In other words, Bourdieu meant for social capital to be used to help untangle the uneven access to various resources embedded in class relations.

As Ben Fine illustrates, by separating "social" capital from other capitals (natural, human, financial, cultural, and physical), productive resources lose their social character. This separation has had consequences for the conclusions made by scholars and institutions regarding the reasons for failed policies in development, particularly those of the World Bank. A lack of social cooperation, trust, and networking is seen as the culprit for failed developmental policies, not other, presumably nonsocial, capitals. Fine argues that this is the ontological framework predominant in neoclassical economic thought: "This conforms to the way in which orthodox economics understands capital, as something capable of generating output and hence utility. As a result, capital is entirely disembodied from the society and context in which it is located. Capital becomes a concept with universal applicability and, thereby, not confined to capitalism. In the hands of mainstream economics, it is the ultimate reification of all social relations."[45]

With such a conceptualization it is possible to convey social capital as being only positive and progressive. Canan and Reichman state, "Like all forms of capital, social capital is productive. Careful investment in relationships produces positive returns to individuals in terms of careers, job earnings, promotions and the like and, at the same time, facilitates the resolution of problems of collective action."[46] Therefore, while Canan and Reichman stress that the TEAP and TOC networks themselves gained power through individual cooperation (achieved by individual desires to advance), such a framework does not focus on the destructive characteristics fostered by unequal power relations affecting individuals, their networks, and access to resources. Social capital is taken as a social fact, leaving the unequal social power structures within and beyond the network rather unexplored.[47]

The MeBr case reveals that members of the MBTOC do not share power equally and that the powerful states and other actors with a stake in the MeBr phaseout affect the TOC network. Such a scenario makes a social capital framework unsuitable; these are conditions that the social capital framework does not consider, being barriers to, not enablers of, progress. Given the MeBr controversy, it is very likely that the Protocol should no longer be seen as "the model of co-operation across industry and government" but most especially not across "NGOs and the academic community."[48] The role the United States has played in stalling the MeBr phaseout speaks to the powerful impact that nation-states have on treaty proceedings. It also reveals the impact that powerful states have on how science is interpreted, which science is legitimate, and which is to be used by the Protocol. Whereas a social capital framework focuses on network cohesion, a critical sociological approach focuses on network tensions that exist between certain scientific claims and the claims of other interested actors. The next section will revisit the 2003

OEWG MeBr CUE proceedings. This occasion was the first time that the MeBr CUEs were discussed in detail at a Montreal Protocol meeting. The debates here illustrate how powerful actors are able to influence the MBTOC network and other MeBr experts. Such influences must be taken as vertically integrated social forces that penetrate the scientific networks at work in the Protocol.

MeBr Controversy in Plenary and Small-Group Sessions

As stated above, some industrialized nations, led by the United States, have refused to give up MeBr in agriculture, asserting that the alternatives do not provide equivalent results. The United States continues to use MeBr, primarily in strawberry and tomato production, through CUEs. The current stalling of the phaseout of MeBr indicates the strong influence that powerful nation-states can have over the rules of procedure, scientific knowledge, and technological expertise. It is increasingly evident that the phaseout of MeBr could negatively affect U.S. agro-industry, particularly California and Florida strawberry and tomato growers, vis-à-vis global competitors, China in particular. Deliberations over MeBr at the Montreal Protocol suggest that such pressures deeply influence U.S. policy and its current relation to the Montreal Protocol.

The members of the MBTOC have been forced to change their scientific assessment regarding the applicability of alternatives to MeBr based on strong pressure from the U.S. delegation and additionally from the scientific evidence selected by California strawberry lobbyists based on their particular circumstances.[49] Such scientific evidence is far from conclusive, with a range of research showing the efficacy of alternatives to MeBr, even some organic ones.[50] Furthermore, the MLF has funded MeBr alternative projects that likewise demonstrate success in the application of MeBr alternatives.[51] Interviews reveal that several MBTOC members believe that the U.S. CUEs are not valid, while other members believe that they are.

The United States has been able to call on the rules of procedure, which in Decision IX/6 of the Montreal Protocol show that the conditions under which funds by the MLF are disseminated are not those that parties need to consider for CUEs. Exemptions must take into account the effect of the alternatives on each *individual user* of MeBr.[52] Thus, by calling on studies that demonstrate even a slight shift in market conditions for U.S. growers, the United States can deny the economic feasibility of alternatives. In addition, the United States has demonstrated its compulsory power by threatening would-be opponents to U.S. demands for continued use of MeBr. For example, when some LDCs raised concerns about the effect that the continued use of MeBr in the United States could have on their economic security, the United States responded: "We would note that, in just three and a half years, all of our Article 5 parties can have the ability to request [critical use] exemptions from this body. The question we would like you to consider is this: Would you like this body to be extremely harsh and critical of your requests, or would instead you like a reasonable standard to prevail?"[53] Such threats reveal the inequalities existing between developed and less-developed countries.

This form of coercion is not limited to LDCs; it is also used on scientific and technical groups when necessary, demonstrating that power penetrates scientific networks in a vertical fashion to assemble scientific knowledge in particular ways. The impact of U.S. claims on changes in the interpretation of scientific knowledge explains that power is vertically integrated into networks that at first blush appear to be organized horizontally.

CHALLENGING CUES, DELEGITIMIZING GLOBAL KNOWLEDGE

In 2003, the Montreal Protocol signatories requested that the Protocol's science and technology experts provide parties with an economic assessment of the MeBr phaseout. Economists Stephen J. DeCanio and Catherine S. Norman performed an assessment of the economic rationality of the CUEs by coming up with a general welfare measure of the economic feasibility of MeBr reductions for the TEAP.[54] At the time, DeCanio was co-chair of the Protocol's AETF. This analysis was therefore an integral part of the 2003 MeBr CUE deliberation process. What parties did not anticipate was that the assessment would present a serious critique of the movement toward CUEs.

The DeCanio and Norman analysis looked at the MLF-funded MeBr projects conducted worldwide as an indicator of what powerful nations were willing to pay to phase out MeBr. The economists used data on the costs of the projects to estimate the median project reduction cost per ozone-depleting metric ton and used this cost as a proxy for the global "willingness to pay" for ODS reduction. They compared this cost to the cost of the alternatives to MeBr reported in the data provided by industries requesting CUEs. Their conclusions were that "many of the MeBr replacement projects described in the [nominations for CUEs] actually are 'economically feasible' using the global willingness-to-pay yardstick."[55] In other words DeCanio and Norman showed that many of the CUEs were in fact not economically efficient from a general social welfare standpoint.

At the 23rd OEWG, DeCanio presented these findings to the Protocol plenary. The report was designed to help the MBTOC decide whether nominations should be granted exemption status. In response to the report, the AETF determined that most requests for CUEs to MeBr were not viable. As DeCanio stated to the plenary, "In defining economic feasibility, it is useful first to consider what that concept cannot mean. It cannot mean no change in agricultural or fumigation practices. Nor can it mean no increase in the cost of production or product prices. Similarly, it can't mean no change unless profitability increases. If it meant any of these things, there'd be no need for the Protocol at all." DeCanio made a further argument about the global welfare effects of the AETF assessment, arguing that "CUEs may lead to requests for exemptions for the same uses in [non-industrialized countries], and thereby dilute the effectiveness of the MeBr control in the [non-industrialized countries]. ... Liberal granting of CUEs will have the effect of protecting MeBr suppliers and customers."[56]

The response from the United States to DeCanio's presentation was extremely negative. U.S. delegates stated that they could not accept an assessment using general welfare, or even general economic costs/savings, when the parties had decided that decisions were based on the impacts on particular users. At a small-group session devoted to the AETF report, U.S. delegate Paul Horwitz stated, "It seems to me that you must not have read the Decision of the Parties, which says that the financial aspects, like the economic aspects and the technical aspects, need to take into account the circumstances of the individual user in each nomination. . . . The decision very clearly states that it is supposed to take account of the individual situation of the nominating user."[57]

The United States strongly questioned the AETF's methods of determining the economic feasibility of alternatives to MeBr. Yet the issue here was not how the general welfare analysis had been carried out but, as Horwitz's statement makes clear, to deny *any* role for general welfare analysis in the discussion of CUEs. Horwitz stated that general welfare improvements are not as important as reinforcing the economic conditions of current agro-industrial systems and those of particular MeBr users, conditions assessed individually by the nominating parties: "You are looking at the issue through an economic prism. . . . But in general governmental policies aren't determined solely through an economic prism. . . . The Parties have always recognized that the circumstances of the individual farmers and users [of MeBr] must be taken into account in the context of the country in which they operate, and the particular economic system in which they operate. The proposal that you made is so far outside of the political reality that we've negotiated and that is being carried out in the Multilateral Fund context that we believe it to be unusable in the context of critical uses."[58] The United States therefore publicly delegitimized the AETF report, saying later in plenary that it should be considered a "learning process."[59] The AETF was dissolved after the 23rd OEWG meeting.

Small-group sessions are designed to help resolve disagreements among parties, to clarify legal interpretations of particular aspects of the treaty, and (as in this case) to help interested parties understand the logic behind the advice scientific panels provide to parties. In the AETF case, it seems clear that the networks achieved within the MeBr scientific community are intricately intertwined with powerful actors operating at the scales of the nation-state and agro-industry. The United States expressed in the small-group session its discontent with the scientific advice offered by the AETF, turning to its own version of science and economic logic to legitimize its position. The U.S. scientific knowledge claims have served to supersede the knowledge of the AETF and the MBTOC for years to come. Here, the social networks of the AETF and the MeBr community in general have been penetrated and manipulated by actors not often considered as being a part of the scientific community. With the inclusion of individualist market-based claims to justify scientific knowledge claims in treaty decision making, scientific networks are increasingly embedded with political and economic actors operating at other scales of power. Market-based claims allow powerful actors to use arguments that justify their claims at the expense of global claims. The more powerful the actors attempting to delegitimize the global knowledge are, the greater their impact.

Instead of using the AETF's knowledge base, the decisions about U.S. MeBr CUEs have relied entirely on an economic analysis based on "market disruptions," and it has been carried out by agricultural economists and scientists at the University of California at Davis and funded by the California Strawberry Commission (although peer-reviewed, as was DeCanio and Norman's analysis).[60] In this case, the analysts presented economic data showing the extent to which the U.S. strawberry industry would experience a market disruption due to the elimination of MeBr or a rise in price due to its reduction.

The Davis economists argued that a MeBr ban would cause market disruptions that would make a portion of the strawberry industry economically unviable. The analysis estimated market disruptions by the percentage of acreage that would go out of strawberry production if the ban were enforced. No attempt was made to measure the concomitant *benefits* of the ban since such a measurement was not part of the analytic criteria. In fact, the funder of the study, the California Strawberry Commission, significantly downplays the health and environmental benefits of the MeBr ban.[61] By emphasizing the economic impacts and denying the benefits of the Montreal Protocol, these private actors influenced public decision makers to extend the use of MeBr.

With these illustrations of the discourse surrounding the MeBr debates, we can see that the case study shows how decision making around MeBr CUEs was based on market disruption as interpreted by a small number of powerful actors. The United States led the effort to delegitimize the AETF report, and in fact to dismantle the AETF entirely, by using carefully selected studies that supported its argument. In other words, under neoliberal governance, there is no general voice of "the public"—only specific voices "in public."[62] In a neoliberal regime, then, decision-making processes are based on stakeholders' individual analyses of regulatory impact, presented in participatory processes.

Social capital frameworks are designed to illustrate how group participation can lead to the empowerment of a particular group. The AETF experience, however, shows that social networks often contain unevenly distributed power. Under neoliberal global environmental governance, the input of global ozone experts and bureaucrats is treated simply as the opinion of another interest group.

The Social Organization of the Montreal Protocol

With such a critical sociological understanding of power, we can conceptualize the Montreal Protocol's social organization. The groups of actors operating at the Protocol engage in social struggles for access to various resources. A group's ability to access resources is contingent upon its access to power in its many forms. In the MeBr case, we see how access to power is increasingly linked to market mechanisms used as indicators for how to handle Protocol deliberations. Powerful groups are able to select scientific claims that match their interests, and those claims have succeeded in challenging the legitimacy of global scientific knowledge on MeBr and its alternatives. Such a vertical integration of power into the MeBr CUE process requires a vertically integrated analysis of social organization.

Few people would argue against the notion that powerful nation-states contain an immense advantage for shaping treaty deliberations, agreements, decisions, and amendments. Other actors also are able to act in ways that provide them with access to power. However, with the Montreal Protocol increasingly organized to use the neoliberalized market as an indicator for how to proceed, as the MeBr case demonstrates, the other actors gaining access to power will continue to be agro-industrial interests with the financial capability to provide their own scientific data to powerful states for representation, thus using their "scalar advantage" to reach from local geographies to the global arena. Global scientific knowledge claims will become less influential, and the networks of scientists operating at the Protocol will become less democratic, less autonomous, and less effective.

Powerful states are able to utilize their inequitable advantage to influence treaty outcomes by distinguishing themselves from other actors. I have attended OEWGs of the Montreal Protocol in which delegates have attempted to disentangle legal interpretations of certain Protocol agreements in small-group sessions. These working groups have operated in English, headed by U.S. delegates with degrees in international law. While LDCs with interest in the policies were often represented by a single delegate, U.S. and E.U. delegations contained numerous lawyers, each with expertise on a specific aspect of the Montreal Protocol. Tilly's sociological work *Durable Inequality* suggests that such inequalities are indeed important and long-lasting. "Social closure," or the process of excluding certain actors from the full benefits of joint enterprises unless their inclusion would benefit those already included, can play out in subtle yet important ways, such as a delegation's having mastery over the language of an OEWG.[63]

For example, the LDCs, which are "Article 5 parties," have a decidedly unequal status that is long lasting in Protocol proceedings for various reasons; these include the fact that English is a second (or third) language for them, racial differences, and their indebtedness to "Article 2 parties" via the MLF funding. As Charles Tilly states, "In many situations the distinction between members of a particular pair does not matter. Where they apply, however, paired and unequal categories do crucial organizational work, producing marked durable differences in access to valued resources. Durable inequality depends heavily on the institutionalization of categorical pairs." While such categories as "Article 5" and "Article 2" have received much praise for the "equal yet different" status awarded LDCs, Tilly alerts us to how such categories can reinforce subordination at the institutional level via extra-institutional means.[64]

That powerful countries provide the most aid to the MLF also reinforces the subordinate status of the LDCs. For example, one delegate of an East European country told me that the countries in his region must comply with all the decisions that the European Union makes, even when such decisions affect East European countries negatively, because they desire membership in the European Union. Another country delegate told me that LDC delegates could never voice opposition to the United States because it provides their countries with aid through the MLF. Therefore, the connection between the powerful nation-states and the MLF is strong, but the uneven power relations are informal, not written into the mandates of the Protocol.

Traditionally, the role of the TEAP has been pivotal, as many scholars stress. As Canan and Reichman state, this is "the workhorse of the treaty," providing nation-states (per Article 6 of the Montreal Protocol) with assessments regarding available scientific, technical, and economic information "through the Secretariat to the Parties." Many scholars praise the flexible role given to the TEAP and TOCs, which are able to adjust quickly to recommendations due to new discoveries "on the basis of available scientific, environmental, technical, and economic information." The flexibility of the scientific committees and the requirement (written in the *Handbook of the Montreal Protocol*) of periodic reevaluation of current knowledge/science "reflect the framers' anticipation of scientific and technological breakthroughs, their faith in creative public-private partnerships, global collaboration, equity and commitment to assessment-based policy-making." Additionally, "The Parties have relied heavily on the TEAP's advice for amending the treaty," and such reliance reflects the "growing centrality of the TEAP in [the] policy-making and implementation process for the Montreal Protocol."⁶⁵

However, in the MeBr case the role of the TEAP and its TOCs appears to have changed. Indeed, the TEAP's legitimacy and power appear to be weaker in this case than scholars previously noted. As the AETF case shows, TEAP and TOC knowledge can be easily shaped to fit the needs of powerful nation-states and well-connected interest groups. Powerful nation-states can accept, reject, delegitimize, and reinterpret TEAP knowledge when it suits their purposes. When the TEAP oversteps its bounds, as powerful states interpret those bounds, the TOCs can be shut down via discursive power. In other cases, the TOCs themselves are dismantled when they threaten the legitimate claims of powerful actors, as the AETF was dismantled. With the Protocol provisions moving toward market disruptions as indicators for phasing out chemicals like MeBr, such power will continue to compromise the legitimacy of TOC scientific knowledge and weaken any opposition from global civil society that makes use of non-market-based arguments. Therefore, it is more appropriate to consider the role of the TEAP and its TOCs in conjunction with the influence of powerful state and other actors (e.g., agro-industry). A discursive approach to social organization contributes here.

DISCURSIVE POWER IN SOCIAL ORGANIZATION

Litfin's work on the Montreal Protocol, *Ozone Discourses,* focuses on "knowledge brokers," or "intermediaries between the original researchers, or the producers of knowledge, and the policymakers who consume that knowledge." Here, members of the EPA, NASA, and UNEP facilitated and influenced negotiations toward an environmentally friendly outcome. Litfin argues that knowledge brokers allowed for the particular outcome of the Protocol, one that was successful in adopting precautionary principles toward the need to phase out CFCs and ODSs. Such an approach, Litfin argues, is necessary because in the Montreal Protocol while "what was accepted as knowledge was tightly linked to the political and economic interests of the principal antagonists, the USA and the European Community, . . . the outcomes were not based primarily on either material interests or material power, for scientific discourse, shaped by distinctive contextual factors, was crucial in defining the range of acceptable policy outcomes."[66]

Coercive and structural power are important but not sufficient to explain the successful negotiation of the Montreal Protocol. One must consider discourse utilized by scientists, institutional actors, and political actors in shaping the possibilities made available to powerful nation-states in order to understand the Protocol, as well as the domestic conditions under which states approach global governance: "The domestic structure of states involved in the Montreal Protocol negotiations influenced the extent to which scientific knowledge was available and appreciated. The nature of the relation between industry and government and the structure of the various national CFC industries were also important factors in setting the political context. Another key element was the strength of domestic environmental groups."[67] Structural dimensions are embedded in treaty negotiations and the social relations among groups as they try to influence the state apparatus. Influential approaches to global environmental governance often focus on the role of science in shaping policy rather than recognizing that *science is a part of the political process.*

It is helpful to think about power-through-discourse in conjunction with structural power. Litfin acknowledges this in the quote above but concludes that the outcomes of negotiations on the Protocol were not based primarily on material interests or power. While I side closely with this interpretation, it can be a misleading conclusion. The role of the state is crucial in this formation of discourse, as Foucault so eloquently illustrated.[68] The United States often legitimates its interests in ways that simultaneously contravene the Montreal Protocol and support its underlying neoliberalized tenets. While many scholars note that the scientific community—the TEAP and its TOCs—holds a great deal of power with its control of "rational" science, Protocol discourse reveals the degree to which science and its interpretation is shaped by powerful actors and the degree to which science is itself political.[69]

For example, at the 15th MOP in Nairobi, the United States desired an "essential use exemption" for salbutamol, a CFC used in some MDIs, to relieve asthma. The European Union opposed the U.S. nomination, stating that there was clear evidence of viable alternatives and that it had recently phased out this very use of CFCs. Additionally, the U.S. Stakeholders Group on MDI Transition, a consortium of leading patient and physician associations representing more than 25 million Americans who suffer from asthma, fully supported the E.U. position.[70] The United States, however, stated that the TEAP had approved its nomination for essential uses of salbutamol: "We, like the E.U., hold the recommendation of decisions of the TEAP in very high esteem. The TEAP has recommended approval of the U.S. nomination [for essential use exemptions for MDIs] for 2006. That is a fact!" The TEAP then stated that it could clarify its recommendation if parties wished, but "it is the parties that decide essential use [nominations]."[71] This, of course, is true. However, the United States did not appreciate that the TEAP avoided the issue. In other words, the United States wanted science to play an active political role at its behest, and in this case TEAP language as written in its report supported a political decision with which the United States agreed, so it wanted the TEAP to "act political" in this instance: "We are quite shocked by the TEAP's interpretation of their [sic] own language. It is not a reasonable interpretation of plain English!"[72] In this case, the United States was all but demanding that the TEAP take a more proactive role, to provide recommendations, as the United States claimed that the TEAP had done in its recommendation. Such discourse suggests that the TEAP is under great pressure from global powers to interpret its findings in a way that supports the positions of those powers.

With MeBr, however, the United States has the TEAP step back, to provide little recommendation, unless it is to recommend the approval of its CUEs to the MeBr phaseout. At the 24th OEWG in 2004, the MBTOC put forward a report that rejected many of the United States' CUE nominations for MeBr. The MBTOC, in effect, recommended smaller exemptions based on current science. According to the United States, the MBTOC assessed the need for MeBr for individual users "based on suspicion" and not on information provided by the parties.[73] In terms of the U.S. accusation that the MBTOC was attempting to apply policy, the MBTOC noted that its recommendations for reductions were *suggestions* and did not go further than that. "But also we realize that the following year it is not appropriate because at that stage the [nation-state] management plans for the phaseout will be part of the nomination."[74] Finally, the MBTOC was forced to revise its final report, granting the United States its entire CUE nomination for strawberries.

How the United States and other countries go about defending their positions on the MeBr issue reveals how the dominant political discourse can shape actor behavior at the international level, but nations' influence on discourse is still based on their uneven political economic positions in the global economy. At the 1st ExMOP, I spoke to an anonymous pro-MeBr lobbyist who stated that the problem with the Montreal Protocol was that it could harm the U.S. economy due to Mexico's ability to produce strawberries cheaply. "Baja [California] is flooding the damn market [with strawberries], as far as I am concerned!" That, according to the lobbyist, was the problem, not the inefficacy of alternatives to MeBr in the United States.[75] As the parties to the Montreal Protocol continuously reiterate, Decision IX/6 of the Protocol notes that the parties decided that all alternatives to ODSs must be both technologically and economically feasible. Therefore, arguments about competition not working in favor of the United States should not be acceptable. But it now appears that alternatives must simply maintain the status quo, not necessarily protect the environment.

The point of this chapter was to apply a critical socio-logical conceptualization of power to the controversy surrounding the phaseout of MeBr, as this case marks a shift in global environmental governance toward neoliberal, market-based solutions that appear to shift power away from global scientific groups.

As Canan and Reichman correctly note, a lack of cohesion, trust, and confidence within the MeBr scientific network likely played a role in setting the stage for the controversy seen today regarding MeBr and the efficacy of its alternatives. U.S. agro-industry penetrated the MBTOC at its inception, and its inclusion brought a political dimension to what was ostensibly a less political situation.[76] However, a social capital framework in the Putnamian tradition is perhaps less equipped to understand the uneven power dimensions at work in the MeBr controversy than Bourdieu's social capital framework. For one, it is difficult to conceptualize social networking as being destructive as well as progressive. For another, it is difficult to incorporate understandings of uneven and geographically contingent power relations into this ontology. Bourdieu's take on social capital provides a better conceptualization of the power dimensions at work within the MBTOC and among other actors operating in the Montreal Protocol. This critical sociological approach, when combined with an understanding of geographies of power and discourse, helps us to understand the social forces at play in undermining the MeBr phaseout process.

"Bourdieu emphasizes the social construction of social capital (what it means and how it relates to practices)," Fine argues, "and that it is irreducibly attached to class stratification and the exercise of economic and other forms of exploitation."[77] In other words, Bourdieu's use of social capital incorporates both structural and institutional power relations into assessing network formation. Nation-states, scientific experts/networks, and global civil society groups are constantly struggling for greater representation in the Protocol. They are also struggling for market share, maintaining control of the interpretation of science and technology, and influencing policymakers to consider the global environment over economic concerns. To understand the uneven power relations *within* the TEAP and TOCs and *between* these networks and other powerful actors, we will examine the links between TEAP and TOC members and their affiliations with powerful states. Here, Bourdieu's approach of assessing "contacts with important people" has the potential to expose the power relations within the scientific networks and understand the effects of these relations on policy outcomes.[78]

In the MeBr controversy, it is not access to and connections within the French bourgeoisie (Bourdieu's problematic), but contact with U.S., E.U., and other powerful state and corporate apparatuses that appears important in scientific decision making in the Montreal Protocol. In other words, it is not just contacts and networks per se, but contacts and networks with powerful actors that matter. An assessment of global environmental governance and the MeBr controversy in particular must include an understanding of how social relations are situated in ways that benefit some individuals, networks, and nation-states more than others.[79] Such inequalities are omnipresent in the social organization of the Protocol.

5
Tensions among Nation-States

I cannot imagine a Mexican farmer producing without methyl bromide who is competing with a U.S. farmer who is using MeBr. Mexico would be at a great disadvantage. . . . We will not eliminate use [of MeBr] if other countries, our partners, don't do so.

—Costa Rican delegation, 1st ExMOP, 2004

As discussed, the CFC phaseout may leave the false impression that nation-states can easily and quickly compromise with industry and civil society groups on how to respond to global environmental concerns. The fact that CFC production was concentrated in the United States and Western Europe was no small component of the successful phaseout of the majority of CFCs over the years. CFC alternatives were concentrated in the hands of a few chemical companies, and the alternatives, while not fully developed at the time of the proposed incremental phaseout of CFCs, were potentially very lucrative. Moreover, considerable domestic pressure early on from civil society groups made the United States a relatively strong supporter of an international phaseout strategy. Later on, scientific evidence strengthening the link between CFCs and bromine and ozone depletion would amplify that support year after year.

However, MeBr use will continue indefinitely in the industrialized world through CUEs and through its growing use in quarantine pre-shipment, which the Protocol does not even attempt to control. In the LDCs, MeBr will be used until 2015, much longer if CUEs are granted. Tensions between the United States and Western Europe on alternatives to CFCs for essential uses ran high in the 2000s, and the political differences sometimes contributed to the stalling of other contested issues, such as the MeBr phaseout, where differences were even greater and concerned a whole host of apprehensive LDCs. What seems clear is that the new focus on solutions compliant with market-based, neoliberal principles in Protocol debates and discourse has exaggerated the tensions that always exist among countries as politicians and their advisers attempt to make sure environmental agreements will be in their countries' best interests.

Here I will illustrate recent configurations of these tensions as they transpired in the 2003–2007 period among Protocol delegates. While I will often refer to the nation-states (e.g., "the United States," "Japan," the "Dominican Republic") and other political units (the "European Union," the "GRU-LAC nations," etc.) as distinct entities, it is important to remember that the delegates representing these entities are speaking on behalf of complex networks of social, political, and economic power that make up "the state." These state and regional political groupings are not removed from their corporate constituents, just as they are not detached from the scientific and other civil society groups with which they constantly interact. Rather, their representatives are linked to such actors via daily routines, laws, discourses, employments, financial ties, political promises, production conditions, shared and contested fears/hopes, ideological (dis)beliefs, and global patterns of socioeconomic and ecological change. Vibrant debates among nation-states at Protocol meetings, we will see, are strongly linked to shifts in global competition and efforts to contest the legitimacy of certain forms of scientific knowledge in the neoliberal context. While utilizing neoliberal rhetoric and associated treaty language, the United States makes demands for the continued use of MeBr that are contradictorily linked to the protectionism of its strawberry agro-industrial complex vis-à-vis competition from Europe and China, both major strawberry producing regions, via the use of its own scientific knowledge claims to counter global knowledge claims regarding MeBr alternatives. Such tensions have an inadvertent effect on participation from the LDCs, which have expressed concern in Protocol meetings about the number of exemptions granted to the industrialized North and the effect these will have on their own terms of trade.

Tension among powerful states is an important factor in determining the phaseout of ODSs. While happening rather smoothly, the transition to CFC alternatives perhaps took too long in terms of resultant ozone-layer loss and the consequential damage inflicted on the planet. What CFC production and consumption remained through essential use exemptions appear to have been strongly tied to legislative concerns in the United States but also to concerns primarily over competition and political maneuvering between the United States and Western Europe.[1]

Regarding the MeBr phaseout, reaching consensus among major players on a plan of action has proved more difficult than the CFC case. Many more nation-states, civil society and industrial groups, and users are involved in the MeBr issue, making the phaseout decision-making process much more complex. Additionally, scientific agreement on the efficacy of alternatives is much further from consensus and much more embedded in the politics of interest groups. The lack of nation-state agreement on scientific knowledge also includes the probability that the global distribution of alternatives might have shifted production of certain agricultural crops away from the United States due to competing "emerging markets," such as in China, and competitors in the European Union.

Scientific experts have been divided in their assessment of alternatives to MeBr in a way that parallels geopolitical tensions between the United States and the European Union. Consequently, the provisions for exemptions to the MeBr phaseout have been much more lenient and much more reflective of neoliberal concerns about market logic than environmental concerns. For MeBr critical uses, concerns for the individual user of MeBr took precedence over concerns for the effect of MeBr on the environment. The reasons behind this shift are intimately tied to concerns within the United States over the potential loss of market share to global competitors in a neoliberal globalizing world.

We will visit here several instances in which tensions among nation-states have stalled progress at Montreal Protocol meetings. In a review of the discourse at Montreal Protocol plenary meetings it becomes clear that issues of geopolitics, economic protectionism, and tensions between industrialized countries and LDCs play major roles in decision making over key issues. In fact, these tensions appear at times much more important than the phaseout of ODSs themselves. The United States and Western Europe play dominant roles in the Protocol, illustrating how these regions often hold the most authoritative position to make adjustments to or interpretations of Protocol provisions. As such, U.S.-E.U. tensions create much difficulty for the less-developed world.

As we know from international relations studies and macrosociological studies, a country's position in the global economy plays a significant role in determining its stance in global environmental governance.[2] In the MeBr case, a major concern for LDCs has been the future phaseout schedule of MeBr in those countries vis-à-vis the number of CUEs requested in the industrialized world, mainly the United States. A major concern with the European Union appears to be the unfair advantage that the exemptions would give to U.S. strawberry producers, and it has had the adverse effect of temporarily increasing exemptions from some E.U. member states (although CUE requests for the European Union ended in 2008). Japan and China appear worried about how exemptions will affect their own farmers, who had to either ban MeBr in 2005 (Japan) or prepare for its ban in the near future (China). China remained relatively silent at Protocol meetings, possibly because the European Union pushed an agenda that likewise benefited China's strawberry production complex, which is much less dependent on MeBr than the U.S. system yet is growing more competitive internationally due to cheap labor and land costs. Indeed, China is in a unique position because cheap labor and huge investment flows make it a hot spot for agricultural production, including non-MeBr strawberry production.[3]

Skepticism is high among LDCs about the "good faith" shown by the industrialized world. Efforts by the European

Union to help LDCs transition to alternatives in a timely manner were cast aside, again due to skepticism with industrialized
country efforts to phase out MeBr on their own terrain. Such
tensions affect how scientific information will be interpreted.
Sometimes, these nation-states either accuse the scientific
community of acting "political" or they accuse each other of
falsely interpreting the scientific community. Sometimes, the
nation-states accuse the scientific community of falsely interpreting its own data! All this tension means that progress in
phasing out ODSs currently is exceedingly slow; at times the
process even moves backward.

Progress toward the MeBr Phaseout to Date

Before delving into the discourse from the Protocol
meetings, it will be useful to note the quantities of MeBr
exempted from the phaseout process and thus granted CUEs.
In 2003, the parties met in Montreal for the 23rd OEWG. The
primary topic of discussion was the looming complete
phaseout of MeBr in the industrialized world in 2005. In 1999,
consumption of MeBr for the United States and other industrialized countries was reduced by 25 percent of 1991 usage, by
50 percent in 2001, and by 70 percent in 2003. Yet in 2003,
the Bush administration made it clear that it would pursue
exemptions to the complete phaseout, mainly in strawberry
and tomato production based, in part, on a report compiled
by the USDA and on the outcome of hearings held before the
U.S. House of Representatives' Committee on Agriculture
stating that the MeBr phaseout would hurt U.S. growers.[4]
Since the mid-1990s, California strawberry farmers
have argued that if they could not use MeBr, competitors in
Mexico would be able to take over the winter fruit market with

superior products.[5] More recently, farmers and U.S. agro-
economists argued that pressure from China would threaten
U.S. producers.[6] MeBr producers likewise put up barriers to
non-MeBr production because there was simply no clear
profit-making venture worth pursuing: "Methyl bromide
producers Albemarle, Dead Sea Bromine, and Great Lakes
Chemical say they are working on chemical replacements, but
administration officials say companies are unwilling to risk
'R and D' investments to develop products that may also be
subject to regulation. 'Chemical companies have to be willing
to spend money to register and then conduct tests for alternatives,' says Ken Vick, coordinator/methyl bromide alternatives
research at the U.S. Department of Agriculture (USDA). Pesticides companies see too many environmental and health
problems or patent hurdles. . . . The main barrier to finding a
chemical alternative is 'the lack of a profit motive.' "[7]

Agricultural groups based in the United States, such
as the California Strawberry Commission, have argued that
scientific progress on improving the efficacy of alternatives
was still lacking. California farmers have argued that there is
absolutely no chance that alternatives to MeBr are effective
enough. The message has been, "If methyl bromide goes away,
we go away."[8]

The parties to the Protocol originally decided that the
exemptions to the phaseout could not exceed 30 percent of a
nation-state's 1991 MeBr baseline use. But that decision was
overturned, largely by U.S. pressure at the 2003–2005 meetings, including an "extraordinary" meeting held in 2004 and a
second one in 2005. At the 15th MOP in Nairobi in 2003, the
United States demanded 2005 exemptions for 37.5 percent
of its baseline, but the international community rejected
the demand. The meeting ended in a standstill, only to be

concluded the following March in the 1st ExMOP, when the international community finally conceded to the full U.S. exemptions request of 37.5 percent.[9] As stated by Mark Murai, president of the California Strawberry Commission, the strong stance against the United States in Nairobi came primarily from the European Union: "The main reason for the breakdown was the opposition of the European Union to any CUE exceeding 30 percent of the baseline."[10] In other words, the reason for the breakdown was that the European Union had struggled to uphold the established laws of the treaty.

The 2005 CUEs allowed the United States totaled almost 10,000 metric tons out of a total 16,050 metric tons granted exemptions in all industrialized countries. The 7.5 percent over the 30 percent limit was to come from existing stockpiles of MeBr. In 2006, the EIA reported that it had discovered private stockpiles of MeBr totaling 10,000 tons, owned by a handful of U.S. chemical companies; in 2006, these stockpiles were more than American farmers needed or had even asked for in the exemptions. In 2007, the NRDC would discover that these U.S. chemical companies actually had 18,500 tons of MeBr in their possession, making the CUE request excessive indeed. The NRDC argued that the exemptions had been demanded because "the U.S. government want[ed] two American chemical companies [Chemtura and Ameribrom] to profit [in the range of $60–$80 million] by producing or importing another 20 million pounds [over 9 million kilograms] of this dangerous chemical."[11]

For 2006, the MBTOC recommended U.S. exemptions at 26 percent of its baseline use. But the United States contested this recommendation. It wanted 35 percent and openly accused the MBTOC of mixing politics with science in its assessment of the U.S. case (see below). The meeting concluded with the parties granting the United States 8,075 metric tons in CUEs, 32 percent of its 1991 consumption baseline.[12]

At the 17th MOP in Dakar in 2005, the United States demanded 2007 CUE nominations for 29 percent of its baseline MeBr use, but the parties, responding to the MBTOC's assessment, approved only 26.4 percent and later a supplemental .3 percent. As the EIA reported, U.S. exemptions for 2006 totaled 70 percent of all exemptions in the industrialized world (worldwide 13,014 metric tons of exemptions were granted for 2006). At the 17th MOP, negotiations among nation-states and among nation-states and private firms took place almost entirely behind closed doors, without any chance for public comment until decisions had been made and voiced to the plenary. The EIA also learned that the United States would seek large exemptions in the years to come: "For 2007, the U.S. is planning to use 6,750 metric tons of methyl bromide [29 percent of the baseline] and it has requested a further 6,415 metric tons for 2008."[13]

For the U.S. reader at least, measures in "metric tons" or even kilograms (the measure the EPA uses in its MeBr reports) might obscure the size of these CUEs. In pounds, the U.S. CUEs for 2005 amounted to approximately 21 million. This quantity is equivalent to over 2.5 million cubic meters of MeBr—enough to fill over 1,050 four-seater hot air balloons, over 450 Goodyear blimps, almost 20 Biospheres II, or the volume of more than 2.5 (former) Houston Astrodomes.[14] U.S. exemptions for 2006 could fill 900 hot air balloons, and so on. This is quite a large figure for an annual exemption for a single country, especially when one considers the effect of MeBr on the ozone layer and the rather inconsequential role that strawberries play in society.

Progress at a Snail's Pace

As anyone familiar with the bureaucratic procedure of global governance can imagine, the process of registering and phasing out any ODS through the Montreal Protocol takes a very long time. Even with relative cooperation among nation-states, the initiation of phaseout procedures takes several years. Since nation-state cooperation is difficult to achieve, the phaseout process often takes even longer than the bureaucratic procedures permit. In reality, the Weberian "irrationality of rationality" in bureaucratic procedure is exacerbated by the political and economic tensions existing among nation-states and their social networks.

At the 24th OEWG in 2004, Alistair McGlone, a lawyer for the E.U. delegation, put forth a proposed amendment to the Protocol designed to expedite the process of ratifying the introduction of ODSs in the Protocol.[15]

> Our view is that the procedure for introducing new substances into the Montreal Protocol regime is too long. . . . First of all, a party will notify the Secretariat of an ODS after a two-year period, which would be required for the submission of peer-reviewed research assessment; then there would be an assessment of the [ozone-depletion potential] of that substance by the [Scientific Assessment Panel] within six years; then the TEAP would take a further one year on its assessment. Following that, the adoption of an amendment for the new substance would take one year. Following that, the amendment would take two years to enter into force, a further three years to bind 50 percent

of the parties, and a further five to seven years to bind 90 percent of the parties. That is quite a long time.

If we look at historic examples we can see, for example, that in the case of HCFCs, they were first discussed in 1986, the London Amendment was adopted in 1990, but it wasn't until September 2003 that the London Amendment was ratified by 93 percent of the parties. So, we are talking, in that case, of a period spanning the years 1986–2003 for HCFCs to be controlled amongst the majority of the Montreal Protocol parties. And there are other examples as well. Methyl bromide, for example: 1989 it was first discussed by the parties, and it wasn't until September 2003 that you had ratification approaching 90 percent. Again, we are talking about a long time. . . .

Quite simply, either as a matter of policy, this long time lag . . . is acceptable, or it isn't. And our view is that, collectively, parties to the Montreal Protocol should be investigating ways to making [sic] this procedure much more quick. . . . We are trying to ensure that new ODSs can be regulated, with all the necessary checks and safeguards, but much more quickly than the current time span of 17 or 18 years. . . .

What causes the problem? There seem to be many causes, but in our book, probably the major cause of the problem is the formalities in international law that are associated with ratification. Clearly, if ratification formalities could be dispensed with, we would not be talking about such a long period before controls entered into force for the majority of parties. . . . In proposing a more informal way of consenting to be bound by legal measures, the European Community is not introducing an entirely new creature in this forum. We are looking at a model that already exists. And it not only exists here, but it exists for example in the Washington Convention on the International Trade of Endangered Species, the International Convention for the Regulation of Whaling . . . the Convention of Persistent Organic Pollutants, the Stockholm Convention, the Convention for the Protection of the Environment in the Northeast Atlantic. There are all manner of conventions that have a procedure for introducing new legally binding measures that do not require formal ratification. . . . We would suggest an amendment . . . which would allow the Protocol to be modified expeditiously it order to control new substances.[16]

The suggested E.U. amendment was never ratified. It was discussed again at the 16th MOP but with no resolution.

There are many reasons why parties would not wish to make the ratification process more expeditious. At the 24th OEWG, Japan, for instance, noted that some parties have yet to ratify past agreements, so making the process more expeditious may be fruitless. Canada and the United States tried to stop any discussion of the issue, pointing to the late arrival of the issue to their capitals, which would make the parties "incompetent" to discuss the proposal. (The Ozone Secretariat, however, was clear that the proposal had arrived to capitals within the timeline set for such procedures under the Vienna

Convention.) The European Union took this as an attempt to avoid its proposal: "There is nothing up our sleeves here. We are just proposing a solution to what many people consider is a problem."[17]

The chief reason, however, for opposition appeared to be related to MeBr, showing again how MeBr served to stall progress in ozone politics in general. The MeBr case made many countries reluctant to support proactive changes to Protocol procedures. The Nigerian delegation, speaking on behalf of all African countries, expressed skepticism that any process of phasing out ODSs could be accelerated: "We are still facilitating back and forth on various decisions that have been ratified. Only yesterday we were experiencing a lot of requests of exemptions [for MeBr]. This gives the impression that, somehow, we are not in full control of the situation. . . . We need more time."[18] The Barbados delegation, speaking on behalf of the Grupo Geopolítico de América Latina y del Caribe (GRULAC, representing the interests of all Latin American and Caribbean countries), also noted skepticism with this proposal due to the issues raised by Nigeria and issues regarding trade complications.

The United States noted skepticism for reasons related to compliance with Protocol ratifications by governments, the effect of quicker ratification on party noncompliance, the effect that would have on trade, and the apparent success of the Protocol to date: "The Montreal Protocol, to us at least, is different. We are not starting from scratch here. We are dealing with what is widely considered the most successful international environmental agreement, under which the most important ozone-depleting substances are already being regulated."[19] For the United States, the lag time of over a decade in registering and ratifying chemicals to the Protocol was what had enabled it to be so successful. In some cases, it simply takes the U.S. Congress a long time to approve of the elimination of a chemical because it wants to make sure the decision will not hinder U.S. producers and consumers. Yet as the African and Latin American countries note in light of the MeBr phaseout, the lag time in phasing out ODSs is often exacerbated by sizable exemptions to chemicals already ratified, so why speed up the process?

The process described by McGlone indeed reflects a problem with the Protocol. The fact that Canada, Japan, GRULAC, and the Group of African Countries agreed in plenary that this was a serious problem was evidence that the ozone-layer issue was in need of expedited action but that it was bogged down in bureaucratic procedure in both national and international policy. The Australian delegation noted that other multinational environmental agreements were able to expedite procedures by using "voting, and some even by secret ballot," a step that would mark "a highly undesirable shift in the culture of the Montreal Protocol because we believe the success of this Protocol is highly dependent on broad-scale unanimous support and transparent understanding of the commitment of all parties."[20] However, as we will see in subsequent chapters, much of the transparency of deliberations in the Montreal Protocol has become veiled as countries increasingly make decisions about how much MeBr should be exempted from phaseout in the industrialized world in special sessions behind closed doors.

Yet the problem as stated by McGlone fails to explain the myriad barriers unrelated to procedural issues. These unrelated issues are strongly associated with disagreement among nation-states on the necessity of ODSs to their various production platforms in the neoliberal political environment.

Nigeria spoke to this issue when it noted that exemptions to the phaseout of even ratified substances can obviate any expedited procedure. Furthermore, for MeBr, disagreement among industrialized countries has led to political strategies to stall progress, sometimes by the use of matters unrelated to MeBr as leverage.

In 2004 at the 16th MOP, disagreement among industrialized nations seemed to increase requests for MeBr CUEs, even in industrialized nations that were visibly strong supporters of a complete MeBr phaseout.[21] Likewise, such disagreement led to a virtual halt in preparations for the 2015 MeBr phaseout in the LDCs. The LDCs simply were unwilling to discuss their own future phaseouts with so much disagreement existing among industrialized nations and the high quantity of MeBr CUEs in the United States. Ironically, these countries sometimes pointed toward global climate change as a source of uncertainty and risk in eliminating MeBr; climate change, they argued, would affect the efficacy of a chemical that even the United States, with its dominant agro-industrial machine, feared to lose. As ozone loss can exacerbate the effects of global warming, such claims seem counterproductive, yet they are practical from a political economic perspective given the U.S. demands for MeBr.[22] Such delays in plenary discussions could postpone any resolutions made by parties for years to come.

The Effect of Powerful Nations on Scientific Knowledge

As noted in chapter 4, at the 23rd OEWG, the MBTOC presented its assessment of CUE nominations to the MeBr phaseout in light of the viability of alternatives. The report, composed by MBTOC and the AETF, was based on current scientific and technological knowledge of MeBr alternatives and their practical application. The MBTOC did not recommend CUEs for MeBr in strawberry or tomato production. It reasoned that recent pilot projects worldwide (over two hundred total projects), funded by the Protocol's MLF, had presented positive results with MeBr alternatives. As stated by then MBTOC co-chair Jonathan Banks, "With two exemptions (control of ginseng root rot and stabilization of high-moisture fresh dates), the complete demonstration projects, for all Article 5(1) locations and all crops or situations tested, identified one or more alternatives comparable to MeBr in their effectiveness in the control of targeted pests and diseases."[23]

The MBTOC noted that many of the nominations for CUEs had been presented without a consideration of the many alternative strategies for growing strawberries and tomatoes. In combination with alternative chemicals, such as chloropicrin, the amount of MeBr could be reduced significantly: "MBTOC noticed there was considerable scope for reduction in MeBr through adoption of MeBr-chloropicrin combinations containing high concentrations of chloropicrin. These are transitional strategies in the sense that they allow time for adoption of non-MeBr containing alternatives, but nevertheless they do appear to be technically suitable in many instances. And in some cases, nominations didn't—had not used—these combinations."[24] The MBTOC noted that by supporting CUEs that did not show an attempt to utilize alternative technologies, growers would hesitate to adopt alternatives and producer/researchers of the alternative technologies would be discouraged from furthering their research. Canada, for one, was using a MeBr-chloropicrin mixture that contained too much MeBr. Some U.S.

nominations did not even bother to attempt a mixture of alternatives with MeBr.

Nation-states, however, were divided on how to interpret the MBTOC's findings. Australia mentioned that the task set before the MBTOC was complex, as the nominations often involved various kinds of data to analyze. It inferred that the task was too complex to lead to any conclusive decision by the MBTOC, stating that the MBTOC, the AETF, and the TEAP more broadly defined lacked guidance from the parties and therefore may have made decisions that went against party consent: "Australia believes that parties should provide greater guidance to MBTOC . . . on the process by which nominating parties' responses to MBTOC and TEAP's queries and recommendations on nominations will be addressed in advance of the 15th MOP. We also believe that parties need to work together to further explore the possible options for assessment of economic viability, recognizing the Agricultural Economic Task Force received minimal guidance from parties."[25] Yet it should be noted that the MBTOC's evaluative process was, ostensibly, *objective* and did not consider the subjective wants of the parties. Indeed, Australia's response to the MBTOC report was more reflective of its national interest to maintain economic output in horticulture, whose industry could lose $300 million due to the MeBr phaseout.[26] Nevertheless, several developed countries questioned the objective methods of the MBTOC.

Canada commented on the specific needs of particular users drafted in Decision IX(6). This decision includes the CUE language that considers the needs of particular users of MeBr and the CFC essential use criteria, which consider the needs of the general population. The implication here was that the alternatives to MeBr that worked in one part of the world did not necessarily work in Canada. In the 2003 TEAP report, the MBTOC reported that Canada had asked for the use of MeBr in the production of strawberry runners. The MBTOC supported this nomination in full (eight metric tons), but only for one year. (Strawberry runner nominations were approved in all cases, the United States included.) Canada was applying a MeBr-chloropicrin mixture in strawberry runner production, and the MBTOC recommended that the proportion of MeBr in the mixture be reduced. Canada, however, believed that the MBTOC needed further guidance to make its decision.

This was a paradoxical comment for Canada to make because the Canadian delegation had not provided the MBTOC with enough information in its own nomination, as indicated in the 2003 TEAP report, where the MBTOC stated, "The [Canadian] nomination does not consider the full range of chemical alternatives reported to be effective by MBTOC. The nomination also contains limited research [one private undisclosed study] to support claims and is relying on research in other countries to support the CUE."[27] Therefore, Canada ironically referred to other countries' ostensibly geographically contingent scientific assessments of the applicability of MeBr to justify its own specific case and support its claim that conditions in Canada were specific and particular to Canada. At the 23rd OEWG, the Canadian delegation stated to the plenary, "Unlike other controlled chemicals, technical and economic feasibility of methyl bromide alternatives could be site specific and account for the specific needs of each user. . . . MBTOC largely assumed that the alternatives used in one place, if approved by a government, might be used everywhere. . . . It cannot be assumed that one alternative that is viable within one region of a country is viable in another region, or that an alternative usable in a modern structure can be applied successfully to one that is a century old."[28] On the one hand, Canada was arguing that for MeBr alternatives, it could not be assumed that geography did not matter, but on the other, its reliance on foreign data supported the notion that for MeBr, it could not be assumed that it did. The total number of CUEs requested by Canada was rather small. The Canadian delegation, however, has a tendency to side with the United States on MeBr issues.

The head of the U.S. delegation commented on the MB-TOC presentation after the Canadian delegation, stating that it would acknowledge the outcomes of the MBTOC report on the CUE nominations only as a "learning process." He stated the official position of the United States: "Climatic and soil conditions vary greatly between countries and between regions within countries. . . . MeBr substitutes . . . that are technically and economically feasibly to one user might not be technically or economically feasible to another user. . . . Regulatory restraints on alternative pesticides can limit their use. . . . In California, there are township caps on the emissions of alternatives. So there are significant special circumstances in the United States in addition to the variation of climate and soil that must be addressed by MBTOC."[29] Here the United States made it clear that geographic and legal conditions inhibited the United States from transitioning to MeBr alternatives, and the conditions were indefinite.

The positions of the United States and Canada were not understood by many nation-states. Some delegations representing the industrialized world, such as those in the European Union, are skeptical of the needs presented by these countries. A delegate from the European Union asked me at the 24th OEWG in Geneva, "You live in California. Does the

U.S. really need all those exemptions? I can't understand why."
Another West European delegate exclaimed to me at the meeting, "If it was up to me, [MeBr] would be phased out right
now!"[30]

The 1st ExMOP was held specifically to handle U.S.
nominations for MeBr exemptions because the parties at the
15th MOP could not agree on whether to allow the United
States the quantities of CUEs it had requested and the United
States refused to budge on the matter. The division at the 23rd
OEWG between the United States and the European Union
was still very much evident. The United States had spent the
previous three plenary meetings proclaiming its particular
need for MeBr. It was at the 1st ExMOP that the MBTOC
finally gave in to U.S. demands.

At the meeting, the California Strawberry Commission—
the spokesperson for roughly six hundred strawberry growers,
together producing California's sixth most profitable agrarian
commodity at the time—noted several aspects that allegedly
separated California from other regions/circumstances.[31]
Roger Wasson, then president of the Strawberry Commission
stated the following to the plenary at the 1st ExMOP:

> We have made significant progress in adopting
> alternatives, but they do not work in every circum-
> stances [sic]. For example, technical issues associ-
> ated with extreme slopes, certain soil types, and
> local regulations have all limited our ability to be
> able to transition any more quickly. . . . Our indus-
> try simply cannot make a change of this magnitude
> in this timeframe without serious consequences to
> an industry with 600 growers. . . . Unless we have
> time to develop the infrastructure necessary to

safely and effectively phase in the alternatives on a large scale, long-term progress in adopting alternatives will likely be jeopardized.[32]

At this point, the U.S. delegation asked the MBTOC to respond to the commission's request for more MeBr. Jonathan Banks explained the new recommendation at the 1st ExMOP:

> The MBTOC has looked at a number of nominations which suffer, shall we say, from the same technical problem as the one mentioned by the Strawberry Commission, and that is that while there may be on occasions technical alternatives available, the speed of transition to those alternatives is a barrier, and it is a very real technical barrier where you cannot turn round a single industry in a single day, or a single season, and therefore MBTOC has been very sympathetic and recommends that parties adopt a flexible approach to this particular issue. ... We would certainly wish to support the suggestion of the California Strawberry Commission and the U.S. delegation. ... We would recommend to parties to grant the [critical use nominations].[33]

This response came as quite a shock to the global community. Not only did it appear that the United States was receiving exemptions that were ostensibly specific to particular regions in California, but it was also doing so by the intervention of a representative of the region with its own scientific expertise. The California Strawberry Commission was claiming that its own science was more applicable to its

case than was the science of the global community. The
E.U. delegation responded at the 1st ExMOP exchanges with
bewilderment:

> Some five minutes ago we heard Mr. Wasson from
> the California Strawberry Commission make a case
> for additional tonnage [of MeBr]. We also heard
> the MBTOC co-chair come on and tell the parties
> that there should be a more flexible approach, that
> this application should be examined, and that it
> [i.e., the tonnage requested] would go up again.
> This is a most unfair process that we are going
> through here! This is unfair on our member states
> who do not have people present to argue the case
> for increases in MeBr. We understood that we had a
> process in place when MBTOC was making the
> recommendations. . . . It is a most unusual process
> that we are going through, where we hear the MB-
> TOC co-chair recommending as though it were
> some kind of auction system![34]

This sentiment was also expressed by some MBTOC
members who wished to remain anonymous. "It is so unfair to
the Article (5) parties," one member told me. "They put so
much effort into the alternatives."

Representatives for the California agro-industrial
complex were in effect claiming that the ozone-friendly alternatives identified by global MeBr experts were not applicable
to California and that they would negatively affect its
strawberry growers. Fitting snugly into the discourse of
neoliberalism, the issue raised by the California Strawberry
Commission was framed within notions of individualism,

the decentralization of scientific knowledge, and competition, which would be made "unnaturally" overcompetitive without MeBr in the United States. Here, private interests were able to provide a market-based argument that obviated the scientific claims of the MBTOC. Parallel to the argument that neoliberalism also involves the usage of private knowledge based on particular sites and expertise networks instead of global knowledge or broad social concerns, the stakeholders themselves were providing a voice for groups in California that required representation in the neoliberal context.[35]

The E.U. dismay over how the MBTOC had responded to the U.S. demands would lead to tensions that carried forward to subsequent meetings, where the European Union would continue to try to reduce U.S. exemptions. At the 16th MOP in Prague in 2004, the European Union was again a strong opponent of the quantity of U.S. CUEs on the table. The issue remained largely unresolved throughout the meeting and ultimately required a second ExMOP.

DEADLOCK THROUGH POLITICS: UNITED STATES VS. THE EUROPEAN UNION

Irresolution on the MeBr issue contributed to another, entirely unrelated, delay. The European Union voiced its opposition to essential use exemptions for CFC-containing MDIs, an issue that it might have readily supported if willing to cooperate with the United States. The opposition was perplexing to the United States, as it had consulted with the European Union over the course of several months about the legal constraints it faced on this issue. A U.S. delegate stated in plenary at the 16th MOP, "We have had more bilateral discussion with the European Union than I have had with my

wife in the last several months. We have told them everything
the United States could possibly tell them about the domestic
and regulatory situation in the U.S. and the concerns that the
U.S. have [*sic*] for public health that we have to balance against
the concerns here in the Protocol."[36] The United States accused
the European Union of stalling on this issue by calling into
question what appeared to be a very straightforward proposal
by noting that some data were missing on emissions quantities
for MDIs. It noted that the parties that had provided emissions data should have their nominations move forward.
Paul Horwitz of the U.S. delegation stated, "If there were any
[countries] that the [European Community] would like to
point to that did not include with their submissions emissions
data, then let us delete them now." The TEAP intervened by
stating that the data were available for some of the nominations, specifically for nominations from the industrialized
countries like the United States. Yet the European Union
refused to budge, wanting to push the entire issue forward to
the next OEWG.[37]

The United States believed this stance was an attempt
by the European Union to stop the United States from
getting what it wanted on the MDI issue perhaps because of
the U.S. position on the MeBr issue—specifically its pending
attempt to obtain multiple-year exemptions to the MeBr
phaseout (see below). The United States stated at the 16th
MOP, "E.C., the data is [*sic*] in the report! Have you had an
opportunity to look at the report? It's been available for a
number of weeks now. ... We don't understand the need
to delay this for another six months or however amount
of time."[38]

When the European Union did not budge, the United
States responded to the plenary:

Just so we understand how we are going to be operating . . . , are we going to be putting brackets
around each other's proposals from here on out
through the meeting, because if that is how we are
going to be operating during the meeting, then we
would like to understand exactly the rules of how
we are moving forward. We thought we had work
to do here and that we were going to be moving
forward on the work that the parties had before
them. We are lacking an understanding of what's
going on. . . . We are wondering if this is part of a
tactic in order to await a final decision on other
outstanding issues that are taking place during this
meeting? And if that is the case, then we just want
to understand because we understand how to move
forward in that way too.[39]

The threat from the United States did not dissuade
the European Union. Instead, it attempted to express the
relative size of the opposition the United States faced. The
European Union, after all, features the world's largest
economy.[40] Rather than simply noting, as it customarily
did, that the E.U. delegate spoke on behalf of its twenty-five
member-states (twenty-seven member-states by 2007), the
delegation instead responded to the United States in the
plenary session by denoting the members in a more flamboy-
ant fashion:

On behalf of Austria, Belgium, Cyprus, Czech
Republic, Denmark, Estonia, Finland, Germany,
Ireland, Italy, Hungary, Latvia, Lithuania, Luxem-
bourg, Malta, Netherlands, Poland, Portugal,

Slovenia, Slovakia, Spain, Sweden, the United Kingdom, France, and Greece, Mr. Co-Chair, we, the E.C. delegation, strongly support this nomination going forward as the essential use nomination for 2005 and 2006. We understand that alternatives are available in the United States, there are CFC-free alternatives available, and therefore in TEAP's suggestion for review in 2006, it's very clear to us that TEAP would like the opportunity of a further review of the CFCs for 2006. We think that the suggestion put forward by the co-chair of TEAP to hold a discussion between the United States and the E.C. is a reasonable suggestion.[41]

The United States was not amused: "On behalf of Maine and Vermont and New Hampshire and Massachusetts, Connecticut and New York [laughter from the plenary], and the other forty-four states of the United States of America and its territories, and its possessions, and its commonwealths, we want to clarify again how we are supposed to have this meeting with the E.C."[42]

The exchanges noted above point to some of the immense obstacles that exist to any efficient resolution. Issues unresolved in one area postpone issues in another. In the cases above, the European Union has taken the position of an environmentalist, aware that alternatives to both MeBr and CFC-containing MDIs exist, but the United States has been slow in adopting them. While the MDI issue may have been valid from a legal perspective—legal procedures in the United States were simply slowing the process—the MeBr problem is more rooted in an economic problem: competition.

COMPETITION IN STRAWBERRIES
CAUSING E.U./U.S. TENSIONS

Historically, the United States has been the dominant player in global strawberry production.[43] With a sophisticated network of research and development, high levels of investment, major research investment from the land-grant University of California, politically powerful grower-distributors, and strong government support to the agro-chemical industry for generations, California became the epicenter of global strawberry production. This system, based on the use of MeBr as a pre-plant fumigant, enabled the "California Model" to dominate both the domestic and high-value global markets.[44]

The advent of MeBr as a chemical technology in the 1960s was instrumental to the creation of California's strawberry agro-industrial complex—the interaction of ecological, technological, social, political, and economic relationships that enabled the intensive regional production of strawberries. The production complex emerged as a result of scientific research by the University of California (and some private agro-industrial companies), the availability of Mexican labor and its communities, and specific ecological conditions. California's share of U.S. strawberry production increased from 53 percent in 1970 to over 80 percent by 2007. Production takes advantage of the area's unique ecology, which permits a long strawberry growing season: well-drained soils, wet and mild winters, and low rainfall amid mild weather in the summer months. Yet these same conditions also create an environment conducive to the pests and diseases that MeBr is designed to eradicate. Strawberries are particularly sensitive to *Verticillium dahliae,* and in the pre-MeBr era, *Verticillium* wilt was a major limiting factor to strawberry production.

Figure 1. Strawberry field tarped for MeBr fumigation, primarily
to prevent *Verticillium* wilt, and view of adjacent community near
Watsonville, California. (Photo by author.)

Today it poses the greatest threat for nonchemical strawberry
production.[45]

Fumigation with MeBr controls multiple pathogens and
weeds, allowing for dense planting of strawberries in large
acreages over many seasons, with little or no crop rotation.
Further, the effectiveness of MeBr has meant that breeding for
disease resistance has not been a major focus of programs at
the University of California or proprietary firms since the
1960s.[46] MeBr-based strawberry growing has provided
sufficiently high returns to enable the agricultural sector to
preserve agricultural land and to discourage land being
converted to housing developments and shopping centers.

Figure 2. Application tractor preparing strawberry field for MeBr injection near Watsonville, California. (Photo by author.)

Coastal California strawberry growing is, therefore, a unique, regional, high-value, fresh-commodity production complex that has depended heavily, if not entirely, on the availability of a particular chemical technology.

California strawberry growing regions are also unique in their strong and multifaceted social and demographic links to particular regions of Mexico. Historically the California strawberry growing has relied heavily on inexpensive Mexican labor, originating from communities in the Mexican states of Michoacan, Jalisco, and Guanajuato.[47] Nonetheless, high wages, coupled with increasing land rents in

Figure 3. Strawberry field post-MeBr fumigation after strawberry transplants were planted into beds near Moss Landing, California. (Photo courtesy of Joji Muramoto.)

Coastal California, have driven California producers to allevi-ate economic pressures by developing export-oriented production in Mexico, accessing inexpensive labor and land costs and extending the growing season to nine months of the year. Also, due to its Article 5 status, Mexico has a ten-year extension in MeBr use beyond that of the United States, making extension into Mexico even more attractive.

Over the years, conventional MeBr alternatives have either not been vigorously sought or have proven difficult to implement. For example, there are township caps on the

Figure 4. Strawberry field with workers harvesting near Watsonville, California. (Photo by author.)

quantity of 1,3-Dichloropropene (trade name Telone) that is allowed due to its toxicity and ability to persist in water; chloropicrin (a World War II war gas) has been the subject of pesticide drift fiascos and is considered an inferior product; and the newest substitute, methyl iodide, is controversial and considered by many chemists to be entirely too dangerous for large-scale use. The California Coastkeeper Alliance has stated that methyl iodide "has been identified as being four times more neurotoxic than the methyl bromide it replaces."[48]

The United States has needed to persuade other countries that MeBr is essential for strawberry production, even though many nations have virtually eliminated it from their own production platforms. The primary reason why the United States needs MeBr, however, is that it helps it maintain an advantage vis-à-vis competitors in Europe and China. European competitors, centered in Spain, have been able to produce and distribute strawberries to Europe's most affluent countries. Yet the European production complex was historically dependent on the California Model. European grower-distributors have depended on U.S.-patented strawberry varieties, which make up the bulk of their production costs. In an attempt to be more competitive, both the California and European production complexes have extended production into adjacent less-developed countries: California into Baja California, Mexico, and Spain into Morocco.[49] Extension farther south in turn extends the growing season with lower labor costs. Conjointly with the U.S. system, the European system is under a great deal of pressure. Because of its history of dependency on the California Model, it suffered from a methyl bromide–dependent production mechanism. Growers in Spain and Morocco claim that the alternatives to MeBr do not work well enough to justify switching to an alternative.[50] Consequently, Spain also appealed to the international community for exemptions to the phaseout of methyl bromide. Due to the successful U.S. request for CUEs, the European Union successfully bargained for CUEs for Spain, although in quantities dwarfed by the U.S. exemptions. While Morocco may continue to use MeBr until 2015, the CUE requests for Spain were terminated in 2008, so production there has become MeBr-free.[51]

 In its own strawberry agro-industrial complex, the European Union has been decidedly more proactive than the United States. In 1998 it established "COST Action 836" to promote the development of strawberry production systems designed to guarantee reliable strawberry production in Europe, secure in economic terms for the producers and in terms of safety and quality for the consumers. Currently, greenhouse companies (such as Viveros California) operating in Spain and Swiss research labs in Hungary are joining efforts to develop strawberry varieties adapted to regional conditions in Spain and Morocco for the European market and to end reliance on costly patented California varieties.[52] Plants are shipped from Huelva, Spain in refrigerated trucks to Morocco, where they are planted using the system that is used in Huelva. In Huelva, strawberry production used to depend entirely on North and West African labor, but recently the government of Spain has initiated a series of state-to-state "guest worker" agreements with Romania and Poland to bring workers to Huelva and Larache. Currently, more than 20,000 workers (primarily women) are transported from Romania, another 8,000–9,000 from Poland, and another few hundred from Morocco. Many of these workers are illegal, a problem that replicates California's dilemma with undocumented agricultural workers.[53]

China has risen rapidly as the site of a third strawberry agro-industrial production complex. In less than five years, it entered full force into the global frozen strawberry market.[54] Frozen production pushed China into a very important position in global strawberry production, where it presently sells in high volume to European, U.S., and Asian markets. Chinese strawberry production is much less dependent on MeBr than is production in the United States, a factor that may work to its benefit. This "emerging superpower" is seen as a serious economic threat to both the U.S. and European strawberry production systems.

Until the 1990s strawberry production in China was very limited, but by 1997 fresh strawberries were available to consumers in every city in the country. In 1985, the total area planted in strawberries was only 3,300 hectares (ha), about 2 percent of the area under cultivation worldwide. By 1995, the area reached 36,700 ha, or 14 percent of that in the world. By 2003, it increased to 77,300 ha, or about 30 percent of worldwide production, making China the world's greatest strawberry producing country. According to the USDA, strawberry production acreage in China in 2009 was estimated at 120,000 ha.[55]

Rapidly increasing strawberry exports from China have instigated protectionism from competitors. On July, 6, 2005, the European Union published a notice of initiation of a safeguard investigation concerning imports of frozen strawberries from the Chinese mainland. The issue was raised by Poland—the other country in the European Union that, along with Spain, requested MeBr CUEs until 2008—which complained that Chinese imports could endanger its domestic production. By 2005 over 25 million pounds (over 11.3 million kilograms) of fresh strawberries were produced annually worldwide, and California growers were struggling to compete in the frozen markets of Europe and China, while China had boosted its own exports. China has at its disposal powerful economic tools—extensive land, cheap labor, high levels of foreign direct investment, and a "market-socialism" system of intense market activity via state-centered development. China can produce strawberries without the plant varieties central to the California Model and is therefore much less dependent on MeBr than the United States.[56]

China is now undertaking an extensive breeding program to increase yields with new varieties tailored to conditions in its major production regions. There are over two hundred different varieties of strawberries grown in China. Most growers propagate plants on-farm or buy plants from other growers who do so. China is also actively developing a higher-value fresh strawberry production platform—a "cold chain" for transporting fresh berries over long distances. In addition, Chinese researchers, in conjunction with U.C.–Santa Cruz researchers, are actively working on developing viable organic varieties that may be important for emerging sustainable regimes of accumulation. Major topics at the nationwide Conference of Strawberry Production in China in 2007 included "Safe Production of Strawberries," "New Variety Breeding," and "Producing Organic Strawberries."[57]

It cannot be stressed enough that China's growth in strawberry production is perceived as a threat to California's hegemony. With a surplus of cheap labor and extensive land and state investment, China can produce lower-yielding strawberries competitively.[58] China's strawberry acreage is already six times greater than California's, albeit with productivity only one-third that of California. Nevertheless, China is now the leading strawberry-producing nation in the world.

As economic threats from China and the European Union have increased, the United States has had to stretch more thinly its interpretation of the Montreal Protocol's Decision IX/6. The alternatives to MeBr will have to do more than simply replace the ODS in a way that avoids market disruptions; they will have to do so in a way that will allow the United States to outcompete foreign producers. While the United States has come nearer to the end of its MeBr usage (receiving just over two thousand metric tons in CUEs for 2012), the lack of a longer vision and pressures from the conventional strawberry agro-industrial complex have forced

Figure 5. Sign warning passersby of an MeBr-treated strawberry
field near Watsonville, California. (Photo by author.)

it to replace MeBr with extremely toxic chemicals such as
1,3-Dichloropropene and methyl iodide. "Market disruptions,"
as understood in Decision IX/6, as well as regional socio-
ecological disruptions, are likely to continue in the United
States.

Tensions among Industrialized and
Less-Developed Countries

As global powers struggled over CUEs, the LDCs grew
more skeptical with each passing Protocol meeting. Indirectly,
the CUE process in the industrialized world provoked the

LDCs to delay any discussion of phasing out MeBr in their own countries until the industrialized world could convince them that the MeBr alternatives indeed worked.[59] Moreover, the LDCs appeared to feel threatened by the position taken by the United States, concerned that CUEs would give it an unfair economic advantage. Whether or not they produced strawberries, many LDCs voiced opposition to the protectionist U.S. position in an ostensibly neoliberal global economy. For example, Costa Rica commented:

> We signed an agreement for the speedy elimination [of MeBr] with the understanding that non–Article 5 countries would do away with the use of MeBr and only leave very small quantities, which we would consider "critical use." . . . I was struck by what was said by Canada, that we should not mix up commercial matters. Well, the whole day we have been talking about commercial matters; when we say that it is not competitive for farmers in any country to use an alternative, we are talking about commerce, trade. We are saying that they will not be able to sell their products, and that is commerce. . . . I cannot imagine a Mexican farmer, producing without MeBr, who is competing with a U.S. farmer who is using MeBr. Mexico would be at a great disadvantage. . . . We will not eliminate use [of MeBr] if other countries, our partners, don't do so. It is a matter of defining what the rules of the game are going to be for everyone.[60]

Debates surrounding MeBr certainly seem reflective of competition among regions in strawberry production, as described above. Both civil society groups and less powerful nation-states have had difficulty influencing decision making to move beyond concerns over competition to address the need to protect the ozone layer. Rather, conventional strawberry constituencies in the United States and MeBr producers/distributors seem the most powerful actors influencing policy.

Although less powerful in decision making, LDCs were able to stall progress on proposals that might have ultimately weakened their political economic positions given the U.S. CUEs. They effectively halted any discussion of strategies to help coordinate the phaseout of MeBr for their target date of 2015. Consequently, the U.S. CUEs indirectly could hinder the phaseout of ODSs worldwide.

While industrialized countries argued over the efficacy of MeBr alternatives, the LDC efforts remained stagnant. Some LDCs argued that the CUEs were an attempt by the United States to extend their dependency on the U.S. market. Others remained mute due to their need to comply with the political positions of global powers. For example, at the 15th MOP in Nairobi in 2003, when interviewing a delegate for a European country hoping to enter the European Union, I asked what his country thought of the U.S. position on MeBr. "It is ridiculous. [The U.S.] claims are ridiculous," was the reply. When I asked why countries that disagree with the U.S. position do not say more in plenary, the delegate stated, "We can't. . . . We received a $500,000 loan from the [MLF]. You know who funds the MLF, yes?" I did. The United States is the most generous donor to the MLF, providing funds to help countries transition to ODS-free alternatives. Sometimes the money is used to buy ODS-free chillers (such as refrigerators, air conditioners, and industrial cooling products) or to test the efficacy of MeBr alternatives in strawberry, date, or tomato production. I asked whether the MeBr issue was really about strawberries. "It is about lots of money," was the reply. If that is the case, I asked, then why was Israel not here, the home of MeBr chemical giant Dead Sea Bromine, supporting its economic interests? (Delegates from Israel had not attended the last two meetings, I observed.) The delegate laughed. "They are represented through other avenues. Their job is done here." He meant that pressure for MeBr exemptions from the United States assured a victory for Israel.

After the United States disagreed with the MBTOC's report on the efficacy of alternatives to MeBr in strawberry and tomato production at the 23rd OEWG, LDCs expressed negative sentiments about what such an impasse would mean for their own economies. Chile noted that the U.S. position seemed contradictory: "Our concern lies in the fact that from a political point of view, this [impasse] is not sustainable at all. . . . You have certain crops in Article 5 countries which are being used in the developed countries, and yet in one they are not critical uses and in the other [industrialized countries] they are critical uses, so we could say that these exemptions should be applied across the board. . . . We cannot imagine that such an important aspect as the phaseout of MeBr, and as it is applied in our country without proper alternatives, could be treated completely differently . . . [in] other countries and that they be allowed to continue using MeBr."[61] In short, Chile was cautioning that it would seek CUEs for MeBr when the time came. Uganda went as far as to question whether MeBr should be phased out at all, proposing to incorporate CUEs into any provision for the scheduled phaseout of MeBr.

The fear of not being able to compete with non–Article 5 (i.e., industrialized) countries without MeBr is indeed a major concern for most LDCs. Chile, Guatemala, Costa Rica,

Uganda, Iran, and Saint Lucia all expressed open concern at plenary about the potential need for future CUEs for certain applications of MeBr. Uganda in particular stated the need for ironclad proof that MeBr alternatives would work in its specific case.[62]

The Dominican Republic expressed some of the most profound criticism of the U.S. CUE nominations. Its response might represent the case for other LDCs in similar situations. For instance, it portrayed a sense of distress over its apparent dependent status as a small-scale producer with a rather weak agrarian-based economy. Noting the extreme dependency it feels in terms of technology transfer and market access to the industrialized North, the Dominican Republic stated:

> Article 5 countries have always been behind non–Article 5 countries; we all know that. Pretty much all the technology that we have in the world, especially methyl bromide technology, has been developed by Article 2 countries really. All the various processes that we use and apply in various models or pilot projects were basically based on a replica of what we've learned from Article 2 countries. And the same could be said when it comes to the search for alternatives. We have some doubts, this being the case, with regard to the increasing demand for CUEs for methyl bromide. *It seems to us as if the very concept of CUE is one way of extending a certain period of domination, if you will.* . . . Article 5 countries are making great efforts to take on and shoulder their responsibilities, finding alternatives for methyl bromide. This scenario could create a direct impact on trading relationships among Article 5

countries and between Article 5 and Article 2 countries. . . . Trade relationships that have been derived
from the purchase and sale of products which require the use of methyl bromide are not necessarily
developing along lines that favor or encourage the
development of the economies in our countries. . . .
It seems to me that TEAP has to not only carry
out very excellent technical work, as they did here,
but also go much more in depth into the issue
of trade and economic issues related to the phaseout of methyl bromide. . . . Nobody can assure us
that this particular mechanism is innocuous,
will not damage our economies. There are many
countries involved in the same situation, and very
few of us are willing to talk about it. . . . We
are coming from a poor country and we are trying
to take on our responsibilities. This is a major responsibility.[63]

The Dominican Republic noted here that the phaseout
of MeBr could be harmful to the LDCs if CUEs were approved
for the developed countries. As reported by the MBTOC, the
MLF had funded projects on alternatives to MeBr that demonstrated promising results. Any country that receives MLF
funding must abide by the phaseout schedule set in place for
LDCs. The LDCs, therefore, were very worried that they would
be bound to a phaseout strategy that could ultimately hinder
their export of certain crops, while the United States would
continue to use the very substance it had funded the MLF to
eliminate.

China likewise expressed profound critiques of the U.S.
nominations that reflected its unique position in the global

economy. Indeed, its comments reflected those of an agrarian economy with large export capability but also with a growing economy that competes on a larger scale with developed countries. In effect, China's response portrays the unique character of a powerful emerging "semi-periphery," demonstrating huge strides in productivity based on a combination of agrarian and industrial production, capital accumulation, increasing middle-class consumption, cheap natural resources, a large labor pool, and influential trading partners.[64] China's response was more straightforward than any other:

> [The MBTOC's] work has enabled us to be aware of the situation we are faced with. . . . Firstly, now we have a lot of non–Article 5 countries that have applied for [critical use] exemptions. I think there must be some objective problems, or difficulties, in obtaining substitutes or replacements [for MeBr], so [the developed countries] ask for some delay in the implementation process; after they find some really replaceable technologies, they will do their job. Now, for the Article 5 countries, I think these countries are going to face some of these problems in the next few years. . . . Secondly, considering the complex nature of this issue, we should be cautious, especially in the first two years. . . . TEAP and Article 2 countries should try to help develop substitute technologies. . . . In that way, I think we can gradually phase out, or reduce, consumption. . . . We fully appreciate and support [the Dominican Republic's] statement. I think their statement reflected a very serious and realistic problem. In the past few years, some Article 5 countries already

started the process of phaseout of methyl bromide. Some of them are even completed! Article 2 countries, they consume a lot, some consume up to sixteen thousand [metric tons] of [MeBr]. I think that may give rise to some unfair practices in terms of trade. . . . If we want to exempt those big consuming countries, while at the same time we ask the Article 5 countries to complete the phaseout, what kind of unfair scenario are we going to be faced with? . . . Article 5 countries seem to be leading the way, and the Article 2 countries are lagging behind! [Laughter among the plenary.] This is not very fair. It should be the reverse order![65]

China's position appealed to those countries and other groups that were interested in eliminating MeBr because it called for CUEs to be eliminated in the United States.

China, as noted, is much less dependent on MeBr than some Article 2 countries. If the alternatives were indeed less viable, China would have a distinct advantage over the United States and would uphold Decision IX/6. However, if there are no significant differences between MeBr and its alternatives and market disruption is simply due to China's "more efficient" strawberry production platform, then the decision would not be upheld, at least as it is interpreted by several delegates and most MBTOC members.

The controversy over the interpretation of the alternatives has resulted in the approval of CUEs year after year. Another deleterious outcome was a halt in any discussion of the phaseout of MeBr in the LDCs. Efforts by the European Union to organize a phaseout strategy have been halted completely, both directly by the LDCs and indirectly by the United States.

TENSIONS CAUSING POTENTIAL PROBLEMS WITH
LDC PHASEOUTS

The European Union not only opposes the United States
on its sizable MeBr CUEs, but it also opposes the LDCs on
their reluctance to discuss their future MeBr phaseouts. It
believes that LDC phaseout efforts would be helpful in several
ways. In one important way, their efforts would help the LDCs
maintain access to European markets, which have a highly
informed, pro-environment and anti-MeBr civil society base
and which would otherwise be closed to them: "There is
a need to avoid developed country boycotts of methyl
bromide-treated imports. According to previous reports, it is
possible that supermarkets and consumers will avoid food
imports known to be treated with methyl bromide. Some large
supermarket chains in Europe now require the growers to be
certified by specialized agencies that food delivered to the
supermarket has been produced without methyl bromide.
Some developing countries with export programs have voluntarily signed into early phaseouts, citing boycotts as one of the
main reasons for doing this. . . . There is a need to continue
this momentum."[66] The European Union has put proposals on
the table that would assist LDCs in organizing their phaseout
schedules. For instance, it submitted a proposal at the 23rd
OEWG to be considered for discussion at the 15th MOP
(CRP.21), and it was discussed there (UNEP/OzL.Pro.15/3/
Add.1) and was subsequently debated at the 24th OEWG.

The E.U. proposal, item 24/6 of the 24th OEWG agenda
(UNEP/OzL.Pro.WG.1/24/6), was an adjustment to the interim reductions in MeBr, and it received a great deal of attention
and controversy. The existing phaseout for LDCs is currently
set at a freeze in consumption based on 1995–1998 averages, a

20 percent reduction in consumption in 2005, and then a phaseout of the remaining 80 percent in 2015. Such a drastic phaseout seemed easier said than done for most LDCs. Tom Batchelor, a previous MBTOC member and then head of the E.U. delegation, presented the E.U. proposal:

> At the Nairobi Meeting of the Parties of November 2003, a contact group decided that smaller reductions of 10–20 percent spaced about two years apart would be more manageable. The three steps agreed in the contact group were reported to that Meeting of the Parties, which proposed a 20 percent reduction in each of the years 2008 and 2010, and then a 10 percent reduction set in 2012. This would leave 30 percent of the MeBr available for the last years until phaseout in 2015. . . . Currently the MLF is funding projects to meet the 20 percent reduction in 2005. There are no other reduction steps in place after this date, except for the phaseout in 2015. The MLF therefore has no requirement to consider funding of the reductions of MeBr after 2005. . . . Many countries agree that it is difficult to go from 80 percent of MeBr. . . . to phaseout in one year. Small downward steps are more manageable and are important for achieving the end result.[67]

The European Union proposed that a contact group be established. However, with the United States requesting enormous exemptions, the LDCs remained skeptical about such a proposal. In fact, the only LDC to voice its support for the E.U. proposal was South Korea, which does not use any MeBr at all. However, South Korea expressed concern for other LDCs "regarding the use of critical use exemptions in non–Article 5 parties" and asked that their concerns be addressed.[68]

Nigeria, speaking on behalf of all African countries, expressed concern for CUEs: "The caveat here is [that] whatever agreement we will have, there should be some provision that will lay out a process for the Article 5 countries for the CUEs." Barbados, speaking on behalf of all Latin American and Caribbean countries, stated that the proposal was untimely: "Since the last Extraordinary Meeting of the Parties, the situation has remained unchanged. There has been no decrease in the level of [CUE nominations for MeBr] requests, and we would wish to see a clear indication of the phaseout of MeBr before making such determinations."[69]

Mexico, the second-largest consumer of MeBr of all the LDCs, consuming almost 1,800 metric tons in 2002 (second only to China's 1,813 metric tons) pointed toward the source of LDC skepticism about any interim reduction in MeBr usage. The LDCs decided that the E.U. proposal would be discussed only when "there was a clear trend . . . particularly when Article 2 countries were ending their use of MeBr. . . . For Mexico, we don't feel that we can make progress if we don't have clear, co-responsibility in the elimination of MeBr, and therefore Mexico emphatically supports the statements expressed by the delegation of Barbados."[70]

Tunisia, Chile, Guatemala, Argentina, Kenya, Peru, Brazil, Jordan, and Colombia all rejected the E.U. proposal in plenary. For Colombia, "the issue of principle is involved. Obviously, we consider it as important to take into account the objective of the Montreal Protocol to reduce, indeed to eliminate, ODSs, including MeBr. . . . We feel that we all need to have the same desire to eliminate the use of MeBr, but we don't feel that it is the time to consider additional timetables for reduction steps for Article 5 countries, taking into account [what effect] this could have for the current efforts of Article 5 countries if extensions for critical uses were accorded to other countries." Argentina likewise remarked, "We are once again faced with a very high volume of critical uses, and therefore . . . we recognize the impact of critical use exemptions. This delegation hopes that when countries which have presented critical use nominations present these strategies for national management . . . the situation will change and that we will then be able to see whether we can move on to adopting such an interim timetable."[71]

Kenya spoke of concerns related to its potential requests for CUEs in the future: "While Kenya supports the proposal in principle, we still feel that there has got to be a fairly level playing ground for all parties involved in this game. . . . As we are struggling with all the attendant problems to meeting these obligations, we also realize that our good development partners . . . are asking for critical use exemptions. . . . We have to be very clear . . . as we are trying to implement the obligations under the convention, [and] we want to be assured . . . that when our time comes for requesting critical use exemptions, there will not be a problem. There will never be a bottleneck put in the way of Article 5 countries. . . . The ground must remain level." Kenya also raised concerns related to the uneven phaseout schedule of MeBr in the LDCs and the developed world, attempting to put forth an amendment that would inhibit parties to the Protocol from restricting trade in products from LDCs solely because the products had been treated with MeBr. Yet some developed countries (i.e., the United States and Canada) felt that the suitable place to raise such concerns was through the WTO, not the Montreal Protocol. Brazil noted that it was understandable that LDCs were adopting a cautionary approach to this proposal "when there is no clear signal that the consumption of MeBr covered by [critical use nominations] will represent a downward trend."[72]

In effect, with CUEs in the developed world, primarily the United States, progress to eliminate MeBr worldwide is greatly threatened. Although the MBTOC reported at the 23rd OEWG that alternatives to MeBr were "comparable," CUEs were still deemed justifiable, especially for the countries that had led the CFC phaseout and contained the most advanced technologies in MeBr alternatives. Moreover, the LDCs were well aware that not only was the United States requesting CUEs for MeBr in strawberry and tomato production, but at the 24th OEWG the United States would also request *multiple-year exemptions*, a proposal it had introduced at the 1st ExMOP with little success. It is very possible that the European Union put forth the proposal for interim reductions in MeBr in the LDCs in order to expose the unsuitability of the U.S. multi-year exemption proposal; it certainly seemed to generate animosity toward U.S. attempts to achieve indefinite high-volume exemptions to the MeBr phaseout.

U.S. ATTEMPTS AT MULTI-YEAR EXEMPTIONS
AND LDC BACKLASH

During the first day of the 24th OEWG, the MBTOC reported on its assessment of CUEs to the MeBr phaseout for 2005 and 2006. This report followed the 1st ExMOP, which had ended in the parties granting the United States its requested CUE amount in full. The LDCs remained highly skeptical of U.S. requests for exemptions, making strong accusations about the apparent U.S. refusal to utilize proven alternatives to MeBr. Previously, the United States had noted that there were legal restrictions on alternatives to MeBr use in California, such as township caps on agro-chemicals such as chloropicrin. This time, however, the MBTOC took into consideration such restrictions: "One area that we do see as needing to allow a critical use nomination is where local regulations prohibit the use of otherwise available alternatives. MBTOC recognized that registration and local regulations can be constraints on the availability of particular chemicals to the end user, in the sense of Decision IX/6, which is the requirement for CUEs. . . . Regulations and local constraints continue to be a major problem with the implementation of alternatives."[73]

Well aware of the constraints parties like the United States were under in terms of local regulations, Japan commented that "we are afraid that . . . parties try to get CUEs as much as possible, resulting in giving less incentive to develop and deploy the alternatives." Barbados, speaking on behalf of GRULAC, expressed concern over the high level of CUEs once again requested by the developed world. The LDCs were aware of "the negative impact that high levels of critical use nominations [had] on the efforts being undertaking by [the LDCs] to phase out MeBr. The volumes being requested of exemptions currently show no sign of decreasing. In this respect, the Group of Latin America and the Caribbean wishes to see a more strict application of Decision IX/6 in the analysis of critical use nominations."[74]

The United States wasted no time in responding. It noted the progress that it and other industrialized countries had made thus far, eliminating the majority of ODSs. It also noted that when dealing with the final amounts of a substance in need of phaseout, "it is axiomatic that it is often the hardest percent to get, and sometimes some countries have problems. So how do we deal with those problems? . . . Countries are going much faster where they can to phase out MeBr. .... We would like the understanding of our colleagues if . . . we are having some difficulties."[75] Yet it was the fact that the LDCs were not moving faster with their phaseout schedules that was so worrisome.

If the risks with alternatives were as great as the United States feared, then the LDCs did not wish to reap that bitter harvest when their time came. As noted by the Dominican Republic, such a situation could recreate a form of dependency on the United States, where competition in strawberries, tomatoes, etc., would be tilted more heavily in favor of the latter. The LDCs appeared somewhat prepared to vote against such large exemptions from the United States, who responded to Barbados in a way that clearly laid out its power: "We would note that in just three and a half years, all of our Article 5 parties can have the ability to request [critical] use exemptions from this body. The question we would like you to consider is this: Would you like this body to be extremely harsh and critical of your requests, or would instead you like a reasonable standard to prevail?" The United States was threatening to stop any CUE nominations from LDCs that opposed the U.S. nominations. Such threats seem counterproductive. The amount that the United States continued to use was only slightly smaller than the total amount of MeBr used by the top fifteen consuming LDCs. The LDCs were well aware of this imbalance.[76]

On the next day of the 24th OEWG at plenary, the United States again made an attempt at passing an amendment for multiple-year exemptions for MeBr. It had put forth this proposal at the two previous meetings, to no avail. Given the U.S. attitude toward the LDCs and E.U. opposition to the high volume of U.S. CUEs, support here seemed unlikely. The

United States, as put by the co-chair of the 24th OEWG, proposed that "when a critical use exemption was agreed with a particular level of production and consumption for 2005, the country could also request the *same exemption for 2006 and 2007.*" The United States commented that there were a number of advantages to multi-year CUEs: "First, multi-year approvals would provide greater certainty to the user community with respect to the availability of needed pest and weed control methods . . . [and] provide advanced notice to farmers on the availability of MeBr so that they can make informed business decisions for the future. Second, multi-year approvals could provide greater certainty to other parties that CUE applicants are taking appropriate steps to phase out MeBr use, and . . . that progress is being made in that process over a longer period of time, rather than simply viewing it on a year-to-year basis as we currently do in evaluating [CUE] applications." The United States also commented that the multi-year approval process would "streamline" the MBTOC's work and "reduce the burden on parties" at the meetings.[77]

Nigeria commented that "[first] we should see in this [proposal] provisions for *declining* consumption. . . . Second, there should be provision for a clear cut-out date. It cannot just continue endlessly." Later, when the United States presented the proposal again in revised form, incorporating Nigeria's (and other governments') concerns with a slight downward trend, the LDCs expressed more skepticism. Indeed, some LDCs remained worried about the effect that such a proposal could have on their UV radiation exposure. Chile cautioned that "we are talking about multi-year exemptions, but we have to see how the situation develops. . . . Chile is a country which is very vulnerable to the depletion of the ozone [layer] because we are in the south and we are at high altitude."[78]

The European Union once again voiced its opposition to the U.S. position. It was worried that the United States was attempting to undermine the MBTOC's scientific expertise:

> We understand that MBTOC is to evaluate the whole multi-year program at the beginning, and then it is the responsibility of the nominating party to reduce the amount of MeBr licensed as alternatives become available. If our understanding is correct, this would set up a system where MBTOC is no longer the single evaluator of whether the use of MeBr complies with Decision IX/6, but rather each party with a multi-year nomination annually licenses MeBr based on its own assessment of Decision IX/6. Effectively, this establishes a different Decision IX/6 evaluation system for single- versus multi-year applicants, which might be seen as unfair by many parties.[79]

Neither the U.S. proposal for multi-year exemptions nor the E.U. proposal for interim steps in phasing out MeBr in the LDCs would be adopted at either the 16th MOP or the 2nd ExMOP. The United States gave up on its proposal at the 17th MOP. At the same meeting, the European Union agreed to defer the topic concerning expedited procedures for phasing out MeBr until 2006. Both proposals faced reciprocal opposition, as well as resistance from the LDCs. The outcome: large exemptions to the MeBr phaseout were granted to the United States and there was little preparation for the phaseout process in the LDCs.

The level of uncertainty regarding the future of MeBr created a large gap and generated tension between developed countries and LDCs. While the European Union cautioned that its consumers and shippers might soon import only Me-Br-free produce, U.S. CUEs gave pause to anyone considering a MeBr phaseout strategy. Many LDCs and some MBTOC members believed that the CUEs were (and continue to be) disingenuous, harming both terms of trade and the ozone layer.

As noted, the United States argued that it and other industrialized countries were responsible for phasing out the majority of the world's ODSs, including MeBr. Yet conflating the CFC phaseout with the MeBr phaseout is problematic. The conditions of the CFC phaseout, where a few actors facing potentially significant economic gains worked on developing comparable alternatives, are hugely different from the MeBr case. Unlike CFC alternatives, the comparative efficacy of alternatives to MeBr is not good enough. What indeed appears to be, as the United States put it, "axiomatic" is that the United States cannot afford to relinquish MeBr too hastily because its entire production complex is historically highly dependent upon it. Due to the unsustainable ecological conditions created by MeBr, the MeBr-specific crop varieties used, and the domestic regulation restrictions on alternatives, the United States cannot easily compete globally without MeBr.[80] These factors, combined with cheaper competitive production platforms in Europe and (especially) China, have forced the United States to fight a protectionist battle to continue to use MeBr as long as is necessary.

Next I will illustrate the effect of these disputes on the scientific community and vice versa. As illustrated by sociologists of science, scientific knowledge is far from objective, both created by and creating political controversies at the global and national scales.[81] Members of the MBTOC and TEAP are

often influenced by their countries of origin and their occupa-
tions. While providing expert advice, plenary meetings and
small session debates demonstrate that science can become
very political and that it involves strategies to protect certain
forms of knowledge from other forms of knowledge. Some
U.S. experts call upon local, particularist cases to defend the
extended use of MeBr, while other experts in the European
Union call upon an alternative knowledge platform to defend
the alternatives to MeBr. Here protectionism is as much
about the protection of the legitimacy of particular scientific
knowledge as it is about the protection of the conditions of
strawberry production that provide the United States with a
competitive advantage.

6

The Coproduction of Science/
Knowledge and Politics

Paragraph 4 basically attacks the fundamental premise under which we operate, which is that parties decide whether there are, for example, critical use exemptions granted or not, and the idea that TEAP would decide is not acceptable.

—*Canadian delegation, 1st ExMOP, 2004*

Contributions in the sociology and politics of science and technology have long questioned the pure objectivity of science, showing that political culture partially determines how science and technology are received and even produced. Differences between U.S. and European receptivity to science and technology, Sheila Jasanoff argues, "cannot be explained in terms of discrepant ideologies, national interests, policy priorities, or states of technological development." The differences, rather, also include "the systematic practices by which a nation's citizens come to know things in common and to apply their knowledge to the conduct of politics." So, in fact, "culturally specific ways of knowing" can shape state politics in ways that do not necessarily reflect state and/or capitalist interests.[1] One has only to read the major newspapers of New York and London to get a sense of the different public attitudes in the United States and Europe toward major issues such as stem cell research, trade in genetically modified organisms, and global climate change; such issues seem to shape political strategies differently in the two regions.[2] Even on the issue of ozone depletion, while there is a sizable reaction to climate change in the United States, there simply is no groundswell of public or private action in defense of the ozone layer, but there appears to be so in parts of the European Union. As we have seen, public opinion in Europe might even lead to citizens rejecting commodities produced with MeBr, a possibility that outrages LDCs, which are scheduled to use MeBr at least until 2015. In the United States, opposition does not exist to a similar extent. U.S. consumers on the whole have appeared rather indifferent to MeBr except where issues of pesticide drift are significant.[3]

When citizens are indifferent (or ignorant) about a particular policy action, the nation-state can often act freely to pursue its political and/or economic interests. Free of citizen awareness, the nation-state might act in ways that remove certain freedoms, or environmental conditions, from its citizenry while bolstering the political economic condition of well-embedded interests, such as the polluter-industrial complex.[4] In such a milieu, the U.S. state would be able to instill a politics of protectionism at the expense of environmental conditions, while the European Union must continue to meet the needs of its political economy *and* address the concerns of its citizenry.

The MeBr case supports claims made by the sociology of science and technology scholars that scientific knowledge and politics are *coproduced* where scientific experts and their findings are subject to political organization, interpretation, dissemination, and legitimization. In global environmental governance, how political actors interpret science can affect how scientists interpret their own work and its applications. In the words of Langdon Winner, the selection of scientific technologies is an "ongoing social process in which scientific knowledge, technological invention, and corporate profit reinforce each other in deeply entrenched patterns, patterns that bear the unmistakable stamp of political and economic power."[5] The MeBr case illustrates how national interests, policy priorities, and states of technological development play significant roles in determining the inclinations of scientific experts housed between U.S., the E.U., and other nations' positions in ozone-related policies.

This is not to say that the social location of scientists, who (it could also be argued) are a part of civil society, is an all-encompassing determination of their political ideologies. Oftentimes, the loyalties of scientists and their networks are not with their home institutions, nor with the politically appointed heads of their institutions, but rather with the broader goals that drive their research. Indeed, the previously formed TOCs were able to maintain their focus on environmental health.[6] The interviews with MeBr experts presented below, however, demonstrate that there is a great deal of pressure on scientists to express the viewpoints of their nation-state delegations, such that scientific knowledge becomes geographically contingent and coproduced with

political and (neoliberal) economic struggles. Thus, although
scientific groups hold a great deal of power due to their
command of "expert knowledge," their capacity to act independently can often be minimal and subject to nation-state
interpretation of science, policy, and economic needs. As
discussed, the delegitimation of the MBTOC reached a low
point in 2003, when the AETF was dissolved, its advice on
how to handle the MeBr CUEs deemed inappropriate and
illegitimate based on the scientific and technical knowledge
of an alternative source provided by U.S. constituents.
Consequently, the MBTOC was forced to change its position
on the U.S. CUE nominations, at the bewilderment of the
European Union and the LDCs.

The MeBr controversy has led to divisions within the
MBTOC itself. Contention between U.S. and E.U. members
reflects a geopolitical division between these two global
powers in a way not evident in previous scientific networks
operating to phase out ODSs. The incorporation of neoliberal
policy into the MBTOC is a primary reason for the tensions.
Also, the tensions reflect the vested interests of some MBTOC
members and put into focus "how science and politics
co-evolve dynamically."[7] The MeBr controversy shows that
the Montreal Protocol is experiencing the intense insertion
of interest group politics more than has been previously
recorded on this global environmental institution.

Particularist Interpretations of
Protocol Decisions

The U.S. court system's interpretation of MeBr science
provides one example of interactions among scientific expertise, national interests, and economically motivated lobbying.

The Montreal Protocol's Decision IX/6 of 1997, allowing for exemptions to the MeBr phaseout (accompanying Article 2H of the Protocol), states that the parties will be granted an exemption to produce or import MeBr only if "methyl bromide is not available in sufficient quantity and quality from existing stocks."[8] However, in 2004 the EPA disseminated a "Final Rule" that allowed noncritical users of MeBr to access the U.S. stockpile. This was clearly a violation of Montreal Protocol rules and prompted the NRDC to file a suit against the EPA "for failure to comply with Protocol Decisions." The Washington D.C. Circuit Court of Appeals sided with the EPA in stating that the Montreal Protocol decision did not contain any language about the "legally binding" nature of CUEs. Therefore, the Protocol decision had not been written into U.S. law, as the court determined that the ambiguity of the language of the decision spoke to the political nature of the agreement, making it less than legally binding: "The D.C. Circuit deemed the CUE Decision a political matter and entertained the idea that if the Decision had legal effect, the CUE process would be unconstitutional."[9]

However, the Montreal Protocol parties do have the legal authority to sanction U.S. products due to the domestic U.S. interpretation of Protocol amendments. But "given the United States' powerful economic and political status, it is perhaps not surprising that the Protocol Parties have failed to use the Protocol's sanctioning provisions against the United States for this continuing practice of using more methyl bromide than approved by the international organization."[10] The stockpile issue was supposed to disappear rather quickly. In 2007, as other countries raised concerns about the large MeBr stockpiles that the United States held and the fact that over 40 percent of them were not actually being used for CUEs, the

U.S. delegation stated that all stockpiles would be used up by 2009. But 2009 came and went, and still, with full knowledge of stockpiles, MeBr continued to be produced in the United States. In 2010, the final rule by parties to the Protocol on MeBr exemptions allowed over two thousand tons of MeBr to be produced by or imported to the United States. This example shows that policy considerations affect the way scientific evidence is utilized and also how geographically contingent political and economic power affects global environmental governance.[11]

From the Bush administration's point of view, it was in the U.S. national interest to remain competitive in agricultural production at the expense of some environmental costs and impact on global environmental governance. In the Montreal Protocol case the reason for doing so via protectionist measures is directly linked to the U.S. MeBr-dependent agro-industrial production complex. Public pressure and scientific knowledge of alternatives could possibly change the policy objectives of the United States, but to this point they have not. Instead, the international community has bowed to U.S. pressure to use MeBr, where, as happened at the 18th MOP in 2006, and in 2011, nation-states sometimes even "spare[d] the United States steeper cuts that were recommended by the treaty's own technical panel."[12]

Further dialogue in U.S. governmental hearings over the MeBr phaseout reveal how such power has an impact on global scientific knowledge:

> The U.S. agricultural industry has long grumbled about this burdensome application process and argues that the process forces users to request more methyl bromide than they actually need. Many

members of Congress have complained on behalf of their constituents that the critical use exemption approval process is unfair and secretive. In a 2006 congressional hearing held by the House Committee for Government Reform, Representative Darrell Issa of California opened the hearing with his statement that "the [critical use exemption] process is lengthy, unpredictable, expensive, and anything but transparent—and I want to emphasize, anything but transparent." In a 2005 hearing, Representatives Tim Holden of Pennsylvania and Frank Lucas of Oklahoma accused the Methyl Bromide Technical Options Committee of being unfair to the United States. Members of the agricultural industry seem to agree with this accusation, as is overwhelmingly apparent from their testimony year after year in congressional hearings on this topic.[13]

The U.S. agro-chemical industry clearly plays an important role in determining the interpretation and legitimization of science surrounding MeBr in the United States. While the European Union urges countries to phase out MeBr due to consumer boycotts of products harmful to the environment, the United States uses arguments of marketability in order to maintain its use. The division between these two powerful economic blocs has a deep impact on the scientific community.

At the Montreal Protocol, the scientific community is given a very limited official role: to advise nation-states. When the scientific community ventures a suggestion on how to move forward, it is often accused of mixing science with politics. Additionally, tensions among nation-states seem to

become embedded within the scientific network. The interviews below suggest that while scientists often comprise a
facet of civil society, there are evident differences in scientific
understanding about the efficacy of MeBr alternatives that
are often reflective of geopolitical competition/tensions and
political sociological differences. U.S. MBTOC members
maintain the U.S. position that MeBr is needed based on
scientific evidence provided by particular cases in the United
States that support the neoliberal environmental turn,
while E.U. members suggest that it is not, drawing on scientific evidence of MeBr alternatives successfully administered
globally—a global knowledge based more on the principles of
precaution and faith in global regulatory control than free
markets and individualism. MBTOC members working
with the developing world insist that the projects conducted
in the global South and funded by the industrial North prove
that MeBr is unnecessary. A major message here, then, is that
politics and science are coproduced but also that political and
economic struggles influence the interpretation of science/
knowledge, and this interplay can have serious adverse effects
on how scientists interpret themselves.

Discourse at Protocol meetings shows that advice based
on science can be changed dramatically to fit the agendas
of the powerful and that science and politics are mutually
created, or coproduced, long before the scientific community
makes any suggestions for policymakers in plenary
deliberations. Drawing from Foucault, Litfin informs us that
"information is incorporated into preconceived stories and
discourses; it is framed, interpreted, and rhetorically commu-
nicated. . . . Knowledge is embedded in structures of power:
disciplinary power, national power, and socioeconomic
power."[14] As we have seen, MBTOC members are embedded

in such structures perhaps more so than other TOCs due to the penetration of antagonistic interest groups into the committee's scientific network from the outset. But when such structures bring about internecine polemic within a scientific advisory group that appears almost perfectly reflective of geopolitical tensions, it seems clear that science has ceased to perform its function as an unbiased advisory group and has taken on an instrumental role for certain interest groups.

The less cohesive a scientific consensus, the more scientific knowledge can be made malleable to fit political interests. In fact, even quite rigorous science with exceptional proof can be shaped to fit political agendas. The MeBr case illustrates that scientific knowledge regarding the alternatives to MeBr is closely tied to the regional location of the scientific community. For example, as noted above, members of the MBTOC with experience working with LDCs on alternatives to MeBr believe the alternatives would easily replace MeBr. E.U. MBTOC members likewise find great promise in the alternatives, while U.S.-based members are skeptical of their efficacy. Such divisions illustrate the close link between politics and science, an increasingly instrumental relationship driven by political economic conditions that, as Jasanoff points out, threaten to move science further away from the real needs of society.[15]

U.S.-Based MBTOC Members

During the 17th MOP in Dakar, Senegal, in 2005, I interviewed two members of the MBTOC. One was a consultant to the U.S. government, the other tied to the U.S. government on a professional basis.[16] The interviews revealed a great deal about the links between politics and science in MeBr decision making.

The two MBTOC members pointed out that the political appointees on the U.S. delegation play a major role in determining the U.S. position and that those are the delegates that industry lobbyists want to talk to. In other words, political appointees try to make sure ozone scientists are doing what they want. In this fashion, the U.S. administration determines how U.S. industry claims are to be addressed, how civil society pressures are to be handled, and how scientific information is to be used from the U.S. perspective. For the United States, "industry and the [strawberry and tomato] growers are the constituents of the government," one of the MBTOC members stated matter-of-factly. This made a great deal of sense to me, having experienced firsthand some thinly veiled animosity from a politically appointed member of the U.S. delegation during a small-group MBTOC meeting open to the public during the 23rd OEWG. "He is a nice guy," I was assured. "He doesn't like nonstate folks in the small groups," the MBTOC member commented.

ACTING POLITICAL

The two U.S. MBTOC members also spoke about how the MBTOC is comprised of various people with disparate talents, some of which are less "valuable," in their opinion, than others. Here I witnessed some of the animosity that existed among MBTOC members across disciplinary and national boundaries. The U.S. members with backgrounds in natural science accused E.U. members with a consultative role of "acting politically," while they themselves were presumably acting on "true science."

One of the members spoke about a particular MBTOC member from the European Union who had spent a great deal of time working on the MLF-funded MeBr alternative projects. The member described this person as "politically minded," as not knowing anything about the science of MeBr and its alternatives. "They push an agenda but don't know anything about the science of the alternatives. They might see the results of MLF projects and say that growers should make the transition [to alternatives], but they don't understand the local situation." The "local situation" in this case referred to the conclusions of particular scientific studies on the impact of MeBr-free strawberry production for U.S. growers. Such a statement attempts to delink the political aspects of the MeBr decision-making process from the science of MeBr and its alternatives. Such a delinking is never fully achievable. As shown in previous chapters, the United States selects which science to bring to the table for negotiation and which science to ignore.

I asked the two MBTOC members about the economic assessment study provided by the AETF.[17] Briefly, the study presented to the Protocol plenary concluded that the alternatives to MeBr should be given top priority and that the U.S. exemptions on the whole should be denied. The study used the MLF projects as a basis for measuring how much parties would be willing to spend on alternatives, and it also considered the rate of success in those projects. However, according to these two U.S. MBTOC members, "The study was a mistake because it didn't take into account the local costs to growers; it only looked at the cost-benefit of MLF spending versus strawberry transition costs." For these members, such a study bears no resemblance to the reality facing growers in the United States. A real cost-benefit analysis, in their opinion, would take into account the local costs to growers, companies, and other stakeholders in the United States. The costs and results of scientific projects in LDCs were irrelevant to U.S. growers.

Turning their accusation of E.U. members "acting politically" on its head, the MBTOC members used a political argument to support their denouncement of the AETF report. The factors that were relevant, they said, were the costs of labor and other costs of production, which are lower in other countries, so any lowering of yields can push out U.S. growers. "In the view of the Bush administration, there can be no loss of competition to other growers, so yields cannot go down with the alternatives," one member stated. It is this plain fact that has driven U.S. MeBr policy since the mid-1990s, but U.S. policy is also legitimized by the evidence of certain scientific reports over others. This policy affects members of the MBTOC associated with the U.S. delegation as consultants or employees of the Department of Agriculture, the EPA, or any other U.S. institution working at the Montreal Protocol. Not all U.S.-based MBTOC members agree with this posture, but there is a great deal of pressure on them to support it.

The pro-MeBr MBTOC members I met with agreed that there have been many successful MeBr alternatives projects in the LDCs. The LDCs have received sizable funding from the MLF to implement projects. However, many of these countries have produced strawberries only since 1995 or so, so their growing platforms are not as path-dependent on MeBr. Such projects support arguments that the United States is fighting a losing battle, that its strawberry production platforms are almost hopelessly dependent on MeBr or require (to this point, at least) extremely toxic alternatives.[18] The United States is embedded in an older production system that is difficult to change due to production-path dependency, protectionist politics, agro-industrial interests, the regulation costs of alternatives, and local regulatory restrictions. Therefore, it has higher economic and political costs than other countries.[19]

The U.S. MBTOC members also spoke at great length about the problems with alternatives to MeBr. Although considering the local environmental effects and regulations on alternatives is not a central concern of the MBTOC MeBr assessments (the committee simply judges the economic and technological viability of available alternatives to MeBr), it is an issue that shapes the U.S. position and that of (some) U.S. MBTOC members. Telone, for example, a registered alternative to MeBr patented by Dow Chemical, contaminates local water sources. The MBTOC members relayed that Telone had contaminated drinking water on Prince Edward Island, Canada, leading to the need for an emergency CUE for Canada to allow it to replace Telone with MeBr. In fact, *all* the alternatives can have very negative local effects. The two U.S. MBTOC members think that their own scientific community and the parties to the Protocol might be too concerned with phasing out every aspect of MeBr without thinking about the impact that alternatives will have on local communities.

One of the MBTOC members concluded that the international regulation of MeBr and its alternatives is a very difficult issue because it involves national politics, national production, and regional debates over production. It includes the issue of whether the U.S. government wants to give certain nation-states a hard or easy time and vice versa. Moreover, it is hard to convince some members of the feasibility of alternatives when MeBr is the pesticide with the least harmful local effects.

It seems clear that the pro-MeBr MBTOC members made decisions and held opinions reflective of the position of the U.S. strawberry production complex vis-à-vis competitors.

With county limits on MeBr alternatives in California, with alternatives producing negative consequences locally, and with the potential loss of market share to competitors, these MeBr experts are unable to support a complete MeBr phaseout for reasons that involve both science and politics. They have direct experience with growers in California, and they utilize certain data presented in scientific journals on the (in)efficacy of alternatives to MeBr.

But considerable work has been done to develop alternatives to MeBr in California. For more than a decade, the United States has invested in research for alternatives through federal and state programs. For example, in 1995 the USDA established an alternatives to MeBr program within its Agricultural Research Service (ARS) that involved researchers spread across ten states, with a budget of $15 million in 2001. The program's goal was to seek both short- and long-term solutions, with short-term strategies (mostly alternative chemical formulations) seen as stepping stones to more integrated long-term strategies. However, the chemical-based alternatives that were being promoted in the last decade still used some quantity of MeBr. Statistics show that in 2006 about 60 percent of California strawberry lands were fumigated with a mixture of MeBr and chloropicrin, 30 percent were fumigated with chemical alternatives, and only about 4 percent were not fumigated at all. Four chemicals—1,3-Dichloropropene (Telone), methyl isothiocyanate (MITC) generators, chloropicrin, and methyl iodide—are currently registered for large-scale use on strawberries in California. However, these alternative chemicals have potentially higher negative health effects during fumigation than MeBr and persist longer in the local environment. For instance, while 1,3-Dichloropropene is considered one of the most effective alternatives, it will not be allowed for use by all California growers as its use has been restricted within townships to address air quality concerns, underscoring the need to develop more benign alternative practices.[20]

Many nonchemical approaches to soil-borne disease management in strawberries have also been studied, including host resistance; small cell transplants ("plug plants"); organic amendments such as compost; high nitrogen organic fertilizers; fungicidal crop residues; microbial amendments; plant growth-promoting rhizobacteria; and crop rotations with broccoli, lettuce, or Brussels sprouts. However, these techniques are more likely to be effective when used in an integrated manner, such as a combination of rotation and the use of disease-suppressive residues and resistant plant material, rather than as individual strategies, While such integrated systems offer considerable promise, they often require significant changes in current fumigation-based production systems, making them less attractive than pesticide solutions for growers accustomed to the current system.[21]

Some have argued that integrated nonchemical approaches generate little attention in the political realm even where chemical alternatives are thought to be unviable.[22] These studies on alternatives are not considered highly by U.S. MB-TOC members. For one, the alternatives cannot help the U.S. strawberry growers outcompete global competitors. For another, they do not help the conventional MeBr agro-industrial complex profit off the chemical side of their economic pursuits.

COPRODUCING SCIENCE AND POLITICS
FOR AGRO-INDUSTRY IN THE MBTOC

I had an informative conversation with two MBTOC members, one from Canada, the other from the United States, in 2005. The reader will recall that both Canada and the United States have been strong supporters of continued MeBr use in strawberry production. At the start of the conversation, I told them that I was conducting an investigation of the relationship between the science disseminated from the MB-TOC and how the parties take that information and use it in the political realm. The U.S. MBTOC member asked sarcastically, "Do you see any science here?" His Canadian counterpart exclaimed, "I think I take offense to that comment!" The offender quickly backtracked to correct himself. He meant, he told us, that the MBTOC is rife with political activity at the very moment that scientific information is discussed within it, before the parties even begin to deliberate. MBTOC meetings can consist of very charged debates in which experts make arguments for or against particular CUE nominations that are oftentimes based on politics, not science. The second MBTOC member felt that the science was indeed objective at the research stage but that as soon as the MBTOC discussed research findings as a group, the science became politically charged. In both their opinions, the alternatives to MeBr were not adequate, and the MBTOC's decisions up to that point did not reflect that "fact" well enough.

But facts can become geographically constituted. For example, it is arguable that the research designs for alternatives in the United States are themselves determined by the local needs of U.S. strawberry growers. Some U.S. growers are simply unwilling to try an alternative to MeBr, or to use MeBr in smaller quantities of MeBr-alternative mixtures, because the risks of crop failure are too high.[23] In other cases, the soil has been degraded to such a state that any emergence of pests can cause complete crop failure. Strawberry is highly sensitive to *Verticillium dahliae* in the soil. Only one microsclerotium per gram of soil can cause deadly wilt on strawberry plants essential to the California Model.[24] MeBr's fumigation power allows dense planting of high-production strawberries over many seasons without an increase in disease, with little need for rotations incorporating less profitable crops.

I mentioned to one MBTOC researcher that some California strawberry growers had made a successful transition to organic production and that initial data on soil-tarping showed promise for making organic farming even more competitive. "Ask them where their plants come from," was the MBTOC researcher's response, referring to the fact that that all the plants are grown from MeBr- or chloropicrin-treated plants in greenhouses.[25] Yet if MeBr were limited to greenhouse production, then the total amount of MeBr would be greatly reduced by many thousands of metric tons.

When we discussed the controversies surrounding the MeBr phaseout, the MBTOC members often contrasted the MeBr case with the CFC phaseout. The CFC phaseout, they commented, involved one industry producing a handful of chemicals. With MeBr, it is more of an ecological issue. The MeBr case is complex and dynamic, and the conditions change from site to site. This complexity has placed a great deal of stress on the whole process. "You can't just substitute this [MeBr] for another when the other has a different effect on the whole system," the U.S. MBTOC member said. The argument here was that changing from MeBr to an alternative chemical would change the whole integrated pest-management strategy; it would change the ecology of the approach to limit pests and pathogens. The phaseout process is different for MeBr because the chemical is part of a larger, dynamic system. Such, at least, is the argument that proponents of the U.S. position are making.

However, as noted in the previous chapters, the position outlined above was not the one originally agreed upon by the MBTOC. In 2003, the MBTOC noted that wide-ranging success in the implementation of alternatives to MeBr virtually debunked claims of local conditions leading to unique needs. Although the registration of alternatives to MeBr might be a serious barrier to their application, these were not the conditions now mentioned by the MBTOC members. Here, they were discussing the local ecological conditions of California strawberry production and its reliance on MeBr.

In 2004, the MBTOC had again advised parties on how to handle MeBr CUEs. Then, the MBTOC changed strategies from previous reports, devising a category, titled "noted," that did not commit it to either reject or accept a nomination. Previously, the MBTOC had recommended either the acceptance or rejection of a CUE nomination. These "noted" CUEs came largely from the United States.

I mentioned to the two MBTOC members that the description of the "noted" category in plenary made it appear that the MBTOC wanted to recommend a rejection of these nominations but needed more information. The two MBTOC members argued that the MBTOC was leaning toward *recommending* the noted nominations but needed more information. But the real issue (I found out later) was that there was no consensus within the MBTOC on the CUE nominations from the United States. Some MBTOC members felt the nominations were not legitimate, and the MBTOC was unable to come to an agreement prior to the next Protocol meeting. Others, such as these two members, felt the U.S. nominations were legitimate.

With such an illustration of the disagreements among MBTOC members, it is difficult to consider MBTOC decision making as not containing political elements. The MBTOC consists of MeBr experts from around the world, but their scientific perspective is significantly affected by the politics of global powers and their employment, geographic location, and relationship to industry or the country to which they are tied. These two MBTOC members, after all, were either employed by a U.S. federal institution or were currently serving as a member of a major pro-MeBr consortium of strawberry growers and had previously been a member of the U.S. delegation when MeBr was incorporated into the provisions of the Montreal Protocol. In addition, one MBTOC member was also a representative for clients that currently received CUEs for MeBr.

CLEAVED SCIENCE

One of the two MBTOC members with whom I spoke, a scientific researcher, believes that the MBTOC utilizes first and foremost scientific evidence in its decision making. The other, with previous employment on the U.S. delegation and a current member of a pro-MeBr consortium, believes scientific objectivity is left at the laboratory. This difference is understandable if we posit that both members' viewpoints follow from their life experiences. How, then, can we expect the MBTOC to be objective? How can we expect it to provide assessments free of political rhetoric? Yet when such a scientific advisory group generates unending debate that reflects geopolitical competition and likewise inhibits the elimination of ODSs, it seems possible that the scientific community has ceased to perform its function as an expert advisory group.[26]

At the 17th MOP, I told a delegate from an East European country that I was investigating the MeBr phaseout. His response was that I was "getting political." Furthermore, two MBTOC members told me that I was "brave" to deal with this political issue right now. These two sets of comments were a "eureka" moment for me because I realized that they had come while the Montreal Protocol was deliberating over who would be the next MBTOC co-chairs. From an administrative and scientific perspective, co-chairs are important for their skills at facilitating meetings, coordinating findings, and reporting those findings to the parties. Yet what was not initially obvious, but became clearer the more I investigated, was that co-chairs—and other MBTOC members for that matter—are also important for their political connections to delegations, industries, scientific networks, and other groups. It became clear to me that these sorts of connections possibly contributed to the political divisions that seemed to cleave the MBTOC in two. As one MBTOC co-chair told me in Dakar, the MBTOC tries to maintain a severance of politics and science, but "Everyone comes to MeBr meetings with an opinion. [Such a severance] is difficult."

For example, in Dakar several countries came forth with nominations for new co-chairs for the MBTOC. The greatest debate was between Canada's nomination and the European Union's nomination. Two U.S. MBTOC members noted to me that this jockeying was due to the different politics the nominated individuals would bring to the MBTOC table for deliberation on what the MBTOC should represent. For that reason the Article 5 parties (i.e., the LDCs) are adamant in making sure they are represented on the MBTOC. Half of the members are supposed to come from the LDCs, but out of forty total members in 2005, only fourteen came from the LDCs. The United States had the most members—seven. As one MBTOC member put it to me, the trouble with the

MBTOC is that the most knowledgeable MeBr experts "come from people in the business," people who work with MeBr on strawberries and know the problems with MeBr-dependence in certain strawberry varieties. Thus, the deeply political atmosphere is a basic norm in MeBr proceedings. Interestingly, one MBTOC member who likewise serves as a consultant for a pro-MeBr consortium agreed with me that perhaps this was not the best way to proceed with environmental issues.

U.S. Pressures on MeBr Science and the TEAP in General

In 2003, the parties to the Montreal Protocol requested that the TEAP provide them with an estimate of how much MeBr is required for use in quarantine and pre-shipment (QPS) and how much could be replaced with alternatives. QPS is currently not monitored under the Protocol. It is easy to foresee a major problem as MeBr is increasingly used for the treatment of wood packaging and for fumigating agricultural and horticultural products for export. In order to get the requested information, the TEAP requested that parties answer a twenty-five-page survey. At the 24th OEWG, parties met in contact groups to discuss ways to make the TEAP's survey less burdensome. However, there was a disagreement between the European Union and the United States over how best to move forward. On the one hand, the European Union felt that the timeline for reporting on QPS uses of MeBr was too long, but on the other, it felt that the workload was too much for the MBTOC. The MBTOC, the European Union felt, had been overloaded by dealing with the MeBr CUE nominations.

The U.S. response to the European Union and the TEAP survey reflects how the difficulties that exist among nation-states can affect relations between nation-states and the scientific experts who provide support for political decision making. When parties—mainly the United States and the European Union—could not agree on a way to make the reporting process easier, the United States exclaimed, "Decision XI/13 never required individual parties to submit to twenty-five pages of detailed questions in order to provide data for TEAP! That decision requests TEAP to pull together an estimate. Maybe we should just go back and ask TEAP to pull together an estimate. . . . If no middle ground can be found, we are fine with reverting back to the language of the last Decision [to] let TEAP make an estimate. We'll submit the best data we have on the basis of that twenty-five-page document . . . but we assure you . . . it is not going to be useful for any decision making! But if that is deemed the appropriate way to move forward, we are fine with it."[27]

In terms of the MBTOC's decision on CUE nominations at the 24th OEWG, the United States was as threatening to the MBTOC as it had been to the LDCs that voiced concern about the high volume of CUEs it and other developed countries requested. It accused the MBTOC of not being scientific in its rejection of certain CUE nominations. The problem, the United States suggested, might come from the "slightly changed" language of the CUE provisions for MeBr from the essential use criteria for CFCs. This "slight change," as the reader will remember, is deeply tied to the neoliberal turn in global environmentalism and involves considering the needs of individuals in the marketplace and the effects of market disruptions on those individuals due to the implementation of MeBr alternatives. According to the United States, the MBTOC had assessed the need for MeBr for individual users "based on suspicion" and not on information provided by the parties.[28]

The United States also accused the MBTOC of attempting to put forward the concept of a transition plan to help countries switch to MeBr alternatives without the approval of the parties. According to the United States, the MBTOC was attempting "to establish policy." Finally, the United States believed the MBTOC reviews did not take seriously the needs of growers and that "we should not look to drive a farm industry, or any other industry, out of business."[29] Some countries, like Australia, noted that their strawberry growers were "unwilling" to accept the low levels of MeBr recommended by the scientific experts of the MBTOC.[30]

The MBTOC responded that this was an "interim report" because it did not have guidance to use national strategies to assess the MeBr nominations until the following round, in 2005. So the MBTOC had "used a standardized weight of reduction, where there were circumstances that might possibly justify this. And if it turned out that this standardized weight was incorrect, and we've always worked on the basis that things should be decided on a case-by-case basis, if this turned out to be incorrect, we would be no doubt informed about this at an early stage." In terms of the U.S. accusation that the MBTOC had attempted to establish policy, the MBTOC noted that the reductions it proposed were a *suggestion* and did not go further than that. "But also we realize that the following year it is not appropriate because at that stage the management plans for the phaseout will be part of the nomination."[31] Clearly, there is great pressure from powerful nation-states on the scientific community and its dissemination strategy of scientific knowledge.

Such pressures as discussed above appear to be increasingly frustrating for non-U.S. MBTOC members. I interviewed one MBTOC member from the European Union with experience in implementing alternatives to MeBr in the LDCs. This MeBr expert had worked previously in the private sector as a distributor of MeBr to Europe and the United States. He sold his company to a buyer interested especially in the U.S. market, to which the company had access. Then, this MBTOC member became involved in helping Europeans grow strawberries without MeBr by using greenhouses and tarping methods, the success of which even rivaled MeBr-dependent Spanish and other European imports (mainly from Poland). Due to his expertise with both MeBr and MeBr-free strawberry production, this member was hired by the UNDP to help coordinate MeBr transition projects and has seen many such projects meet with success. He helped with alternative projects for cut flowers as well as strawberries, both of which are large import-export markets for much of Europe. (The market in cut flowers has helped the economies of African countries such as Uganda and South Africa.)

This MBTOC member firmly believes that the MBTOC scientific community lacks "practical experts on the ground." This is an odd deficiency when one considers that the MeBr critical use language calls for a scientific and technical understanding of MeBr and its alternatives in very specific circumstances. Nevertheless, one of the problems facing more practical approaches is the need in the MBTOC for data from recent findings in particular geographic settings and presented in scientific journals. Not surprisingly, the most available and reputable reports on MeBr effectiveness come from the United States. The MBTOC member felt that the use of reports from the United States slowed down the promotion and dissemination of alternatives at the MBTOC discussion table and thus at the Protocol in general. Of course, U.S. corporations have an important role to play in the MeBr issue, as does growers' unwillingness to try alternatives, as other MBTOC members noted. This particular MBTOC member believed "there are alternatives if you try hard enough to find them" and that the alternatives are more economically viable and yield a better product.

The MBTOC member noted that civil society pressures also help with the transition to alternatives. For example, Europe has a special label for cut flowers that shows "no methyl bromide" was used in their production, although several LDCs regard such a label as a real problem.[32] "This label can now be found in New York!" he exclaimed. Cut flowers are a success story of transition to MeBr alternatives because certain companies with expertise in MeBr alternative technologies are able to use computers to disseminate the technology to growers around the world. This is "real globalization," in the MBTOC member's own words, where technology is provided instantaneously via the Internet and where soil content analyses are sent to experts in the industrialized world who then analyze the data and send them immediately back to the growers with the necessary combination of chemicals for successful flower cultivation. According to this MBTOC member, there is "no difference" between this sort of success and what could happen with strawberries, were it not for the difficulties discussed above.

The issues raised by this MBTOC member and the pro-MeBr members speak at different levels of analysis. The E.U. member points to successes that have been achieved due to changes in production practices, while the U.S. members stress that their current systems would not be viable without MeBr. These viewpoints speak to the disparate ways that MBTOC members view science and the potential for changing science in order for production to be more environmentally sustainable. U.S. MBTOC members are concerned about existing patterns, while the E.U. members are concerned about changing existing patterns. Both groups acknowledge the successes in MeBr alternatives worldwide, but the U.S. members maintain that the U.S. system must remain the same. Decision IX/6 allows the U.S. model to remain the same and to use MeBr as long as non-MeBr substitutes would adversely affect individual users. E.U. MBTOC members appear to approach the situation from a different perspective, which is perhaps reflective of dissimilar sociopolitical conditions in the European Union, as Jasanoff points out.[33] However, the comments made by U.S. MBTOC members regarding global economic competition and the political-mindedness of their global colleagues suggest that sociopolitical conditions are always-already coproduced with political economic conditions, and this coproduction shapes how science/knowledge is interpreted and disseminated by all actors involved.

Political and economic issues play significant roles in shaping how science is both constructed and interpreted at the international regulatory level. Science/knowledge and politics are coproduced where scientific findings are subject to political organization, interpretation, and dissemination in ways that politicize science. In global environmental governance, how political actors interpret science affects how scientists interpret their own work as well as its applications. The MeBr case illustrates that national interests, policy priorities, and the history of technological development can play significant roles in determining the inclinations of scientific experts housed between the United States, the European Union, and other nations in ozone-related policies. The social location of scientists is not a unicausal determination of their political ideologies. Nevertheless, the interviews with MBTOC members demonstrate that there is a great deal of pressure on scientists to express the viewpoints of their nation-state delegations and the conditions of production of particular geographic sites.

The division between some MBTOC members indeed seems to be partly a result of geographical and political differences. MBTOC members in the United States appear to believe there are significant barriers to the transition to MeBr-free strawberry production. MBTOC members in the European Union believe the transition is less difficult. Nation-states in powerful positions often pin the MBTOC between themselves and their competitors, denouncing MBTOC interventions when they do not serve their purposes. Moreover, MBTOC members' connections to national delegations and/or grower/ agro-industry groups clearly play a role in determining their outlook on the possibilities of MeBr-free strawberry production. The data used to support claims for the need for MeBr in the United States are predominantly found in selected articles from U.S. scientific journals and test plots in California. The issue here is that California strawberry production is likely, and was at its inception, dependent on MeBr like no other strawberry agro-industrial complex. It is arguable that the U.S. system will never be able to find an input that replicates MeBr completely and with as few locally constituted problems because it is truly MeBr-dependent. Any conventional substitutes—such as Telone and methyl iodide—are likely to generate costly local opposition as pesticide drift and environmental contamination become problems that MeBr reasonably avoided due to its "chemical character."

In the next chapter, I will focus on how the coproduction of science and politics affects those facets of global civil society most often associated with keeping nation-states on the path toward better modes of environmentalism at the Montreal Protocol—the NGOs. We will see how some NGOs make their arguments on the basis of "true science," while others offer appeals to public health and security, to the global environment, and to other issues of "environmental ethics" and justice. But science is subject to politics, while public health concerns are irrelevant to the neoliberalized (de)regulation of the MeBr exemption process. Thus, the global environmental concerns reflected in the early days of command-and-control and precaution in environmental governance have only limited standing in the face of market-based neoliberal knowledge. This shift, in turn, shapes the ways that civil society groups engage in Protocol deliberations.

7

The Limited Influence of Global Civil Society

One has only to attend a Montreal Protocol meeting to get a sense of the skepticism that the majority of ozone-policy-savvy people have about the U.S. position of supporting MeBr. Not only are MeBr experts and nation-states skeptical, but NGOs are as well. In the history of global environmental governance, NGOs have been in a position to present arguments in plenary deliberations to help shape policy. However, some NGO interventions in the MeBr issue seem to go unnoticed. This indifference appears to be a serious flaw in the attempt to create global environmental governance that is—as regime scholars might put it—a vehicle through which knowledges and norms are established via interactions between nation-states and other interlinked actors, such as NGOs, scientists, and other civil society groups.[1] Yet when NGOs do participate in the Protocol, we can see clearly how their involvement actually reflects what studies of scale in human geography describe as the "social reproduction" of "socio-ecological processes" through which certain ways of engaging with environmentalism become "normal." As we have seen throughout the book, those processes are never "fixed" to a particular scale of activity but rather ebb and flow via the networks of actors that penetrate, retreat, and regroup for further interventions in order to affect global policies. National delegates might intervene in the scientific dissemination of knowledge, strawberry lobbyists might account for locally specific conditions of production at Protocol meetings, NGOs might call attention to successes with CFC alternatives in Europe, and new chemicals developed in California might change the geopolitics of agricultural production and environmental decision making. It is a multiscalar, evolving process through which global environmental governance is achieved. Yet overarching—and acting from within—such processes is the global process of the neoliberalization of social life.[2]

It will be useful to reintroduce the term "governmentality" here and map out some of the interventions by civil society groups, demonstrating that they are often successful only when they expose the underhandedness of U.S. dealings by shedding light on U.S. protectionist policies, which are a contradiction of the neoliberal discourse of free and open markets. Interventions that argue for a promotion of "the general welfare" or protection of the ozone layer and human health above individual grower concerns have become irrelevant in a neoliberal political and economic environment. Interventions, however, that illustrate serious flaws in arguments made to justify the continued use of ODSs seem to have some effect on deliberations. Exposing existing U.S. stockpiles of MeBr by NGOs seems to have generated preliminary moves toward a shift in MeBr policymaking, but we must be cautious and avoid overestimating the efficacy of such interventions.

Unlike civil society that "takes to the streets" in open, public settings, international NGOs operating in global environmental governance (IENGOs) specialize in "information, lobbying, and service provision" and are composed of complex structures, divisions of labor, and interests.[3] While IENGOs are institutionalized more than other social movement organizations, scholars still believe that they represent a "critical communicative link between citizens and government" in such settings.[4] Yet we must not think of these groups as completely distinct from the nation-state, or other institutions for that matter. Rather, IENGOs are a part of the governance process, and that includes being part of the state-making, scientific network–forming, and civil society–making processes. Their participation involves the reproduction of certain styles of action and the dissemination of certain ways of knowing deemed appropriate to the governance process. Thus, their role is perhaps best thought of as being more limited than traditional studies of global governance portray because they are more integrated and coproduced through governance than is widely assumed. Since the neoliberal turn, their role appears more limited than ever.

IENGO interventions in the MeBr controversy are shaped by the neoliberalization framework of the Montreal Protocol. Throughout the MeBr controversy IENGOs, primarily U.S.-based, have attempted to persuade Protocol actors to implement precautionary regulatory processes that had heretofore achieved exceptionally successful ozone-layer protection. As we shall see, such efforts did not lead to many substantive deliberations among states during plenary sessions. Attempts by IENGOs to highlight the various social and global ecological impacts of a delayed MeBr phaseout were also limited. Rather, IENGO influence was most salient when documenting the unfair market practices of U.S. firms. Therefore, we can say that IENGOs contribute to global environmental governance, yet their impact changes as treaty rhetoric and policy changes, and such shifts can also influence the agendas of IENGOs themselves.

What I mean by this last statement is that some IENGOs operating in the Montreal Protocol have learned to "govern themselves" in ways that legitimize powerful state agendas, including the U.S. push for a neoliberal rationale to continue MeBr use beyond the phaseout date of 2005. The reader will remember that these "tenets" of neoliberalism are written into the MeBr CUE language of the Montreal Protocol and thus indicate the insertion of neoliberal discourse and rationality into this environmental treaty.

Below we will map out how U.S.-based IENGOs, such as the NRDC and the EIA, have made use of neoliberal discourse to make effective interventions. The NRDC, an influential environmental watchdog with over six hundred thousand members and renowned for its "litigation and regulatory negotiations approach," often works to improve global environmental governance through its demands for a more environmentally conscious position from the U.S. government.[5] The EIA, another U.S.-based organization with global reach, has utilized neoliberal discourse more centrally to similar effect but only after disbanding its early concerns for the global environment and adherence to the precautionary principle. Other IENGOs, such as Greenpeace International, with its mandate from over 2.8 million supporters to "ensure the ability of the earth to nurture life in all its diversity," and the U.S.-based California Certified Organic Farmers organization (CCOF), did not abandon their discourse of concern for the global environment, precaution, and global social welfare.[6]

As a result, Greenpeace and the CCOF interventions appear to have had little effect on Protocol actors.

Global Civil Society and Neoliberal Governmentality

As we know, global environmental governance is a process through which many of the world's direst environmental problems are tackled. Global climate change, stratospheric ozone depletion, biodiversity loss, and many other environmental problems are handled chiefly through the global institutionalization of environmentalism. Through this process, governments, industry, and facets of civil society (including the scientific community) work to achieve some level of consensus on how to soften the impact of what Speth describes as "the Great Collision"—the convergence and contradictory needs of the global economy and the global ecosystem.[7]

As we saw in previous chapters, in global governance today a predominant "normalized" discursive framework has stabilized around neoliberal concerns of market efficiency, individualism and individual responsibility, citizen-as-consumer, transparency/accountability, entrepreneurialism, and faith in private as opposed to public/state knowledge. While neoliberalism never manifests perfectly, these values are pursued by powerful states either through rhetoric or application in decision making. Of course, values such as transparency and accountability are not strictly neoliberal (they are also democratic and legal considerations), and in practice they can often be used to veil protectionism of powerful state interests. Yet they nonetheless are rhetorical goals of the neoliberal project—establishing free/fair market transactions whereby all actors may gain through efficiency. In addition, global civil society often plays a significant role in reinforcing and relegitimizing the tenets of neoliberal governance. By adopting neoliberal discourse, global civil society may actually shape its agenda to fit the neoliberalization process.[8]

Traditionally, global governance scholars have emphasized the role that nonstate actors play in the governance process, especially in their ability to wrench power away from the state.[9] In fact, Ole Sending and Iver Neuman contend that for governance scholars, the increasing influential power of civil society actors and the decreasing power/authority of the state "are at the core of what global governance is all about."[10] While the margins between states, markets, and civil society are often blurred, here, we are told, civil society groups articulate a relatively unconstrained representation of the desires of various social groups. Similarly, some environmental sociologists emphasize the important status of NGOs in global environmental governance as more socio-ecological problems are tackled in the global arena. In fact, NGOs are seen as being "at the forefront of environmental reform in the advanced industrial democracies," and yet their role is limited to "pressuring the traditional political agents—national environmental authorities—into action."[11]

NGOs are oftentimes compelled to modify the very doctrines and belief systems upon which they operate at the behest of state and institutional agendas. More influential than simply "green washing" the image of environmental governance or assuaging protests through inclusive reforms, increased NGO participation *disciplines* such groups to reproduce the global neoliberal context.[12] NGOs begin to "govern themselves" in ways that comply with neoliberal environmentalism.

Foucault's conception of governmentality, the "art of government," can help us understand the intimate links between governments and IENGOs operating in global governance. "Governmentality" is understood as the process through which certain ideas, discourses, and social practices take on mentalities of rule that are necessary in order to reinforce state power. Rather than our perceiving of IENGO involvement as a loss of state power, governmentality urges us to analyze how such involvement reinforces, or relegitimizes, the rationality of state power at the global scale.[13] In this theorization, IENGOs can be analyzed as part of the process of governance, their increased presence and participation contributing to "changes in the practices and rationality of governing."[14] Rather than simply pressuring the state into action, IENGOs participate in the dissemination of certain knowledges/discourses that sustain powerful states' influence and agendas. In the age of neoliberal globalization, such maintenance legitimizes neoliberal resolutions to global environmental problems.[15]

Through the concept of governmentality, we can simultaneously consider "microcircuits of power" along with the "macropowers" at play in governance.[16] Market logic is enforced through global governance and (re)produces subjects that reinforce that same logic via everyday practices. While a strictly Marxist approach might focus on the hegemonic institutionalization of capitalist logic in global environmental governance and its impact on nonstate actors, the Foucauldian approach concentrates on practices of governing that embrace certain knowledges, expertise, and discourses while excluding others.[17] And while civil society advocates might see IENGOs working against state hegemony, neo-Foucauldians see the reinforcement of state power as working through these groups rather than merely against them, compelling them to act in ways constituted through the process of "the production, accumulation, circulation, and functioning of discourse."[18] It is important that an eye toward governmentality allows us to analyze the links between site-specific socio-ecological conditions (e.g., those of California strawberry production) and the otherwise placeless influences of global systems of governance (e.g., the Montreal Protocol).[19]

In the global arena, actors—state and nonstate, public and private—"act" in ways that become normalized by the institutional rules of global environmental governance. With neoliberalism being the dominant overriding political discourse, or discursive frame, its tenets act as principal threads guiding self-management. Ironically, neoliberal concerns for individual responsibility and private-over-public knowledge can often link global environmental governance to localism and individualism, thus weakening the legitimacy of global expertise while reinforcing state-sanctioned expertise at the national scale (at least for powerful nations). The devolution of global environmental governance to the local scale can be successfully supported by IENGOs interested in maintaining the legitimization of neoliberal knowledge at the national and not the global scale. Powerful states support this process, not through the imposition of specific outcomes, but by creating frameworks that rationalize certain behaviors and involve IENGOs in the process of defining problems, solutions, and modes of intervention. In Foucauldian parlance, some IENGO interventions are deemed "sane" (i.e., bearing legitimate insight and knowledge) and others "insane" (i.e., backed by illegitimate knowledge and logic). Governmentality, then, helps us understand how the various groups operating in global environmental governance are themselves a part of the same process of creating and shaping modes of state control. Such involvement naturally supports the powerful states' interest in maintaining control of knowledge and scientific expertise.[20]

IENGO interventions during Montreal Protocol deliberations on the MeBr phaseout show again (1) that the agenda and rationality of ozone governance has shifted over time to a neoliberal position, and (2) that U.S.-based IENGOs have helped to ensure that this neoliberal agenda has come to dominate. While the powerful states (mainly the United States) have not directly imposed a solution to the MeBr phaseout issue, they have aided in the creation of a framework in which certain behaviors and discourses were legitimized. IENGO deliberations supplement state control in ways similar to how expertise at the local and regional scales helps bring territories under state control.[21] The most successful IENGO interventions fit snugly into the agenda of neoliberal governmentality in that they promote the powerful liberal states' "idea of freedom through the encouragement of [open and fair] competition."[22] Alternative IENGO interventions have been less effective in generating debate/discussion, and such groups have either altered their approach or sought other scales of contestation.

While the MeBr CUE process has been discussed above, here I wish to explore in detail (1) the neoliberalization of the Protocol via MeBr CUEs, and (2) the impact of neoliberalization on global civil society operating in the Protocol. To accomplish this task I draw from studies that understand this new neoliberal regime as "historically specific, ongoing, and internally contradictory."[23] Thus, neoliberalism is understood as a process, what Jamie Peck and Adam Tickell call "neoliberalization."[24] The incorporation of MeBr into the provisions of the Montreal Protocol marks a moment in which neoliberal policies became embedded into the global environmental governance of the ozone layer.

As we have discussed, during the 1990s global environmental governance began a wholesale transition to "liberal environmentalism," to pursuing environmental protection undergirded by a free-market order. The George H. W. Bush administration focused global and domestic policy on market-based incentives for environmental protection (e.g., expansion of the Clean Air Act to include a permit system for sulfur dioxide) in lieu of command-and-control legislation, spearheading such change in global environmental governance as well.[25] And the Montreal Protocol was no exception. The conditions in which CFCs were incorporated into the phaseout process were clearly different from those of MeBr. Some CFC uses were excluded from the earlier ban because they were deemed "necessary for the health, safety or [were] critical for the functioning of society (encompassing cultural and intellectual aspects)."[26] Based on these criteria, three extremely limited "essential uses" were exempted from the CFC ban. The criteria for the CFC phaseout implied that the benefits of these applications to society outweighed the environmental costs.[27]

As we have seen, the more recently contrived criteria for exemptions to the MeBr phaseout reflect the rhetorical concerns of neoliberalism. Under much U.S. pressure/support, the "Critical Use Exemption" clause, drafted in 1997 and found in Decision IX/6, reflects a movement toward greater participation by private experts and civil society groups that inform states of the economic consequences of global environmental decision making, as well as a reliance on private assessments of market mechanisms to determine qualification for exemptions.[28] Here, parties focused centrally on the economic impact of the MeBr phaseout on specific interest groups, even on individual users of MeBr, not on the general health or welfare of society.

How the United States has convinced the global community to allow for the continued use of MeBr, despite the global risks, is tied to discourses of individual rights, competition, and criticism of public global scientific knowledge. Below I will illustrate IENGO interventions in this process as they have attempted to persuade the global community to restrict U.S. MeBr use.

IENGO Interventions Based on Socio-Ecological Concerns

As we have seen, the United States made use of selected scientific reports specific to the California strawberry agro-industrial production complex to support its claims that non-MeBr ozone-friendly alternatives proven effective worldwide were not applicable in California and would negatively impact the economic condition of a number of strawberry growers. The issue raised by the California strawberry industry was framed within notions of global competition: the market would become "unnaturally" competitive without MeBr. The California Strawberry Commission, a quasi-private interest group, provided a market-based argument that obviated the scientific claims of the global community of MeBr experts, the MBTOC. Here, the stakeholders themselves provided a voice to groups requiring representation in the neoliberal context. Other California actors attempted to shed doubt on the claims made by this nation-state/agro-industry alliance. Most of these initial counterarguments, however, did not fit the neoliberal agenda and did not generate much response from the delegates.

At the 1st ExMOP (2004), which was designed primarily to deal with U.S. MeBr CUE nominations, Vanessa Bogenholm, then spokesperson for the CCOF, attempted to delegitimize the U.S. requests. The CCOF's intervention used the tactic of a practitioner, as Bogenholm herself had phased out MeBr: "True farmers are stewards of the land. . . . Farmers [do not] need to use materials that are destructive to the environment, harmful to the employees, or dangerous to anyone who may come into contact with the farm operation. . . . Financial concerns of individual farmers cannot be considered more important than environmental concerns or the health of human beings."[29] Unlike the U.S. argument about economic feasibility, Bogenholm raised concerns of environmental stewardship and the health of farm workers and human beings in general.

In a similar vein, the tactic of the EIA was to connect the prolonged U.S. MeBr use to global socio-ecological harms. At the 1st ExMOP, the EIA highlighted global socio-ecological concerns that had brought parties together to ratify the Montreal Protocol to begin with: "The Montreal Protocol threatens to turn away from a phaseout of a chemical that is as dangerous to human health on the ground as it is in the stratosphere. Exposure to MeBr gas has been shown to cause prostate cancer, nervous system damage, and death."[30] In addition, the EIA pointed to the problem of U.S. MeBr stock-piling, which was not being considered along with the U.S. MeBr requests. It highlighted social concerns related to global security threats as well as to general environmental and human health concerns regarding stockpiling: "At a time of increased security efforts around the world, . . . we know less and less who's stockpiling [MeBr], where it is, or where it is going. This is despite the fact that . . . MeBr [is a] potential target of . . . terrorist attacks. . . . In countries such as the U.S., MeBr is imported in large tanks, transported via its railway system through large population centers, and stockpiled with minimal oversight. The U.S. government has to date offered no clear information on existing stockpiles."[31]

Later, the EIA argued that the U.S. request for exemptions would baffle anyone aware of the threat that MeBr causes and the lack of precaution in making decisions:

> A reasonable person might ask, ' "Why are any CUEs handed out—particularly of a dangerous chemical that could be used in terrorist attacks, when by a party's own admission, they have little control over the stockpiles or the businesses that keep them?" . . . Before the parties effectively decide to . . . continue to endanger the global environment and our immediate health and security, we need to know how much we have, where it is, and we need measures to control trade. . . . *The Montreal Protocol is threatening to abandon the precautionary principle on which it is based.* A clear understanding that human lives would be lost because of emissions of ozone-depleting chemicals brought this body together. And a consistent precautionary approach has rightfully made this the most successful environmental agreement in history.[32]

Here, the EIA was recalling the preamble to the Montreal Protocol that deliberately states, "For the protection of the ozone layer, precautionary measures should be taken."[33] At the 2nd ExMOP in 2005, again designed to deal with the sizable U.S. MeBr requests, Greenpeace also made use of the discourse of general global environmental concern, precaution, and social health: "The ozone layer is now in its most vulnerable phase, and we know from our scientists that we may well be in

for some more nasty surprises, such as the ozone hole over
central Europe this past week. . . . We urge the parties to be
mindful of the fact that the [exemptions] recommended
for . . . 2006 represent over 130,000 tons of more [ozone-
depleting] tons being produced in the world."[34]

Interventions from the CCOF, the EIA, and Greenpeace
are indeed tied to a certain arrangement of science/knowledge
deemed legitimate in a number of circles. For example, the
EIA is well known for its role in exposing illegal ODS trade
worldwide, in 2007 receiving the prestigious "Best-of-the-
Best" Stratospheric Ozone Protection Award from the EPA.[35]
Arguments for precautionary measures and global environmental conditions, however, do not fit into the MeBr phaseout
exemption language, which considers the effect of the MeBr
phaseout on individual MeBr users first and the general
environment second. Consequently, the CCOF's comments
regarding the need to achieve environmental sustainability
in agriculture and to be proactive by switching to less socio-
ecologically harmful alternatives did not visibly influence
Protocol deliberations. The CCOF's claims centered on the
lack of foresight of the California strawberry industry regarding the MeBr phaseout process and the implications for the
global environment and human health. True, the CCOF's
position is based upon actual successes with MeBr alternatives, both those of its constituents and those reported in
scientific studies in California and Florida.[36] But the California
strawberry agro-industrial complex, as a specific site of knowl-
edge/power legitimized by the U.S. government, selects
particular scientific studies to influence Protocol proceedings.
Despite the growing evidence for comparable alternatives
to MeBr, that science/knowledge discourse claims that the
alternatives are ineffective and that there are significant legal

barriers to the broad usage of conventional alternatives. The CCOF's claims about the general welfare of the global community versus that of some six hundred California growers are not a viable counterargument when local knowledge regarding the fairness of competition is a priority in global environmental governance.

The EIA's reference to a global security threat and general environmental/health concerns received little attention from the plenary as well. The precautionary principles upon which the Protocol was based are not written into Decision IX/6, which deals almost entirely with the economic impact that alternatives will have on individual MeBr users. Environmental health, global security, and the general welfare of society are not considered a part of that economic impact. A longer-range economic analysis using a lower discount rate might indeed incorporate changes in global climate, loss of lives, and/or global terrorism into assessments of the MeBr phaseout for U.S. growers. But the shorter-range economic models used to legitimize the science/knowledge position of the United States are concerned with the immediate impact of a MeBr phaseout on immediate users.[37]

The disappearance of socio-ecological welfare from the Protocol in the neoliberalized MeBr discourse has frustrated some IENGOs seeking U.S. support, as this concern is important to their constituents. For example, some of the EIA's concerns coincide with those of the U.S. Department of Homeland Security, which acknowledges that MeBr is sought by global terrorists, naming it a "chemical of interest" that requires increased vigilance from federal authorities, and medical research reports increased rates of certain cancers due to MeBr exposure.[38] Yet these threads of knowledge are not recognizably sustained components of the MeBr discourse.

An IENGO representative told me at the 17th MOP, "The Montreal Protocol doesn't work anymore," because, she argued, the precautionary principle was no longer utilized. This participant expressed frustration because the very raison d'être of the Protocol was to identify and eliminate potential ODSs, regardless of the economic impact on individuals. Global environmental governance in the neoliberal milieu discourages civil society groups from emphasizing broad structural problems within the designs of the treaty. Rather, the current rules encourage interventions to use the rationale agreed upon by parties and reified in Decision IX/6.

Neoliberalized Interventions Gaining Recognition

Above, we saw that neoliberalization sometimes "constrains and depletes activism" to the point that alternative discourses are overlooked.[39] The global MeBr community is increasingly dependent on the science of particular sites, and the sites with the highest "scientific capital" due to their position in the capitalist global economy are the most influential. IENGO discourses of global environmental concern are less effective because they do not fit with the principal mandates of the MeBr CUE criteria. To be effective, some IENGOs have developed a neoliberal discourse strategy. One IENGO that has generated reactions from the Montreal Protocol plenary is the NRDC. Using a discursive strategy that fits neatly within the neoliberal environmental model, the NRDC is the most effective of the IENGOs working on the MeBr issue. As such, it appears to make an impact on Protocol deliberations by maintaining a focus on market fairness, transparency, and other economic considerations.

At the 24th OEWG in 2004, David Doniger, policy director of the NRDC Climate and Clean Air Program and one-time director of climate change policy at the EPA, commented to the plenary on the sizable U.S. MeBr stockpiles, which were more than enough to supply U.S. CUE needs: "Although the U.S. government has not yet disclosed exactly how much, we know that it is at least ten thousand tons [of MeBr]. . . . And it may be much higher. Decision IX/6 and the ExMOP Decision both require parties to use available stocks before they nail on more MeBr production. . . . The fact that it's been possible to accumulate a stockpile . . . underline[s] the need for far better data collection on this critical question of stockpiles." The United States felt obliged to explain the NRDC's comments from its perspective: "Methyl bromide stockpile numbers are considered confidential business information by our Environmental Protection Agency; it is a legal judgment that they make."[40]

At the 15th MOP in 2003, a representative of the Coalition of Pest Managers for the Replacement of Ozone-Depleting Substances spoke about the MeBr phaseout exemptions and the impact of stockpiling on the Protocol's efforts. This intervention also made use of a neoliberal discourse of free markets/competition, noting that CUEs hindered fair competition. Stockpiles potentially harm corporations that have invested in MeBr alternatives, so "why should the companies that have met the challenges of searching for MeBr alternatives be punished by these exemptions? . . . Why should the companies with the 'wait and do little' strategy get favored treatment? Excessive critical use exemptions are simply unfair! . . . The second problem . . . is stockpiling. . . . This 'legal smuggling' . . . will add to these exemptions."[41]

The NRDC's comments at the 15th MOP also highlighted how U.S. exemptions created an uneven economic playing field while opposing the Protocol's mandate to reduce ODSs. The NRDC noted the apparent contradiction between the U.S. exemption requests and the litigation of the Protocol: U.S. requests would temporarily increase its MeBr quantities. "There is really only one [party] that ... is now seeking to reverse itself and increase its use and production of MeBr. . . . The U.S. [request] is larger by volume than all other requests combined," David Doniger stated.[42] Additionally, the NRDC connected the U.S. request to other tenets of neoliberalism, as well as to democratic concerns: accountability and transparency. It claimed that the U.S. public had not been made aware of the exemption requests through the appropriate channels, as required by U.S. law. If true, not only would this be illegal by U.S. law, but it would also contradict the principles of good faith and democratic openness upon which the mandates of the Protocol are based: The U.S. critical use exemption request "was made without any public awareness. . . . There's been no opportunity domestically to test whether the applications really have merit. The MBTOC . . . specifically finds that there isn't adequate support for [the majority of the U.S. requests]. . . . This is a question of whether the Protocol is going to be faithfully carried out or abused by one large party."[43]

The NRDC's comments drove Mark Murai, chairperson of the California Strawberry Commission, to retort with rhetoric of individualism in the strawberry economy and devolution of global governance to the local scale and private sphere: "How can we possibly make decisions in Nairobi or even in a United Nations committee that propose to address all situations in all farming communities around the world? The answer can only be [to] let the regulating agency in each country work closely with their farmers to make the necessary progress."[44] Murai identified an inefficacy in global environmental governance that could not handle issues of local concern. He argued for the devolution of governance to the local scale so that local circumstances supported by locally specific scientific knowledge devised by the private sector could examine "legitimate" knowledge claims and circumstances. This discursive strategy has succeeded in supporting the U.S. MeBr exemptions.

IENGO interventions are most effective when exposing contradictions between a nation-state's rhetoric of good faith and its actual material conditions. U.S. MeBr stockpiles clearly trouble countries not host to large MeBr-producing firms. The NRDC and other groups that have repositioned their strategy along neoliberal lines (such as the EIA; see below) have provided nation-states with a way to address the U.S. protection of its stockpiles, its strawberry growers, and its agro-industry in general.

By 2005, the EIA had begun to focus full force on the stockpile issue with the NRDC, while ceasing to intervene in deliberations with calls for greater attention to global socio-ecological issues. For example, at the 25th OEWG in 2005, the EIA hosted a small-group session with the NRDC to provide evidence of the U.S. MeBr stockpiles discussed above; they included pictures and video of MeBr stored on railway cars and in canisters by private companies. Many country delegates attended the small-group session. Questions asked pertained to U.S. democratic procedures on public comment (Norway), and the NRDC claimed the United States had violated these (see above); the likelihood that the NRDC lawsuit would lead to access to stockpile data (New Zealand); and whether there was a limit on how much MeBr the U.S. companies could feasibly stockpile (South Africa). Some countries would use this information in interventions during Protocol deliberations.

At the 17th MOP, for example, New Zealand commented on the ambiguous definition of what constitutes a stockpile across countries and that the legal considerations in some countries (i.e., the United States) continued to "frustrate parties" as they decided what to do with MeBr CUE requests.[45]

The NRDC, and afterward the EIA, efforts to make stockpiling clearer and fairer, economically speaking, will possibly lead to the adoption of some legal parameters on MeBr stocks. The European Union has made use of the NRDC-generated issue to streamline the MeBr stockpile debate and resolve the stockpile issue. LDCs, such as Kenya, concerned that "there are no accounts of available stocks"; that "this is a problem" that threatens the LDC economies; and that parties "need to provide an estimate of available stocks to facilitate the MBTOC decision" were pleased to hear the European Union address this issue.[46] At the 17th MOP, the European Union stated that a "framework report" would become available the following year with details on the MeBr stocks of every E.U. country, and it was working with the United States to provide the same. At the time of this writing, however, the stockpile issue is unresolved.

During a small-group session at the 17th MOP, the European Union stated that it would forthwith consider existing MeBr stocks for CUE requests, and it expected other parties to do so as well. Argentina raised the question of why the United States found it so difficult to account for stockpile amounts. The United States admitted that it was not sure how much MeBr went to U.S. growers and/or was exported. At this point, Australia raised concern about the presence of IENGOs in the session, and nonparty observers were asked to leave the room. Indeed, all decisions thereafter related to MeBr were discussed behind closed doors. Several IENGOs expressed disappointment with this decision, one representative shouting that "this is supposed to be an open process!"[47] Therefore, while IENGOs had raised the stockpile issue and brought it to the table, their impact stopped at the point of entry.

By 2005 it seemed clear that IENGO input was waning further. After the closed-door deliberations at the 17th MOP, the NRDC attempted to present its closing comments to the plenary. David Doniger began, "On behalf of NRDC, I am disappointed in the decisions reached this week on MeBr and on CFCs and metered dose inhalers." The co-chair of the meeting (a U.S. delegate) interrupted Doniger: "Point of order! I asked for an intervention only on MeBr [CUEs]!" Doniger continued, "All right. Point taken. I apologize. . . . The negotiations on MeBr have been conducted on a fundamentally uneven playing field. One country possesses crucial information on its stockpiles that it does not disclose. . . . So other countries are forced to negotiate with blindfolds on. . . . We still do not have the transparency of accounting for stocks."[48] I later spoke with a prominent member of the TEAP. This ozone scientist told me that there was no ground for the co-chair's demand for an intervention by the NRDC focused exclusively on MeBr. He worried that the unilateral position of the United States could have long-lasting effects on the Protocol itself and on the impact of IENGOs in the process; he felt IENGO participation was essential to the success of global environmental governance.

Likewise, the EIA maintained its newly concentrated focus on stockpiling, made sure "to keep [its] statement brief," and discussed exclusively the economic issues of stockpiling. It stated that "as a matter of priority MeBr stockpiles must be quantified and considered before granting any further CUEs," urging parties to cease to "continue to represent a protection of stockpiles [because] this will have harmful consequences for the phaseout." Thus, by 2005, the EIA had abandoned its concerns with general socio-ecological welfare, security, and global health and instead focused on the economic implications of stockpiling.

The EIA has chosen to seek solutions to ozone depletion by targeting the MeBr users in California specifically. Arguably a form of devolution of global environmental governance by an IENGO, in 2006 the EIA efforts were concentrated at the national scale as it launched a public relations campaign against the California Strawberry Commission for contributing to the approximately 130,000 new annual cases of melanoma skin cancer because of its insistence on using MeBr. Rather than drawing attention to the socio-ecological effects of MeBr at the global scale, for the first time the EIA directed its efforts at the strawberry producers themselves, calling on the California strawberry industry to stop contributing to the deaths of children due to elevated radiation levels.[49]

The reasons why the EIA changed tactics and sought alternative scales of political intervention are clear: counterclaims from IENGOs stressing global socio-ecological concerns are rather unsuccessful in neoliberal global environmental governance. Such claims seldom penetrate the dominant discourse of science and politics and the rhetoric of neoliberalism established around U.S. claims. However, the EIA's devolution of governance to the national scale also supports neoliberal states in their efforts to relinquish state responsibility of environmental conditions. Concentrating blame for environmental harms on strawberry growers via a national campaign while maintaining the market-efficiency approach of governance at the global scale fits well with neoliberal governmentality.

IENGOs are an intricate part of neoliberal global environmental governance. As such, they "are constituted and reconstituted, sometimes through the very agency that, at first glance, appears to be a means of opposition and resistance."[50] IENGOs that seek change from within the neoliberal context often reinforce that logic, playing an important role in legitimizing or normalizing a neoliberal mode of governance. Such groups "govern themselves" in the image of neoliberalism in order to participate effectively.

The NRDC has been successful in intervening in Montreal Protocol deliberations and in causing verbal and even some agenda-setting reactions from parties. But other concerns, such as the health of citizens, ozone depletion due to phaseout exemptions, and other measures related to global social/environmental justice remain relatively unaddressed. IENGOs like the NRDC have generated interest from nation-states by focusing on MeBr stockpiles, which contradict U.S. (and neoliberal) rhetoric of competition, transparency, and economic fairness. Yet IENGOs that are successful in exposing the contradictions of U.S. protectionism by utilizing neoliberal strategies of their own must neglect broader concerns. The NRDC's neoliberal discourse of a level competitive playing field and antipathy toward protectionism might please LDCs with similar economic concerns, but such interventions are unlikely to provoke states to consider the condition of the global environment and those most affected by ozone depletion.

The NRDC has concentrated its efforts on exposing the contradiction between U.S. claims for consuming and (in 2003) even producing more MeBr and the material condition of U.S. firms, which, the NRDC has shown, have enough MeBr to meet U.S. critical use needs. Other IENGOs, such as the EIA, have joined the NRDC and begun to concentrate on similar neoliberalized interventions. The EIA/NRDC small-group meeting at the 25th OEWG represented an alliance across identities in order to increase their saliency in deliberations. While we cannot conclusively determine whether the EIA's change in tactics is strategic or a form of disciplining, it is clear the EIA learned from 2005–2006 to make less use of rhetoric related to the precautionary principle in favor of the neoliberal discourse it used on the stockpile issue, which proved more effective. While this has meant sacrificing other (global) concerns, it has served to expose a contradiction of neoliberalism—protection of the U.S. agro-industry. As such, NRDC and EIA influence might grow in response to these neoliberal contradictions via a politics based on the laws of the market.

IENGO interventions at the Protocol, however, also demonstrate that general concerns about the environment and normative concerns of individual rights to a healthy and safe environment will probably not be addressed in the neoliberal context. Interventions calling for improved environmental stewardship from U.S. citizens or safeguards for local health, terrorist concerns, or precautionary measures in the name of global environmental health will continue to have little impact on Protocol deliberations. Some groups, such as the EIA, have chosen to focus such campaigns at the national scale in order to generate change in production practices.

To resolve the contradiction of continued MeBr use and nation-state responsibility for a healthy environment for its citizenry, it is quite possible that interventions working from within the provisions of the Protocol will not be enough; a more participatory set of democratic actions might be necessary. Operating within the confines of governance "greatly restricts the range of possible policy considerations" on the table.[51] The discursive frame that exists in global environmental governance has a way of shaping possibilities, of providing what scholars have described as a certain "style of reasoning" that characterizes the neoliberal era.[52] On the other hand, facets of civil society that are more solidly based in "communicative action" are able to propose actions less hindered by "the limitations of institutions based in either the market or the state."[53] Due to these limitations, "new forms of global environmental (sub)politics" are emerging outside the confines of international law.[54] Yet even (especially) here, Foucauldian governmentality cautions us to be mindful of the impact that state agendas, discursive strategies, and neoliberal logic can have on social movement agendas/approaches/ discourses. Due to neoliberal governmentality, the effects of the Great Collision—of market parameters colliding with the need to protect ecological processes—are unlikely to be debated centrally in global environmental governance as a result of IENGO interventions. And IENGOs need to be aware of their active role in this governance process.

8
Conclusion
Is a Better Future for Global
Environmental Governance Possible?

I have emphasized that the Montreal Protocol is often touted as an exemplary model of how to combat global environmental degradation. To be sure, the Protocol has rightfully earned this reputation by eliminating the majority of ODSs from global consumption in just twenty years. The MeBr controversy, however, reveals a significant flaw, or a "dangerous hole," in ozone governance. The process of turning to market-based solutions to resolve the MeBr problem has deeply impacted the way that scientific knowledge, policy making, and ozone governance in general are formed and acted upon. I am convinced that this "hole" is not limited to the politics surrounding the ozone layer. Rather, this neoliberal turn is affecting global environmentalism, including the environmental politics of global climate change. It is no wonder that a global agreement on climate change has not been achieved because the solution needs to make complete economic sense for all participants. There is hope that the

Montreal Protocol can help guide climate politics, but the MeBr case—which marks the latest "style" of ozone governance—shows why such guidance is not going to be easy to achieve, nor necessarily effective.

In the MeBr CUE decision, the signatories to the Protocol decided to join the "neoliberal turn" and incorporate market-based parameters to determine whether certain MeBr practices could be exempt from the MeBr phaseout. I have argued that these parameters reflect the logic and political rhetoric of neoliberalism, where the fate of environmental conditions rests on the economic impact of actions as opposed to the direct regulation of the conditions of agro-industrial production. Additionally, I have argued that the neoliberalization of ozone politics includes a turn to particularist knowledge claims, where local private actors call upon local conditions and sponsor particular scientific studies to justify their claims. Other ODS phaseouts and their exemptions, such as that for CFC essential uses, included parameters to consider the general welfare of society in decision making. The shift to neoliberalism has allowed powerful interest groups in the United States to call upon their own scientific knowledge base to delegitimize the global knowledge base.

Recently scholars have begun to investigate how the successes of the Montreal Protocol could help with another major issue of global importance: global climate change.[1] While I agree with these scholars (some of whom have been involved in the Protocol since its inception, others who, unfortunately, were a part of the AETF debacle) that there are indeed lessons to be learned from the Protocol, those lessons must include the failures experienced in the MeBr phaseout and its links to neoliberalism. I will conclude by explaining the intimate link between ozone-layer depletion and global climate change. Then, I will explain why the MeBr case needs to be considered when the focus is on global climate change. There is a possible way forward to make the successes of the Montreal Protocol compatible with climate politics, but that way involves proactive, activist scientists and a greater range of participation from NGOs than allowed for by the neoliberal turn.

Global climate change has relied on neoliberal measures of its own—in particular the trade in pollution permits in the European Union—with unsatisfactory results. The results have been so paltry, in fact, that some scholars are looking to the Montreal Protocol to phase out ODSs with global warming potential (GWP) and thus synthesize greenhouse-gas-reduction efforts with ozone-reduction efforts and avoid the MeBr controversy all together.[2] Such a synthesis is a long way off at this point. More likely we will continue to see debates over the phaseout of MeBr, which will hit the LDCs in 2015, and as parties consider incorporating quarantine and pre-shipment MeBr uses into the Protocol. We have seen why such debates will continue to threaten the safeguarding of the ozone layer if policies are not changed, if global scientific knowledge remains delegitimized, and if U.S. CUEs and U.S. particularistic scientific knowledge claims maintain their dominance.

Linking Ozone-Layer Protection and Global Climate Change

By the late 1990s, it had become overwhelmingly clear that ozone-layer destruction and global climate change were intricately linked.[3] Ozone-layer recovery is affected by global climate change, and global climate change is shaped by changing weather patterns caused by ozone-layer losses. Additionally, CFCs and some replacements for CFCs—such as hydrofluorocarbons (HFCs)—and MeBr are greenhouse gases. In *The Weather Makers,* Tim Flannery notes the serious issue that remains: "At the moment, Earth is experiencing both stratospheric cooling (due to the ozone hole) and tropospheric warming (due to increased greenhouse gases)."[4] Studies show that this cooling could delay ozone-layer recovery by 10–15 years. Ozone-layer depletion affects weather patterns, increasing ocean winds and raising temperatures in the Southern Hemisphere. On the other hand, global climate change will alter precipitation patterns and temperatures, which will likely increase both the effect of ozone depletion on plants and animals (e.g., skin cancer) and the costly degradation of various man-made materials. Other studies show that global climate change and ozone-layer thinning simultaneously affect aquatic animals at the base of food chains (such as mollusks). These studies show that increased UV radiation (caused by ozone-layer thinning) and increased ocean temperatures (an effect of climate change) work synergistically to increase mortality rates of marine organisms in early stages of life by as much as 90 percent. Other studies show that the ability of oceans in the Southern Hemisphere to absorb carbon has diminished over the last decade, likely a consequence of the increased intensity of ocean winds resulting from ozone-layer depletion and changes in sea-surface temperatures caused by global climate change. Of course, the exact negative effects of climate change and ozone-layer depletion are very difficult to predict. Nonetheless, evidence is building that international environmental governance needs to consider the synergistic effects of global environmental change and ozone-layer depletion/recovery.[5]

The notion of linking ozone-layer depletion/recovery and climate change is not as outrageous as it might seem at first. While the primary concern of the Montreal Protocol was certainly to protect the ozone layer, the preamble to the agreement expresses that the negotiators were "conscious of the potential climatic effects of emissions of these [ozone-depleting] substances." In 2002, parties to the Vienna Convention, which set the stage for Montreal Protocol negotiations in 1985 by committing parties "to protect human health and the environment against adverse effects resulting from modifications of the ozone layer," passed a decision directing "the World Meteorological Organization and the United Nations Environment Programme to draw to the attention of the Parties opportunities for meeting common objectives among conventions, in particular the United Nations Framework Convention on Climate Change."[6]

In response, the Protocol's TEAP and Scientific Assessment Panel collaborated with the IPCC on a report to assess the ozone–climate change interface. The report, presented at the 25th OEWG in 2005, found that reductions in CFCs and other ODSs had already had a significant impact on greenhouse gas emissions. At this meeting, Marco Gonzales, executive secretary of the Ozone Secretariat, praised the Protocol's contribution, stating, "It is gratifying to know the contribution that the Montreal Protocol has made to prevent climate change."[7]

Referring to the IPCC report, Norman, DeCanio, and Fan state, "The Montreal Protocol has accounted for [greenhouse gas] reductions to date equivalent to approximately five times the reductions that would be accomplished by meeting the first Kyoto [Protocol] target." Yet despite the obvious interface between the ozone layer and climate change, "co-investment to realize joint benefits has been difficult to accomplish under the current treaty frameworks."[8] At present the Montreal and Kyoto Protocols simply do not contain the language for coordination. This disconnect between the two treaties has had negative consequences.

THE TROUBLE WITH DISTINCT OZONE/CLIMATE GOVERNANCE PROCESSES

In December 2007, parties to the Montreal Protocol agreed to accelerate the phaseout of HCFCs produced in industrialized countries by ten years, with incremental reductions in 2015 (95 percent phaseout year), 2020, 2025, and full phaseout in 2030.[9] UNEP executive director and U.N. undersecretary general Achim Steiner praised the Protocol parties for this "important and quick win." "Historic is an often over-used word," Steiner stated, "but not in the case of this agreement made in Montreal. Governments had a golden opportunity to deal with the twin challenges of climate change and protecting the ozone layer and governments took it."[10]

While the accelerated HCFC phaseout may have short-term appeal, in the long term, the agreement may have less impact than the Kyoto Protocol could have with U.S. support. After all, the parties to the Montreal Protocol had already agreed to a phaseout of HCFCs in 2040. The accelerated phaseout simply pushes that agreement ahead ten years. In climatological terms, ten years is not a great deal of time. After 2030, the Montreal Protocol HCFC phaseout will have virtually *no effect* on climate change, leaving carbon dioxide (CO_2) reduction still the major concern for global climate change. Thus, while the Montreal Protocol has indeed led to reductions in greenhouse gases (more than the reductions requested in the first Kyoto target), the Kyoto Protocol would require signers to set *new* emissions reduction levels, not change the schedule of emissions levels already agreed upon. The Kyoto Protocol, then, has the potential to change long-term behavior by setting guidelines for future emissions.

More important, the accelerated phaseout has allowed the United States to draw attention away from its lack of commitment to the Kyoto Protocol. The U.S. support of the accelerated HCFC phaseout was likely connected to the Bush administration's desire to tackle climate change on its own terms. As the Earth Negotiations Bulletin noted, "The United States displayed particular enthusiasm for taking climate-related action outside of the climate regime. According to some, their delegation had marching orders to bring climate into the ozone process before the upcoming high-level meeting in Washington and New York on climate change. More skeptical observers suggested that the agreement may also serve to draw attention away from the UNFCCC."[11] Indeed, after the 19th MOP, the United Nations hosted the UNFCCC meeting, designed to "jump-start talks on how to replace Kyoto, saying an agreement needed to be reached by 2009 to avoid 'any vacuum' after its restrictions lapse." President Bush decided to skip the climate change talks, committing only to the dinner reception. It seemed clear that the United States planned to handle global climate change in this unilateral way: "It's our philosophy that each nation has the sovereign capacity to decide for itself what its own portfolio of policies should be," the president's chief environmental adviser, James Connaughton, stated. U.S. deputy national security adviser Dan Price alluded to the U.S. desire to handle global climate problems in a way appropriate for the nation first and foremost, not in a way that benefits global health first and foremost: "It [sovereignty] requires each to make a contribution consistent with its national circumstances."[12]

Unfortunately, the accelerated HCFC phaseout might actually be negative for global climate change.

The provision of the Montreal Protocol's phaseout process that allows developing countries to increase their production and use of HCFCs through 2013 was decided from an ozone-only perspective, but in conjunction with provisions of the Kyoto Protocol it can create perverse incentives. A developing country can expand production of HCFC-22 beyond its needs, in order to obtain [with the clean development mechanism (CDM) of the Kyoto Protocol] credits under Kyoto by destroying the HFC-23 . . . that is a byproduct of the HCFC-22 production process. The IPCC/TEAP Special Report notes that "destruction of byproduct emissions of HFC-23 from HCFC-22 production has a reduction potential of up to 300 [metric tons (Mt)] CO2-equivalent/year by 2015 and specific costs below 0.2 U.S.$/ton CO2-equivalent according to two European studies in 2000." . . . Revenue from the CDM was expected to promote the development of cleaner energy infrastructure in developing countries, which was presumed to be cheaper than retrofitting existing developed world energy generation. Instead, the bulk of the CDM monies have gone to relatively expensive subsidies for the destruction of chemical byproducts like HFC-23. Proper coordination of the two Protocols would entail simultaneous accounting for the impacts of the HCFC-22 and HFC-23 that are jointly produced. It would not then be possible to exploit the provisions of one protocol at the expense of the other.[13]

While combining protocol concerns might be beneficial in this case, in the short term at least it is unlikely to happen. It is important that the United States is not a signatory of the Kyoto Protocol, and this and other major greenhouse emitters that ratified the Montreal Protocol, such as China and India, are not a part of the E.U. plan for 20 percent reductions of the 1990 baseline after the Kyoto provisions expire in 2012.[14] More likely, the protocols will continue to work separately on many, perhaps all, issues.

LOOKING FOR HELP, CARBON ECONOMY?

Controversy surrounding MeBr CUEs should give pause to policymakers and scholars looking to the Montreal Protocol for assistance in reformulating a successful global climate change regime. Indeed, Norman, DeCanio, and Fan's proposal of increasing synergy between the Kyoto and Montreal Protocols would involve avoiding the MeBr controversy all together by swapping MeBr with other ODSs that could be phased out without the political turmoil that erupts with each MeBr CUE request. Having experienced firsthand the AETF fiasco, Norman, DeCanio, and Fan are well aware of how powerful states are able to override global scientific knowledge claims made on the economic and social viability of alternatives to MeBr.

However, avoiding the MeBr CUE process is currently not possible under Protocol rules and likely will not be possible for years to come. True, the MeBr issue is only one aspect of the Protocol. But as a signboard of the new attitude toward an ODS phaseout process, the MeBr controversy illustrates the direction in which policy is moving in the ozone regime and in global environmental politics in general: toward neoliberalism. The MeBr case provides evidence of the harm that market-based approaches can cause when employed the wrong way, with significant effects on levels of cooperation among nation-states, the legitimacy and cohesiveness of global scientific knowledge, and protection of the global environment. Attempts to link these global regimes will need to include rethinking the market-based approaches they both utilize.

The neoliberalization of ozone policy has had a deeply negative impact on the Montreal Protocol. Discussion from the less-developed world on how to prepare for its MeBr phaseouts in 2015 has been difficult. The scientific and technical experts that advise the parties on the MeBr issue, the MBTOC, and other technical committees that have worked on the CUE issue, such as the Economics Options Committee and the AETF, have experienced a moment of delegitimacy in their ability to disseminate sound advice on how to deal with the MeBr phaseout and its exemptions. The United States has been able to call upon specific knowledge claims in order to delegitimize the claims made by the global ozone scientific community. Additionally, global civil society groups, traditionally hailed for their role in pushing the industrialized countries to commit to the ozone effort, have had difficulty convincing governments to reduce or withdraw their CUE nominations. Here, the neoliberal criteria for CUEs have rendered ineffective calls to protect the global environment from groups such as Greenpeace, the EIA, and the NRDC, as they do not reflect market-based concerns written in Decision IX/6. In contrast, the neoliberal criteria have strengthened the ability of protectionist governments, such as the United

States during the Bush administration, to stall the phaseout of MeBr. To date, the Obama administration has shown no sign of changing the strategies laid down by its Republican antecedents.

Possible Solutions

In the short term, the global community may wish to rethink its strategy of leniency with regard to U.S. demands to continue producing and consuming MeBr and, for that matter, other substances that cause environmental harm. Allowing the United States to maintain the status quo may inadvertently prolong its economic dominance of the strawberry sector via environmentally destructive policies and agrarian technologies. However, the United States is gradually switching to alternatives on its own terms (especially since the highly toxic chemical iodomethane—or methyl iodide—became available in California), and so this rethinking will have only minimal effect.

More significant, the MeBr issue is a microcosm of a larger pattern of the clashing environmental policies between the European Union and the United States. The differences are not limited to a single chemical, or group of chemicals, but rather are based on different levels of environmental commitment, most likely intensified by civil society pressures. The differences are also likely influenced by the varying positions of the two powers in the global economy. The United States finds itself in a position of declining dominance in certain sectors (e.g., agriculture, industrial manufacturing, and textiles), whereas the European Union, as well as China and other zones, may foresee growing potential in adopting sustainable alternatives and/or attracting investment counter to the U.S. industrial complex.

For example, the European Union tried to pass legislation that would accelerate the process of declaring chemicals ODSs and consequently phasing them out of existence. It commented at the 24th OEWG in Geneva that the procedure for introducing new substances into the Montreal Protocol regime took too long and needed amendment. While the United States strongly opposed the E.U. proposal, the only solution open to it may soon be to agree to such amendments, reducing MeBr CUEs and other pro-ozone measures, or withdraw from this legally binding agreement—a step it has threatened in plenary and that is a distinct possibility. In the current global political economic milieu, the United States is ostensibly attempting to repair its environmental relations with Europe. As a delegate to the European Community stated, "At the 2006 E.U.-U.S. summit in Vienna, the European Union and the United States have agreed to establish an E.U.-U.S. High Level Dialogue on Climate Change, Clean Energy and Sustainable Development to build on existing bilateral and multilateral initiatives and further advance implementation of the G-8 Gleneagles Plan of Action for Climate Change, Clean Energy and Sustainable Development."[15] Therefore, pulling out of the Montreal Protocol is perhaps an implausible option, as this agreement is the only one committing the United States to multilateral global climate issues.

Many political pundits hoped that U.S.-E.U. environmental relations would improve in the post–Bush administration era, where even the Republican nominee, John McCain, wished to improve U.S.-E.U. cooperation on climate change. Yet that has not happened. The Obama administration's strategy at the fifteenth session of the Conference of Parties (COP-15) to the UNFCCC was one of private decision making and little commitment. The Copenhagen Accord was simply "taken note of" but not adopted, and it was drafted by the United States, China, and a handful of other countries behind closed doors. The document was deemed a "meaningful agreement" by the U.S. government, yet it is not legally binding, and it was not passed unanimously. This stance is similar to the closed-door strategies employed by the United States in the MeBr discussions in 2005, where civil society groups were completely excluded from the decision-making process even as observers to deliberations.[16]

It may be possible to reconfigure the organization of ozone governance so that the entire scientific community and global civil society have more influence in ozone decision making. For one, it might be beneficial to allow the MBTOC to extend its role in *discovering* alternatives and not just assessing ones presented to it. At present, the MBTOC relies on the parties to report which alternatives are viable to their particular circumstances. As Jonathan Banks responded to the Chinese delegation at the 17th MOP in 2005, "MBTOC is not in the process of discovering alternatives. . . . It is expected that individual MBTOC members should be very aware of the progress that is carried out and indeed that would be the subject not only of our annual report, but of the assessment report that is due in December of 2006. So we are not in the process ourselves of being a discovering organization, however we would be very appreciative of any party that brings to our attention the progress in this area."[17]

The MBTOC could be restructured to actively seek alternatives and assess their long-term effects both in the air and on the ground. Alternatives evaluated by the MBTOC could be registered by the parties if they met certain criteria that went beyond just being available. Many countries would likely support such a solution, as they face phaseouts of their own. China noted that the less-developed world often relies on the innovations manufactured in the industrialized world. With industrialized countries like the United States unhurriedly pursuing alternatives, the less-developed world is placed in a difficult position. If the MBTOC were given authority to evaluate and propose alternatives on a proactive basis, this might help it find and justify the need for implementation of MeBr alternatives in all countries. As China put it,

> A lot of [less-developed] countries use the technologies [originating in the industrialized countries]. ... Who is responsible for these alternative technologies? Nobody. The critical use exemptions, when can they be stopped? When can [they] stop without alternative technologies? How can [less-developed] countries phase out MeBr, to have confidence to continue doing so? ... The Meetings of the Parties will face a very serious problem we have never encountered in terms of compliance, in terms of MeBr. ... In MeBr, we'll have encountered such a problem because the parties have spent a lot of time discussing two conflicting policies. One is ... two countries [United States and Spain] have given a lot of reasons [for their need for CUEs]. ... We discuss the exemption procedures and rules and the parties are deadlocked, and the issues are getting more and more complicated, and MBTOC, until today, has been unable to solve these problems. And the other policy is for the [less-developed] countries to phase out MeBr, and ... for [less-developed] countries these party discussions are conflicting with each other. ... Who is

responsible for the screening, the assessment, confirmation, and the widespread examination of the alternative technologies? Tell me, what are the alternative technologies so we can [use them] with confidence, and those technologies which can be used by [less-developed] countries *must also be used by [industrialized] countries.* There cannot be two policies. Now, I regret to say that the TEAP policy report from 2006 to 2008 . . . does not intend to make any effort in terms of MeBr alternative technologies substitution procedures and that nobody cares about these alternative technologies, so that's a very strange phenomenon which is apparent between parties.[18]

It is possible that providing the MBTOC with the role of discovering alternatives would help reinstate its authoritative role over MeBr knowledge, thus returning the legitimacy of MeBr knowledge to the global scale. Providing the MBTOC with the proactive role of seeking alternatives also would fit with the comments made to the 2003 plenary by Stephen DeCanio (at the time co-chair of the AETF) that the promotion of alternative technologies would provide incentives for investments in the alternatives and disincentives for a lack of investment.

This sort of role for the MBTOC could perhaps improve the range of possibilities available for growers. At present, alternatives are promoted primarily by the agro-industrial complex. For example, Arysta LifeScience strongly advocated for the MeBr replacement chemical methyl iodide, arguing that the continued use of MeBr will kill up to an additional eight hundred people in the United States alone due to skin

Figure 6. Author with daughter picking organic
strawberries, a chemical-free alternative to methyl bromide in
Davenport, California. (Photo by Tara Pisani Gareau.)

cancer directly caused by MeBr's ozone-depleting effects,
while this alternative has no ozone-depleting properties.[19] A
proactive scientific community, however, would be able to
weigh the local toxicological effects of methyl iodide against
the global effects of methyl bromide in a more robust way
than a chemical company with profit interests. In such a
scenario, organic alternatives might achieve mainstream
status, as research, incentives, and civil society become capable
of voicing alternative, yet legitimized, discourses in ozone governance. Research in organic strawberries has been performed

for decades, but funding in the area has been scant in comparison to that of conventional MeBr alternatives.

As with climate-change negotiations in Copenhagen in 2009 and Cancun in 2010, it seems clear that the MeBr process has ceased to be transparent.[20] As a lobbyist working on the MDI issue expressed to me at the 17th MOP, "The problem now is that the regime is not equipped, or structured, to handle the issues it currently needs to handle." The entire range of MeBr and MDI deliberations at the 17th MOP took place in small groups closed to the public, frustrating interest groups in both arenas. Both ODS deliberations have led to prolonged, stalled phaseouts.

One way to allay the disconnect—and at times heated disagreement—between NGOs and nation-states would be to provide more transparency. But because deliberations from 2005–2007 were conducted primarily at the bilateral level (European Union vs. United States; United States vs. agro-industry actors), the situation is less about global consensus and more about bilateral and multilateral political decision making. Such was not always the case. According to the MDI lobbyist, "With the CFCs phaseout, folks got involved with the phaseout because they all knew where everyone stood, and they were moving toward alternatives already in the pipeline." Indeed, when I asked a member of the U.S. delegation if I would be able to attend the bilateral meetings between the United States and agro-industry lobbyists, I was told that I could not attend any chemical industry meetings because they were bilateral at this point and not open to "outsiders."

Finally, it appears that one of the best ways to change the closed-door policy that has typified the MeBr controversy is to exert pressure from civil society positioned *outside* the rules of procedure of the Protocol. The neoliberalization of Protocol rules for exemptions to the MeBr phaseout has generally weakened the ability of civil society groups to push governments toward a phaseout. NGOs must utilize a neoliberal discourse in order to be heard, and that discourse encourages them to work with market logic and concerns for the effect of policies on individual actors. "Neoliberal governmentality" is increasingly geared toward drawing on market disruptions to search for ways that parties are evading the reliance on market mechanisms (e.g., stockpiling, the EIA complaint; use of stockpiles for noncritical uses, the NRDC complaint) and not drawing parties' attention to the concerns that led to the agreement in the first place—the impact of industrial production on the global environment (e.g., Greenpeace's complaint).

It is possible that a shift in the U.S. position on the MeBr issue will have to come from civil society groups operating at the nation-state or regional levels. Here, citizens can participate in all manner of activities that demonstrate to the U.S. government that it is in the interests of the U.S. people to phase out MeBr and to participate in an intricately designed global environmental policy that reflects the synergistic relations between ozone depletion and global climate change. MeBr activists could increase U.S. citizen participation by focusing on both the local impact of MeBr and conventional alternatives *and* the global impact of ozone depletion. Increasing awareness would improve chances of involving powerful actors interested in exposing the health impacts of unsustainable and dangerous farming practices in court hearings and other venues costly to the agro-chemical industry. Industry leaders that have switched to MeBr alternatives could be played against industry laggards, where the threat of receiving compensation for injuries could help push the entire industry in a better direction. This approach helped in the CFC case, and it could here as well.[21]

The U.S. civil society base is in a unique position. It is located in a site with immense potential for changing the production activities of the largest national economy on the planet. Many ozone scientists and scholars would agree that to change ozone and climate governance, change must come from within the United States. Civil society groups less fettered by the rules and procedures of neoliberal governance might be able to lead the way.

However, it seems critical that any gains made by civil society external to Protocol rules and procedures be coupled with the re-enfranchisement of activist scientists and other actors working within the Protocol proper. The reemergence of precautionary measures, concerns for global society, and global ecological conditions amid broad-based neoliberalization can occur only with liberated insider support as well.

Afterword

In late March 2012, I received an e-mail from a colleague who has spent many years working as an environmental economist on (among other things) the methyl bromide issue. It had been a few years since we last corresponded, but recently we had exchanged a string of e-mails because her work and mine were suddenly generating a number of "hits" on the Internet, and she wanted to know if I was aware of any new developments on the methyl bromide phaseout. Our work was very different but related: hers systematically evaluated the economic effects of methyl bromide alternatives on strawberry growers and the strawberry industry more generally, and my work largely concentrated on the science/ policy interface and the effect of the methyl bromide contro- versy on civil society groups working at Montreal Protocol meetings. The latest e-mail shed some light on what was causing such a stir among methyl bromide scholars and ozone policymakers.

"Wow!" was all she wrote in the e-mail, with a story for- warded from the *New York Times*. The story, by Malia Wollan, was titled "Maker Pulls Pesticide amid Fear of Toxicity." The maker, Japan-based Arysta LifeScience Corporation, had with- drawn methyl iodide from sale in the United States, it stated, due to concerns with its "economic viability in the U.S. marketplace."[1] Wollan reported that Arysta's decision to pull this "controversial pesticide from the American market [was] surprising [for] both growers and environmentalists who have warned that it poses serious hazards."[2] Indeed it was surprising.

After reading through the story, I couldn't help remembering a conversation that I had had with a California strawberry grower in 2003 about methyl iodide. We were talking about comments made at the time by the California Strawberry Commission about how methyl bromide alternatives didn't work as well as this "perfect chemical." Most important, the commission argued, there were township caps on how much of the alternatives could be used within specific regions in California. In short, the alternatives had negative local effects that made it necessary to limit their use. Telone (1,3-Dichloropropene) is a carcinogen that persists in water supplies, and chloropicrin is extremely toxic when inhaled, is lethal to aquatic life, and isn't safe to touch (if splashed in the eye, it could literally liquefy the cornea). Also, the California Strawberry Commission argued that the alternatives were most commonly applied with water, making their use on hillsides presumably more difficult, if not impossible. (Incidentally, both the EPA and Erin Mayfield and Catherine Norman found expansion of strawberry acreage in Watsonville, California, a major strawberry-producing region containing a great deal of strawberry acreage on hillsides.)[3] Methyl iodide would solve the problem of usage on hillsides. I remember the grower stating that "everyone is waiting for methyl iodide to be approved" for use in California. Then methyl bromide would not be needed.

In 2007, the growers got their wish when methyl iodide became registered for use in the United States, and it became available to California growers in 2010. But the chemical never

achieved large-scale use in California. In 2012, methyl iodide
was evaluated by the EPA's Science Advisory board as the
"the near perfect substitute" for methyl bromide, "the most
economic alternative ... for California strawberries," and
"financially feasible according to the criteria set out by the
MBTOC."[4] But growers simply were not willing to use it, likely
due to the environmental backlash from environmental
groups operating in California (also noted in the EPA report).
The *New York Times* story explained quite clearly: "One member of the [California Department of Pesticide Regulation's]
own scientific review committee called [methyl iodide] 'one of
the most toxic chemicals on earth.'" Environmental groups
such as Pesticide Action Network of North America (PANNA)
had mounted a vibrant campaign to alert Californians to the
imminent introduction of this chemical into their daily lives.
Along with sixteen other groups, PANNA sued Arysta and the
state of California for failing to review methyl iodide properly
for agricultural uses of the toxin. As PANNA reported after
Arysta's withdrawal of the chemical, "This is a tremendous
victory for scientific integrity in the face of corporate pressure,
especially for rural communities and farmworkers."[5]

So while methyl iodide might not deplete the ozone
layer, it could most certainly harm the environmental conditions of the landscape where it was used. And while it could
replace methyl bromide almost effortlessly, the political backlash of its use could potentially be very problematic. This
chemical had led four Nobel Laureates in chemistry to state
that they were "perplexed that [the] U.S. EPA would even consider [introducing it] into agricultural use," and the California
review panel for the case had stated that it was "too toxic to be
used safely outside of a laboratory."[6] How it was approved
for use in strawberry fields is astonishing. Tom Phillpot, food

and agriculture blogger for *Mother Jones*, thinks he has the answer:

> In 2006, the Japanese chemical giant Arysta pre-
> sented [methyl iodide] to the EPA as the perfect
> candidate to replace methyl bromide. The pitch: It
> works just as well on [strawberry plant pathogens],
> but it doesn't harm the ozone layer. . . . Arysta had
> friends in high places while the EPA pondered
> methyl iodide: In 2006, then-EPA director Stephen
> Johnson [himself appointed by the Bush Adminis-
> tration] appointed Elin Miller, then-CEO of the
> North American arm of Arysta, to a high post with-
> in the agency [as EPA Administrator for Region 10].
> Before her stint at Arysta, Miller had worked at
> Dow Chemical, "overseeing the company's public
> affairs, global pest management, and Asia Pacific
> operations," according to an EPA press release.[7]

Coincidental circumstances? Perhaps. But there are too many investigations linking the passage of certain chemicals to political maneuvering within the EPA to dismiss such a link entirely.

More important, however, the methyl iodide withdrawal speaks to a much larger problem linked more directly to glob-al environmental governance of the ozone layer. It is this: what good is global environmental governance if the outcome is greater local environmental harm? Is this the best we can do? Are the choices before us to further deplete the ozone layer or to worsen the environmental conditions of rural communities and farmworkers? Must we accept the introduction of new dangerous agro-chemicals in order to successfully remove others? If the bottom line is principally maintaining economic output, then there might be no other choice.

No ethic, only yields. I'm reminded here of C. S. Lewis's masterpiece, *The Abolition of Man*, where Lewis expresses concern with scientific applications used to debunk value judgments in the name of "progress" devoid of moral guidance or, in this case, applications guided by mere profit. Lewis feared that the application of science and technology without an ethical base could threaten the integrity of our whole civilization. Yet we have seen in the global scientific community a backlash against forces interested in maintaining the status quo, and we see with the methyl iodide backlash more scientists unwilling to leave their ethical concerns at the door of the laboratory. In fact, they want to keep these dangerous chemicals *in* the laboratory, where they can be controlled. But at the end of the day, profit is still the primary concern of the agricultural establishment (after all, the methyl iodide backlash came from outside the agro-industrial community). The issue remains that alternatives must be profitable, and anything is possible as long as it is approved by the EPA and growers are willing to adopt it. Chloropicrin—a part of the chemical warfare arsenal of World War I—and its ilk might be the best we can hope for if profit is the only moral guide.[8]

But the outcome of the methyl bromide controversy shows some promising signs that less harmful alternatives might be more viable than the agro-chemical industry suspects. The best signs come from the new article published by Mayfield and Norman in the *Journal of Environmental Management* and from the 2012 U.S. Critical Use Nomination for methyl bromide in 2014.[9] The reports show that the post–methyl bromide world is much less dismal for strawberry growers than the industry anticipated and that work on alternatives—including nonchemical alternatives—is finally entering the predominant discourse.

Mayfield and Norman's research is the most striking. To put it simply, they find little indication that California strawberry growers have been negatively affected by the methyl bromide phaseout. In fact, it seems that the entire California strawberry industry has grown despite the minimization of methyl bromide on strawberry fields. "Contrary to ex-ante industry claims," they write, "the years of declining methyl bromide use have been years of rising yields, acreage, exports, revenues and market share for California growers, even when faced with a global recession and increased imports from Mexican growers who retain the right to use the chemical [until 2015] under the Protocol."[10]

Astounding. After years of internecine polemic among Protocol delegates, after years of denigration of the soundness of the global scientific establishment, after hundreds of hours of intense negotiations and additional expenditures to host not one but two extraordinary meetings of the Montreal Protocol, it turns out that methyl bromide reductions actually didn't affect California growers too badly. On the contrary, the industry actually *grew*. My first reaction after reading Mayfield and Norman's report was outrage; my second was unbewildered acceptance that the agro-industrial complex will always fight to maintain the status quo if there is any chance that its profit machine might be at risk. Now that it is completely clear that the available alternatives are feasible, we will likely see momentum toward their complete adoption. But even here we are left concerned with the effects that the alternatives will have on local socio-ecological conditions.

The U.S. Critical Use Nomination report for 2014 is promising for different but related reasons. Within the

document we see a rather honest engagement with the literature on alternatives, including nonchemical ones. The report
discusses various treatments that either reduce or promise to
eliminate the need for chemical applications altogether, such
as the use of different landscape fabrics, anaerobic soil disin-
festations, and better buffer zone management in strawberry
production, to name but a few possibilities. The report states
that "transition from methyl bromide is expected to continue
with the refinement of these new technologies being funded
by the USDA nationwide."[11] Yet if most of these techniques are
still only in the trial stage and strawberry acreage, yields,
and profits are increasing regardless, then does this report not
inadvertently inform us that greater acreage could very soon
be devoted to nonchemical strawberry production, perhaps
even organic strawberry production, than the U.S. agro-
industry would have us believe? Is it possible that the inclusion
of information on these projects and the authors that are cited
in this report—many of whom are organic agriculture advocates—could lend support to research and civil society groups
that support solutions that are more sustainable and less toxic
to both global and local ecologies? Such a step would get us
closer to the scientific/civil society advocacy that is necessary
for real change in environmental governance.

The alternative technologies are there, but sometimes it
takes a push from society to get them implemented. We have
seen the strength of civil society in pushing methyl iodide off
the landscape (at least for now). Can it go a step further and
push off other locally harmful toxins as well? There are a few
barriers to such an outcome from the production side of the
equation. First, the growers risk everything; if an alternative
does not work as hoped, they lose their crop, their land,
and their livelihood. It seems possible to incorporate into the

global governance structure a financial mechanism that would allow growers (even U.S. growers) to make use of the recommendations from activist and forward-thinking scientists to adopt cutting-edge alternatives that are not only profitable but also beneficial from social and ecological perspectives. The Montreal Protocol provides such a mechanism for less developed countries, but the United States has seriously undermined it domestically due to the undercutting of land grant extension programs designed to help American growers (programs that remain often rely on the chemical industry to foot the bills). To continue to provide such a mechanism, it would be necessary to weigh the total benefits of nonchemical growing techniques against the long-term socio-ecological costs of chemical use. Supporting this sort of approach is what environmental protection from a precautionary perspective is all about.

Appendix
Note on Methods

I obtained information for the book from several sources: (1) in-depth formal and informal interviews; (2) direct observation at Montreal Protocol meetings; (3) historical and archival research, as well as extensive research on previous work on the Protocol. I attended Montreal Protocol meetings as an "observer." From 2003 to 2007, I attended each of the annual MOPs, the two ExMOPs, and the annual OEWG meetings, which are held to prepare for the annual MOPs. Protocol meetings are attended by nation-state delegations, scientists, international organizations such as the World Bank and the GEF, NGO and industry representatives, nonsignatory countries (as long as no country objects to their attendance), and observers.

Attendance at Montreal Protocol meetings provided me with firsthand information regarding the decision-making process of the Montreal Protocol in general and the MeBr phaseout specifically; such information is often inaccessible due to the structure of UNEP documentation, which is often written in the passive voice. Nation-states have the opportunity to speak at the plenary meetings in the order that they request the floor. Scientific committees give presentations during plenary sessions on updates in ozone science and recommendations for how parties should handle cases of noncompliance or requested exemptions to the phaseout of ODSs. NGOs may speak as well; however, they are typically allowed to speak only once the floor is clear and then only if time permits. It was clear to me that NGOs that had gained favor with their governments were given the floor quite easily, as interventions by the California Strawberry Commission indicated. At these meetings, I took tape-recorded notes of all plenary deliberations (which were later transcribed) and interviewed key nation-state delegates, NGO and industry representatives, and MeBr scientists. Official documents of the meetings, reports published by the UNEP scientific community, and other supplementary information were also used to support the claims made here.

Prior to conducting interviews at MOPs and other meetings, I established contact and rapport with the majority of interviewees, an important step for interviewing success.[1] Interviews were kept anonymous but in general included MBTOC members, industry and NGO lobbyists, and other key scientific figures. From these interviews and from seminal monographs on the Montreal Protocol,[2] I was able to assess how scientific knowledge "flows" in the Montreal Protocol governance process and how it is "packaged" for dissemination and linked to the political and economic struggles of nation-states and other actors.[3] Drawing from Canan and Reichman's broader-based structured surveys of scientists operating in the Montreal Protocol, I designed my formal and informal interviews to gather basic information on MBTOC members and other actors and discover actors' feelings about the history of the MeBr phaseout, levels of involvement of key participants and countries, and levels of cohesiveness among MBTOC members and other actors.[4] In-depth interviews with these participants were also used to gather information on how MeBr scientific research is collected, organized, used, and presented by the global ozone scientific community at Protocol meetings. Informal interviews with state, industry, and NGO representatives were designed to discover the links between MeBr science and politics and as a triangulation tool to verify other gathered information.[5]

Assessment of the trends in strawberry production in each of the three primary competing regions (United States, European Union, and China) proved necessary in order to gauge actors' claims about MeBr and its alternatives. I analyzed data on historical trends in MeBr use and levels of strawberry production in each of the three regions, compared these to research on and promotion of alternatives, and evaluated these data with information gained from the analysis of surveys and in-depth interviews.[6]

To assess the effectiveness of global civil society groups at influencing state and regional policy in the United States and the European Union on the MeBr issue, I used direct observation of interventions at Protocol meetings (which I tape-recorded) and interviewed the civil society groups mentioned above and additional members of the MBTOC who were either consultants to MeBr-based growers or were involved in alternative MeBr projects. For research on the apparent differences between the E.U. policy to accelerate the MeBr phaseout and the U.S. interest in slowing it down, I did the following: (1) performed an archival search of the history of national policy in each region vis-à-vis its ozone policies and MeBr policies in particular; (2) interviewed key actors mentioned above; and (3) attended Montreal Protocol meetings, tape-recording and transcribing plenary discussions.

Notes

Introduction

1. The phrase "ozone hole" is used to refer to ozone thinning or when ozone levels fall below 220 Dobson Units (DU), rather than an actual hole in the ozone layer.

2. Gutro, "NASA"; Hofmann quoted in Newman, "Annual Records."

3. "The average UV-B [a type of UV radiation that can cause sunburn and skin cancer] measured at the South Pole during spring between 1991 and 2006 was 55–85% larger than estimated for the years 1963–1980." Fahey and Hegglin, "Twenty Questions," 52. The ozone layer is so effective at absorbing harmful UV-B rays out that with a 1 percent loss of the ozone layer, "2% more UV-B is able to reach the surface of the planet." S. Wells, "Ozone Depletion."

4. WMO, "Record," and Black, "Arctic Ozone."

5. Dell'Amore, "First North Pole Ozone Hole Forming?" and Earthsky, "Record Depletion."

6. Murray, "Arctic Ozone Hole Moving South."

7. Expatica, "New Ozone Hole over Germany Poses Health Risks."

8. Lorente et al., "Climatology of Ozone 'Mini-Hole' Events," 65.

9. Rivas et al., "Ultraviolet Light Exposure," 567. The strength of UV rays hitting earth's surface is more profound at both poles, where ozone is weaker. The number of melanoma cases follows this pattern, with annual cases of Cutaneous Malignant Melanoma (CMM) ranging from five to twenty-four per 100,000 within Europe and the United States and increasing dramatically to "over 70 per 100,000 in higher ambient UV radiation regions of Australia and New Zealand." Norval et al., "The Human Health Effects of Ozone Depletion," 202.

10. Esty and Winston, *Green to Gold*, 53–54.

11. Hobson, "Gobal Warming," 525.

12. S. Wells, "Ozone Depletion."

13. American Cancer Society, "Cancer Facts"; Staples et al., "Non-Melanoma Skin Cancer"; Australian Bureau of Statistics, "Causes of Death"; Australian Institute of Health and Welfare (AIHW) and Australasian Association of Cancer Registries (AACR), "Cancer"; National Cancer Control Initiative, "The 2002 National Non-Melanoma Skin Cancer Survey"; Australian Institute of Health and Welfare (AIHW), "Health System Expenditures"; and Flannery, *The Weather Makers*.

14. Rivas et al., "Ultraviolet Light Exposure," 567.

15. Flannery, *The Weather Makers*, 218–219, and van der Leun, "The Ozone Layer."

16. Skin Cancer Foundation, "Ozone and UV."

17. Quoted in BBC, "Ozone Hole 'Can Be Fixed by 2080.' "

18. Hadekel, "Montreal Protocol Outshines Kyoto," B1.

19. Quoted at http://www.theozonehole.com/montreal.htm.

20. Mulroney, Benedick, and Hufford quoted in ENB, "20th Anniversary Seminar."

21. Hunter, Salzman, and Zaelke, *International Environmental Law and Policy*, 624.

22. Goldberg, "As the World Burns."

23. E.g., Parson, *Protecting the Ozone Layer;* Benedick, *Ozone Diplomacy;* Haas, "Banning Chlorofluorocarbons"; and Canan and Reichman, *Ozone Connections.*

24. Parson, *Protecting the Ozone Layer,* and Litfin, *Ozone Discourses.*

25. BBC, "An Animated Journey"; IPCC. "Climate Change 2007"; and Benedick, *Ozone Diplomacy.*

26. My.barackobama.com.

27. To emphasize this point, the Reagan administration's secretary of the interior was James G. Watt, who was "described by the chief environment counsel at the House Energy and Commerce Committee . . . as one of the two most 'intensely controversial and blatantly anti-environmental political appointees' in American history." The other, according to Freudenberg and Gramling, was Anne Gorsuch, who was appointed by Reagan to run the EPA. Freudenburg and Gramling, *Blowout in the Gulf,* 128 and fn. 19.

28. Saad, "Increased Number Think Global Warming is 'Exaggerated.' "

29. Black, "Arctic Ozone." See also Lubchenco, "Entering the Century of the Environment," 492, and IPCC, "Climate Change 2007."

30. Quoted in Carlowicz and Ecochard, "Arctic Ozone Loss."

31. Black, "Arctic Ozone."
32. Quoted in ibid.
33. Eyring et al., "Multi-Model Assessment," 9468.
34. Clark, "Illegal Trade," 1.
35. BBC, "Whistle Blown."
36. Hayman and Trent, "New Challenges," and Ning, "Illegal Trade," 6.
37. EPA, "Methyl Bromide," and Kegley, Katten, and Moses, "Second-hand Pesticides."
38. Faber and McCarthy, "Neo-Liberalism," 53.
39. B. Walker, "California Study."
40. Faber, *Capitalizing on Environmental Injustice.*
41. Three popular alternatives to MeBr used in strawberry production are chloropicrin, a highly toxic product used in World War II for chemical warfare; 1,3-Dichloropropene (trade name Telone), a carcinogen that persists in water and is being phased out by the European Union; and the recently EPA-approved methyl iodide, a chemical so toxic that some scientists (including three Nobel Laureates) "concluded that use of the fumigant would result in acute public health risks because tests on rats and rabbits have shown that airborne exposure to the chemical causes thyroid cancer, miscarriages and damage to the nervous system. Scientists also found it can pollute air and water." Wozniacka, "Neighbors."
42. TEAP, "Report," 7.
43. Quoted in BBC, "Ozone Hole 'Can Be Fixed by 2080.'"
44. Stephen O. Andersen, director of Strategic Climate Projects in the EPA Climate Protection Partnerships Division and longtime Montreal Protocol contributor, attributes early Montreal Protocol successes to the "Stockholm Group," policymakers working with these principles of precaution and global cooperation on environmental issues. Andersen, Sarma, and Taddonio, *Technology Transfer.*
45. Canan and Reichman, *Ozone Connections.* But see also Grundmann, *Transnational Environmental Policy.*
46. E.g., Arrighi, *The Long Twentieth Century;* Burawoy, *Global Ethnography;* Meyer, "The World Polity"; Tilly, *Durable Inequality;* Marx: *Capital* and *Grundrisse;* Wallerstein, *The Modern World-System;* Bourdieu, "The Forms of Capital"; and Foster, "Marx's Theory."
47. Bourdieu, "The Forms of Capital," and Castells, *The Rise of the Network Society.*
48. Litfin, *Ozone Discourses,* 3.
49. Lipschutz, "Power, Politics and Global Civil Society"; Harvey, *Spaces of Hope;* Watts, "Green Capitalism"; and Goldman, *Imperial Nature.*

50. See, for example, Heynen, McCarthy, Prudham, and Robbins, *Neoliberal Environments;* Liverman and Vilas, "Neoliberalism"; Okereke, *Global Justice;* and Robbins, *Political Ecology.*

51. McCarthy, "Privatizing Conditions of Production"; McCarthy and Prudham, "Neoliberal Nature"; Harvey: *A Brief History of Neoliberalism* and *The New Imperialism;* Perreault and Martin, "Geographies of Neoliberalism"; Williams, *The Roots of the Modern American Empire;* Brenner and Theodore, "Cities"; O'Connor, *The Fiscal Crisis.*

52. Friedman, *Capitalism and Freedom;* Friedman and Schwartz, *A Monetary History;* and Hayek, *The Road to Serfdom.*

53. Brenner and Theodore, "Cities," and Gareau, "Dangerous Holes"; see also Polanyi, *The Great Transformation.*

54. Gareau, "We Have Never Been 'Human,'" 129–132.

55. Harvey, *The Limits to Capital;* O'Connor: "The Second Contradiction" and *The Fiscal Crisis.*

56. Mansfield, "Rules of Privatization"; O'Connor, *Natural Causes,* 307; Peck, "Neoliberalizing States"; and Polanyi, *The Great Transformation.*

57. Goldman, *Imperial Nature;* Babb, *Behind the Development Banks;* Diaz-Bonilla, Frandsen, and Robinson, *WTO Negotiations;* and Conca, "The WTO."

58. Cf. Goldman, *Imperial Nature.*

59. Cf. ibid.; Gareau: "Dangerous Holes" and "Ecological Values"; Bakker, *An Uncooperative Commodity;* Conca, *Governing Water;* Peluso, "Coercing Conservation"; Liverman, "Who Governs?"

60. McCarthy and Prudham, "Neoliberal Nature"; Peck: "Neoliberalizing States" and "Geography and Public Policy"; and Peck and Tickell, "Neoliberalizing Space."

61. Cf. Faber, *Capitalizing on Environmental Injustice,* ch. 5, and O'Connor, "Capitalism, Nature, Socialism," 27, 37.

62. In line with his earlier work, in *The Fiscal Crisis of the State,* O'Connor means by "social capital" investments by the state in social institutions and infrastructures. O'Connor, *The Fiscal Crisis.* He does not mean the kind of "networking-for-success" common among social capital scholars. Cf. Coleman, "Social Capital." For goods and services, O'Connor includes infrastructure, a labor force with certain characteristics and abilities, and given environmental conditions and services. McCarthy, "Privatizing Conditions of Production," 335; see also O'Connor, "Is Sustainable Capitalism Possible?"

63. Foucault, *History of Sexuality.*

64. O'Connor, *Natural Causes*, 307.

65. Polanyi, *The Great Transformation.*

66. Gareau, "We Have Never Been 'Human,'" 137–140, and Goodman, Sorj, and Wilkenson, *From Farming to Biotechnology.*

67. Swyngedouw and Heynen, "Urban Political Ecology," 912, my emphasis.

68. Foucault: "Truth and Power," 116, and "Two Lectures," 98.

2

From Public to Private Global Environmental Governance

1. See for example, Babb, *Managing Mexico;* Campbell and Pedersen, *The Rise of Neoliberalism;* Fourcade-Gourinchas and Babb, "The Rebirth of the Liberal Creed"; Henisz, Zelner, and Guillen, "Worldwide Diffusion"; and Marglin and Schor, *The Golden Age of Capitalism.* Others refer to the Golden Age period as that of "embedded liberalism." See Ruggie, "International Regimes."

2. Keynes, *General Theory.*

3. Fourcade-Gourinchas and Babb, "The Rebirth of the Liberal Creed," 535. "Government is not the solution, it is the problem," President Reagan famously stated. True to the emergent anti–Club of Rome (i.e., limits to growth) rhetoric emerging at the time, during his 1985 Second Inaugural Address, Reagan stated that "there are no limits to growth and human progress when men and women are free to follow their dreams." Quoted in Clarke and Cortner, *The State of Nature,* 301. See also Reagan, "The American Sound." Today, references to Hayek's *The Road to Serfdom,* the anti-Keynesian, anti-socialist, anti-government-regulation economic manifesto, is being cited by American conservatives as being influential in their political choices. Conservative political pundit Glenn Beck discussed the text on the Fox News Channel in June 2010. Republican presidential hopeful Rick Perry stated that "Friedrich Hayek's book is one that had an impact on me, understanding that John Maynard Keynes absolutely knew nothing about economics." Republican hopeful Michele Bachmann mentioned that she frequently reads the works of Milton Friedman and those of Hayek's mentor, Ludwig von Mises. See Keith, "Austrian School Economist Hayek Finds New Fans."

4. Adapted from Henisz, Zelner, and Guillen, "Worldwide Diffusion," 871.

5. See Cohen and Centeno, "Neoliberalism," and Boli and Thomas, "World Culture."

6. See Harvey, *A Brief History of Neoliberalism,* 69–73.

7. Bourdieu, "The Essence of Neoliberalism."

8. Dunlap and Mertig, *American Environmentalism;* Szasz, *EcoPopulism;* and Conca and Dabelko, *Green Planet Blues.*

9. Compare, for example, Dunlap and Mertig, *American Environmentalism;* Hoffman, "Institutional Evolution"; Eckersley, *Environmentalism;* Olzak and Soule, "Cross-Cutting Influences"; Frank, Hironaka, and Schofer, "The Nation-State"; and Schofer and Hironaka, "The Effects of World Society."

10. See the second section of *Blueprint for Survival,* http://www. theecologist.info/page32.html.

11. See Eckersley, *Environmentalism,* 20–21, and Speth and Haas, *Global Environmental Governance,* 56–60.

12. Ophuls, "The Scarcity Society," 60.

13. Ophuls, "Leviathan or Oblivion," 224.

14. Hardin, "The Tragedy of the Commons," and Commoner, *The Closing Circle,* 296. Some, like Hardin, would go even further, arguing that the industrialized world needed to sever ties with the global South so that it would not industrialize and thus increase its impact on the global ecosystem. See Hardin, "Lifeboat Ethics."

15. Lipschutz, "Global Civil Society," 233.

16. Dunlap and Mertig, *American Environmentalism,* and Szasz, *Ecopopulism.*

17. U.N. General Assembly 1972 A/RES/2581, XXIV.

18. Hunter, Salzman, and Zaelke, *International Environmental Law and Policy,* 170–174.

19. Rowland and Molina, "Chlorofluoromethanes," and NAS, "Carbon Dioxide and Climate."

20. Bankobeza, *Ozone Protection,* 27, 36, and Litfin, *Ozone Discourses.* While it is possible to trade CFC quotas internationally under the Montreal Protocol, the strategy is seldom employed. Instead, governments and CFC producers negotiated the transition to non-CFC production largely via command-and-control mechanisms not directly tied to market conditions. Parson, *Protecting the Ozone Layer.*

21. Fest Grabiel, "Crucial Crossroads," 21.

22. Havel, "Democracy's Forgotten Dimension," 9.

23. Palmer, "New Ways," 262; see also Hunter, Salzman, and Zaelke, *International Environmental Law and Policy,* 234–244, and Esty, *Greening the GATT.*

24. World Commission on Environment and Development, *Our Common Future,* and Lélé, "Sustainable Development."

25. Hunter, Salzman, and Zaelke, *International Environmental Law and Policy,* 199.

26. Bernstein, *The Compromise,* 37, 106–107, and Speth and Haas, *Global Environmental Governance.*

27. Meadows, *The Limits to Growth;* Goodland and Ledoc, "Neoclassical Economics"; and Lélé, "Sustainable Development."

28. See Moses, "Abdication," 125.

29. World Commission on Environment and Development, *Our Common Future.*

30. Goldman, *Imperial Nature,* 91, emphasis in original; see also Babb, *Behind the Development Banks,* and Bernstein, *The Compromise.*

31. Harvey, *A Brief History of Neoliberalism;* Castree, "Neoliberalising Nature"; DuPuis and Gareau, "Neoliberal Knowledge"; and Gareau, "A Critical Review."

32. Boswell and Chase-Dunn, *The Spiral;* Evans, "Is an Alternative Globalization Possible?"; and Gill, "Constitutionalizing Inequality." The United States promised a paltry $250 million, mostly for reforestation efforts, a key concern for its environmentally minded citizenry. See Hunter, Salzman, and Zaelke *International Environmental Law and Policy,* 182–183.

33. Brown, "Time Is Running Out," 13.

34. Speth and Haas, *Global Environmental Governance,* 80, my emphasis. See also Tickell and Peck, "Making Global Rules," 167.

35. Introduction to first two editions of Dorfman and Dorfman, *Economics of the Environment.*

36. Tietenberg, "Transferable Discharge Permits."

37. Dorfman and Dorfman, *Economics of the Environment.*

38. Stavins, *Economics of the Environment,* 4th and 5th eds.

39. Bernstein, *The Compromise,* 81.

40. Schelling, "The Cost of Combatting Global Warming," 510.

41. Ibid.

42. Lowenfeld, *International Economic Law,* 316–317.

43. Http://www.unep.org/geo/geo1/ch/ch3_2.htm.

44. Http://www.unep.org/geo/GEO4/report/GEO-4_Report_Full_en.pdf.

45. UNEP, "Economic Instruments," 1.

46. UNEP, "Statement by Dr. Klaus Töpfer," 2.

47. Ibid., 1.

48. Stigson, "Walking the Talk," 266, my emphasis.

49. Hunter, Salzman, and Zaelke, *International Environmental Law and Policy*, 198.

50. UNEP, "Earth Report."

51. Http://www.nobelprize.org/nobel_prizes/peace/laureates/2009, and my.barackobama.com; accessed September 3, 2008.

52. See http://environment.yale.edu/climate/files/SixAmericasJan2010.pdf.

53. Monbiot, *Heat*, 215.

54. Okereke, *Global Justice*, 53. See also Newell and Paterson, "The Politics of the Carbon Economy"; Yamin, Burniaux, and Nentjes, "Kyoto Mechanisms"; Helm and Hepburn, *The Economics and Politics of Climate Change*; and Bodansky, "Prologue to the Climate Change Convention."

55. Hepburn, "Carbon Taxes."

56. Speth, *Red Sky at Morning*.

57. Ekins and Barker, "Carbon Taxes."

58. Cf. McKibbin and Wilcoxen, "The Role of Economics."

59. Parson, *Protecting the Ozone Layer*; Andersen, Sarma, and Taddonio, *Technology Transfer*; and Canan and Reichman, *Ozone Connections*.

60. Norman, DeCanio, and Fan, "The Montreal Protocol at 20."

61. Flannery, *The Weather Makers*, 215; Environment News Service: "Developing Countries Funded for Ozone Safe Technology" and "South Pole Ozone Recovery"; and UNEP, "Report of the 19th Meeting."

62. Benedick, *Ozone Diplomacy*, 239.

63. Ibid., 240.

64. EPA, "Essential Use Exemptions."

65. Decision IX/6, UNEP, *Handbook of the Montreal Protocol*.

66. Ancarani, "Globalizing the World"; Decision IX/6, UNEP, *Handbook of the Montreal Protocol*; Diaz-Bonilla, Frandsen, and Robinson, *WTO Negotiations*; and "The Right Time to Chop."

67. Ancarani, "Globalizing the World," 668–669.

68. Forsyth, *Critical Political Ecology*, 104.

69. Yearly: "The Environmental Challenge" and *Sociology, Environmentalism, Globalization*; Guston, "Boundary Organizations"; and Yeates, "Social Politics."

3

A Critical Review of the Successful CFC
Phaseout versus the Delayed MeBr Phaseout in
the Montreal Protocol

1. See, for example, Andersen and Sarma, *Protecting the Ozone Layer;* Benedick *Ozone Diplomacy;* and Parson, *Protecting the Ozone Layer.*

2. Center for Civil Society, "What Is Civil Society?"

3. Breitmeier and Rittberger, "Environmental NGOs," 138, and Wapner, "The Transnational Politics of Environmental NGOs."

4. Rittberger, "(I)NGOs," 85.

5. Bernstein, *The Compromise,* 148, and Litfin, *Ozone Discourses.*

6. Yearly, "The Environmental Challenge," 459.

7. Beck, *Risk Society,* and Yearly, "The Environmental Challenge," 458–459.

8. Mol, "The Environmental Movement," and Sonnenfeld and Mol, "Ecological Modernization."

9. Mol, "Ecological Modernization," and Mol and Spaargaren, "Ecological Modernization."

10. Goldman, *Imperial Nature;* Faber, *Capitalizing on Environmental Injustice;* and Bailey and Wilson, "Theorising Transitional Pathways."

11. Hajer, *The Politics of Environmental Discourse;* Mol, "Ecological Modernization"; Mol, "The Environmental Movement"; and Murphy and Gouldson, "Environmental Policy."

12. Bailey and Wilson, "Theorising Transitional Pathways," 4.

13. Conca, *Governing Water,* 8.

14. Ibid; Lipschutz and Mayer, *Global Civil Society;* and Young, *International Governance.*

15. Parson, *Protecting the Ozone Layer,* viii. Some other notable contributors to this line of thought include Bankobeza, *Ozone Protection;* Benedick, "The Diplomacy of Climate Change"; Canan, "The Problem of Ozone Depletion"; UNEP, *Protecting the Ozone Layer;* Haas, "Banning Chlorofluorocarbons"; and Litfin, *Ozone Discourses.*

16. See, for example, Jänicke and Jörgens, "New Appoaches."

17. Parson makes the interesting observation that this was the first time that a chemical's inertness, and not its reactivity, was a serious environmental threat. That CFCs could remain nonreactive until they reached the stratosphere was the very attribute that threatened life worldwide. Parson, *Protecting the Ozone Layer,* 31–32.

18. Ibid., 20–21.

19. Ibid., 36.

20. Ibid., 58, and DeCanio, "Economic Analysis."

21. By 1984, the United States had reversed its position again: "The United States, previously the most forceful advocate of binding and compulsory arbitration, had reversed its position after being sued in the World Court for mining Nicaragua's harbors and losing its procedural bid to avoid the court's jurisdiction." Parson, *Protecting the Ozone Layer*, 121.

22. Andersen and Sarma, *Protecting the Ozone Layer*, 63.

23. Parson, *Protecting the Ozone Layer*, 126–127. See also Litfin, *Ozone Discourses*.

24. Litfin, *Ozone Discourses*, 94–95.

25. Hunter, Salzman, and Zaelke, *International Environmental Law and Policy*, 573–574.

26. Http://ozone.unep.org/Ratification_status/.

27. Parson, *Protecting the Ozone Layer*, 137.

28. Hunter, Salzman, and Zaelke, *International Environmental Law and Policy*, 544–545.

29. Breitmeier and Rittberger, "Environmental NGOs," and Huber, "Upstreaming Environmental Action."

30. Litfin, *Ozone Discourses*, and Farman, Gardiner, and Shanklin, "Large Losses."

31. Bernstein, *The Compromise*, 149.

32. Parson, *Protecting the Ozone Layer*, 145.

33. Ibid., 158.

34. *Chemical Week*, and Whitney, "20 Nations Agree to Join Ozone Pact."

35. Parson, *Protecting the Ozone Layer*, 177–180.

36. Butler et al., "A Decrease in the Growth Rates."

37. Parson, *Protecting the Ozone Layer*, 144.

38. Synthesis Report, UNEP/OZL.Pro.WG.II(1)/4 (89–1-11), 9.

39. Benedick, *Ozone Diplomacy*, 117–125; Andersen and Sarma, *Protecting the Ozone Layer;* Bankobeza, *Ozone Protection;* Haas, "Banning Chlorofluorocarbons"; Litfin, *Ozone Discourses;* and Parson, *Protecting the Ozone Layer*.

40. Parson, *Protecting the Ozone Layer*, 192.

41. Van der Leun, "The Ozone Layer."

42. "Ozone Loss Hits Us Where We Live."

43. UNEP, *Environmental Effects Panel Report;* Parson, *Protecting the Ozone Layer*, 223, fn. 137.

44. UNEP, "Progress Report [2003]."

45. Hajer, *The Politics of Environmental Discourse.*

46. Parson, *Protecting the Ozone Layer,* 211.

47. Ibid., 336, fn. 105.

48. Ibid., 218. The ODP of a chemical compound is commonly described as the ratio of global ozone loss in the atmosphere caused by the chemical over the loss of ozone caused by CFC-11 of the same mass: "CFC-11 is typically defined as the standard reference compound and is assigned an ODP of 1.0." See http://www.ciesin.org/TG/OZ/odp.html.

49. UNEP, "Scientific Assessment of Ozone Depletion," xxii.

50. Parson, *Protecting the Ozone Layer,* 225.

51. Ibid., 227–228.

52. UNEP, "Report of the Methyl Bromide Technical Options Committee," 3.

53. UNEP, "Report of the Seventh Meeting." Both environmental groups and—later and anonymously—members of the MBTOC criticized the 1995–1998 average given to developing countries, worried that it would increase consumption of MeBr over that period in order to get the base figure at a higher level. It is likely true that this happened, and, as Parson relates, it likely greatly benefited the chemical companies, which were responsible for up to 85 percent of ODS usage in places like Thailand. Parson, *Protecting the Ozone Layer,* 231, fn. 187. See also Gareau, "Dangerous Holes."

54. Parson, *Protecting the Ozone Layer,* 233.

55. UNEP, "Report of the Ninth Meeting."

56. Www.epa.gov/ozone/MeBr_exec_summary.pdf, and Bailey and Wilson, "Theorising Transitional Pathways," 15.

57. U.S. Committee on Agriculture, *The Implications of Banning Methyl Bromide.*

58. Borrego, "The Restructuring of Frozen Food Production"; R. Walker, *Conquest of Bread;* and Gareau, "Dangerous Holes."

59. FAO, "Fresh Strawberry Production Statistics." On July 6, 2005, the European Union published a notice of initiation of a safeguard investigation concerning imports of frozen strawberries from the Chinese mainland. The issue was raised by Poland, which complained that China imports could endanger its domestic production. USDA, Foreign Agricultural Service, "Gain Report: China Frozen Exports," 4. See also USDA, "Gain Report: Strawberries in Poland."

60. California Strawberry Commission, "California Delivers"; FAO, "Fresh Strawberry Production Statistics"; Carter, Chalfant, and Goodhue, "China's Strawberry Industry."

61. Goodhue, Fennimore, and Ajwa, "The Economic Importance of Methyl Bromide."

62. DeCanio and Norman, "Economics of the "Critical Use' of Methyl Bromide," and DuPuis and Gareau, "Neoliberal Knowledge."

63. Fisher, Fritsch, and Andersen, "Transformations."

64. Norman, "Potential Impacts," 175, my emphasis.

65. UNEP: "Progress Report [2009]" and "Report of the 19th Meeting"; and U.S. Department of State, "Methyl Bromide Critical Use Nomination."

66. Banks, "Methyl Bromide Technical Options Committee," 168. See also Canan and Reichman, *Ozone Connections.*

67. Parson, *Protecting the Ozone Layer,* 228.

68. Ibid., 175.

69. DeCanio and Norman, "Economics of the "Critical Use' of Methyl Bromide."

70. Gareau and DuPuis, "From Public to Private Global Environmental Governance," and Bernstein, *The Compromise.*

71. Claudia McMurray, U.S. delegation, 15th MOP, Nairobi, November 14, 2003, tape-recorded notes.

72. Dryzek et al., "Ecological Modernization."

73. Parson, *Protecting the Ozone Layer,* 106–107, my emphasis.

74. Wapner, *Environmental Activism.*

4

Social Capital and the Vertical Integration of Power

1. Trask, "Montreal Protocol Noncompliance Procedure"; Patlis, "The Multilateral Fund"; Mulder, "Innovation by Disaster"; Ha-Duong, Megie, and Hauglustaine, "A Pro-Active Stratospheric Ozone Protection Scenario"; Hahn and McGartland, "The Political-Economy of Instrument Choice"; Leaf, "Managing Global Atmospheric Change"; Litfin, *Ozone Discourses;* Morrisette, "The Montreal Protocol"; Næs, "The Effectiveness of the E.U.'s Ozone Policy"; Oberthur, "Linkages"; Ogden, "The Montreal Protocol"; Rutgeerts, "Trade and Environment"; Shende and Gorman, "Lessons in Technology Transfer"; Swanson, "Negotiating Effective International Environmental Agreements"; Auffhammer, Morzuch, and Stranlund, "Production of Chlorofluorocarbons"; Bryk, "The Montreal Protocol and Recent Developments"; Capretta, "The Future's So Bright"; Haas: "Banning Chlorofluorocarbons" and "Epistemic Communities"; Parson, *Protecting the*

Ozone Layer; Young: *International Governance, Global Governance* and "Political Leadership"; Young, Levy, and Osherenko, "The Effectiveness of International Environmental Regimes"; Sims, "The Unsheltering Sky"; Mitchell and Keilbach, "Situation Structure"; and Beukel, "Ideas, Interests, and State Preferences."

2. Murdoch and Sandler, "The Voluntary Provision"; DeCanio, "Economic Analysis"; Hammitt, "Are the Costs of Proposed Environmental Regulations Overestimated?"; Jonathan Harris, "Review of Duncan Brack's *International Trade and the Montreal Protocol*"; Luken and Grof, "The Montreal Protocol's Multilateral Fund"; Mason and Swanson, "A Kuznets Curve Analysis"; Munasinghe and King, "Implementing the Montreal Protocol to Restore the Ozone Layer"; OECD, "Multilateral Environmental Agreements and Private Investment"; Beron, Murdoch, and Vijverberg, "Why Cooperate?"; Barrett, "Self-Enforcing International Environmental Agreements"; Auffhammer, Morzuch, and Stranlund, "Production of Chlorofluorocarbons"; Agee and Fah, "Social Discount Rates"; and Arce M., "Leadership."

3. Canan and Reichman, *Ozone Connections;* UNEP, "Scientific Assessment of Ozone Depletion"; Munasinghe and King: "Accelerating Ozone Layer Protection in Developing Countries" and "Implementing the Montreal Protocol to Restore the Ozone Layer"; Andersen and Sarma, *Protecting the Ozone Layer;* WMO/UNEP, "Executive Summary"; IPCC, "Safeguarding the Ozone Layer"; Benedick: "The Diplomacy of Climate Change" and *Ozone Diplomacy;* Luken and Grof, "The Montreal Protocol's Multilateral Fund"; and DeCanio and Norman, "Economics of the 'Critical Use' of Methyl Bromide."

4. Powell, "CFC Phase-Out"; Roscoe and Lee, "Increased Stratospheric Greenhouse Gases"; van der Leun, "The Ozone Layer"; Doolittle, "Underestimating Ozone Depletion"; Flannery, *The Weather Makers;* Yokouchi et al., "Recent Decline"; Staehelin et al., "Ozone Trends"; and Ha-Duong, Megie, and Hauglustaine, "A Pro-Active Stratospheric Ozone Protection Scenario."

5. Koike et al., "Verticillium Wilt"; Bolda et al., *Sample Costs;* EIA, "Opportunity Wasted"; Schneider et al., "Pre-Plant and Post-Harvest"; Carter et al., "The Methyl Bromide Ban"; NRDC, "The Bush Record"; Offner, "California Strawberries"; Agricultural Research Service, "Excerpt of Remarks by David R. Riggs"; Bull et al., "Strawberry Cultivars"; and Miller, "Much Ado about MB."

6. Canan, "The Problem of Ozone Depletion"; Canan and Reichman, *Ozone Connections;* and Grundmann: "The Strange Success of the Montreal Protocol" and *Transnational Environmental Policy.*

7. Among others is Parson, *Protecting the Ozone Layer.*
8. Litfin, *Ozone Discourses.*
9. See Heynen et al., *Neoliberal Environments;* Liverman and Vilas, "Neoliberalism"; McCarthy and Prudham, "Neoliberal Nature"; and Perreault and Martin, "Geographies of Neoliberalism."
10. See Swain, "Social Capital."
11. Quotation taken from the Preamble to the Montreal Protocol.
12. Canan and Reichman, *Ozone Connections,* 42; see also Shende and Gorman, "Lessons in Technology Transfer."
13. Http://unep.org/ozone/Treaties_and_Ratification/index.asp.
14. Canan and Reichman, *Ozone Connections,* 58; see also Hunter, Salzman, and Zaelke, *International Environmental Law and Policy.*
15. Canan and Reichman, *Ozone Connections,* 54. Countries that do not qualify under Article 5 but need assistance have utilized the government-funded GEF. Between 1991 and 2004, the GEF allocated more than $177 million to projects to phase out ODSs and a co-financing of $182 million. See UNEP, "Brief Primer on the Montreal Protocol," and www.gef.org.
16. Canan and Reichman, "Montreal Protocol."
17. Canan and Reichman, *Ozone Connections,* 57; see also Shende and Gorman, "Lessons in Technology Transfer," 99.
18. For a thorough account of Montreal Protocol rules and procedures, see Canan and Reichman, "Montreal Protocol."
19. Field notes, 16th MOP, Prague, November 2004; and Hunter, Salzman, and Zaelke, *International Environmental Law and Policy.*
20. E.g., Paterson, *Understanding;* Mitchell: "International Environment" and "Of Course International Institutions Matter."
21. UNEP, *Handbook of the Montreal Protocol,* 96–97; Benedick, *Ozone Diplomacy;* Morrisette, "The Evolution of Policy Responses"; EIA, "Opportunity Wasted"; NRDC, "The Bush Record"; Parson, *Protecting the Ozone Layer;* and EPA, "Protection of Stratospheric Ozone."
22. EPA, "Essential Use Exemptions"; Federal Register, "Protection of Stratospheric Ozone."
23. UNEP, "Report of the Ninth Meeting," 27.
24. IIED, "Reshaping Local Democracy," 1.
25. Bankobeza, *Ozone Protection.*
26. Canan and Reichman, "Montreal Protocol."
27. Statement of Greenpeace at 2nd Extraordinary Meeting of the Parties to the Montreal Protocol (ExMOP), tape-recorded notes. For ecological impacts of ozone depletion, see van der Leun, "The Ozone Layer";

van der Leun and Gruikl, "Climate Change"; and van der Leun and Weelden, "Light-Induced Tolerance."

28. Twenty-third OEWG, Montreal, 2003, tape-recorded field notes.

29. Ibid.

30. Ibid. Responses to the U.S. CUEs from the less-developed world, including fuller quotations, are discussed in more detail in chapter 5.

31. First ExMOP, Montreal, 2004, tape-recorded notes.

32. Pellow, "Review: *Ozone Connections*," 68.

33. Canan and Reichman, *Ozone Connections*, 15, 60; Benedick, *Ozone Diplomacy*; and Haas, "Banning Chlorofluorocarbons."

34. Canan and Reichman, *Ozone Connections*, 35–36.

35. Ibid., 103, 114–115, my emphasis.

36. Ibid., 86.

37. Banks, "Methyl Bromide Technical Options Committee," 168.

38. Ibid., 169.

39. Canan and Reichman, *Ozone Connections*, 101.

40. Fine: *Social Capital*, "Callonistics," and "Social Capital for Africa?"; Swain, "Social Capital"; and John Harris, *Depoliticizing Development*.

41. Portes, "Social Capital"; Coleman, "Social Capital"; Becker, *Accounting for Tastes;* and Putnam, "Bowling Alone."

42. Canan and Reichman, *Ozone Connections,* 102–103. See also Putnam, "Bowling Alone."

43. See, for example, Swain, "Social Capital"; Fine: *Social Capital* and "Those Social Capitalists"; Fine and Lapavitsas, "Social Capital"; John Harris, *Depoliticizing Development;* Foley and Edwards, "Escape from Politics?"; and Edwards and Foley, "Social Capital." For more on the intellectual origins of social capital, see Fine and Lapavitsas, "Social Capital."

44. Swain, "Social Capital," 212, and Bourdieu, "The Forms of Capital."

45. Fine and Lapavitsas, "Social Capital," 27–28. See also Fine, "Social Capital for Africa?"; John Harris, *Depoliticizing Development;* and Fox, "The World Bank and Social Capital."

46. Canan and Reichman, *Ozone Connections*, 102–103.

47. Foley and Edwards, "Is It Time to Disinvest in Social Capital?"; Swain, "Social Capital."

48. Canan and Reichman, *Ozone Connections*, 60.

49. Goodhue, Fennimore, and Ajwa, "The Economic Importance of Methyl Bromide"; Gareau, "Dangerous Holes."

50. Cf. Millner, Ringer, and Maas, "Suppression of Strawberry Root Disease"; Muramoto, "Nutrient Dynamics"; Bull, Koike, and Shennan,

"Performance"; Schneider et al., "Pre-Plant and Post-Harvest"; UNEP, "Case Studies on Alternatives"; Arnault et al., "Soil Behaviour"; Duniway, "Status of Chemical Alternatives"; and Norman "Potential Impacts."

51. UNEP, "Synthesis of the 2002 Reports."

52. UNEP, *Handbook of the Montreal Protocol.*

53. Paul Horwitz, U.S. delegation, 24th OEWG, Geneva, 2004, tape-recorded notes.

54. DeCanio and Norman, "Economics of the 'Critical Use' of Methyl Bromide."

55. Ibid., 387.

56. DeCanio presenting the DeCanio and Norman report to the 23rd OEWG, Montreal, 2003, tape-recorded notes.

57. Horwitz of the U.S. delegation speaking at the small group session at the 23rd OEWG, Montreal, 2003, tape-recorded notes.

58. Ibid.

59. Tape-recorded notes, 23rd OEWG, Montreal, 2003.

60. See Goodhue, Fennimore, and Ajwa, "The Economic Importance of Methyl Bromide."

61. On http://www.calstrawberry.com/research/mbromide.asp.

62. Bonanno, "The Crisis of Representation."

63. See Tilly, *Durable Inequality*, 6–7, quoting Weber in *Economy and Society.*

64. Tilly, *Durable Inequality*, 8.

65. Canan and Reichman, *Ozone Connections*, 54–57, 161. See also Article 6 of the Montreal Protocol in UNEP, *Handbook of the Montreal Protocol*; Benedick, *Ozone Diplomacy*; Parson, *Protecting the Ozone Layer*; and Litfin, *Ozone Discourses*, 117.

66. Litfin, *Ozone Discourses*, 4, 11.

67. Ibid., 80.

68. Foucault: "Two Lectures," 78–108, and *Discipline and Punish*, 333.

69. Haas: "Banning Chlorofluorocarbons" and "Epistemic Communities"; Benedick, "The Diplomacy of Climate Change"; Jasanoff and Martello, *Earthly Politics*; and Goldman, *Imperial Nature.*

70. Intervention by the U.S. Stakeholders Group on MDI Transition at the 15th MOP, tape-recorded notes.

71. Statement of U.S. delegation and response by the TEAP, 15th MOP, tape-recorded notes.

72. U.S. delegation, 15th MOP, tape-recorded notes.

73. U.S. delegation, 24th OEWG, Geneva, 2004, tape-recorded notes.

74. MBTOC, 24th OEWG, Geneva, 2004, tape-recorded notes.

75. Chapter 5 will also investigate the perceived threat of China's growing strawberry production platform to U.S. growers.

76. Canan and Reichman, *Ozone Connections,* and Banks, "Methyl Bromide Technical Options Committee."

77. Fine, "Those Social Capitalists," 797.

78. Bourdieu, *Distinction.*

79. Swain, "Social Capital and Its Uses," 212. For a similar argument about the use of social capital in the World Bank, see Fine and Lapavitsas, "Social Capital," 22–23.

5

Tensions among Nation-States

1. At the 16th MOP, the European Union attempted to block the passage of essential use exemptions for U.S. MDIs for 2006, as it understood that "alternatives [to CFC MDIs] are available in the United States, there are CFC-free alternatives available, and therefore in TEAP's suggestion for review in 2006, it's very clear to us that TEAP would like the opportunity of a further review of the CFCs for 2006." The Stakeholders Group on MDI Transition fully supported the E.U. position, expressing in plenary the adoption of "the E.U. draft decision on essential uses. . . . In the U.S. two CFC-free albuterol MDI products have been on the market for over two years, and a recently approved third product is expected to be available next year. Even the U.S. Food and Drug Administration, in an ongoing rule-making process, has tentatively concluded that patients are adequately served by the available [CFC-alternative] HFA albuterol products." 16th MOP, Prague, 2004, tape-recorded notes. For a discussion of the need to reconfigure Protocol rules that presently allow governments to call upon the domestic needs of their financially poor citizens, such as the excuses made by the United States to continue using CFCs in MDIs, see Norman, DeCanio, and Fan, "The Montreal Protocol at 20."

2. Mitchell, "International Environment"; Boswell and Chase-Dunn, *The Spiral;* and McMichael, *Contesting Development.*

3. TEAP, "Report," and Borrego et al., "Agents of Change."

4. Osteen, "Methyl Bromide Phaseout Proceeds," 23, and U.S. Committee on Agriculture, *The Implications of Banning Methyl Bromide.*

5. Leinwand, "Farmers, Environmentalists Battle over Ban on a Chemical."

6. Sideman, "Strawberry Growers Seek China Market."

7. Franz, "Methyl Bromide Users Clamor for Alternatives," 55.

8. U.S. Committee on Agriculture, *The Implications of Banning Methyl Bromide;* USDA/ERS, "Economic Implications"; Carter et al., "The Methyl Bromide Ban"; and Dinnage, "Pesticides."

9. At the 1st ExMOP (2004), parties set a cap for new production at 30 percent of 1991 levels. Any amount over the 30 percent figure must come from existing stockpiles of MeBr. For the United States, this cap meant that 2 percent of 2005 MeBr use had to come from existing stockpiles.

10. Quoted in Environment News Service, "U.S. Demand for Methyl Bromide Blocks Ozone Accord."

11. NRDC, "Chemical Companies." The 1991 baseline for the United States is 25,528 metric tons. EPA, "The Phaseout of Methyl Bromide," and EIA, "Opportunity Wasted."

12. EPA, "Fact Sheet."

13. EIA, "Opportunity Wasted," 3. See also EPA, "United States Nomination for Critical Use Exemptions," and Gareau, "The Limited Influence of Global Civil Society."

14. MeBr is three times heavier than air, at 7.9 pounds [3.6 kilograms] per cubic meter. A typical four-seater hot air balloon holds 2,500 cubic meters of air; 21,000,000 lbs. MeBr/7.93664 lbs. per cubic meter = 2,666,667 cubic meters; 2,666,667 cubic meters/2,500 cubic meters = 1,067 hot air balloons. The GZ-20A Goodyear blimp has a volume of 5,740 cubic meters (www.goodyearblimp.com). Biosphere II has a volume of about 150,000 cubic meters. See Turner, "Building an Ecosystem from Scratch." The former Houston Astrodome has a volume of about 1 million cubic meters. See http://www.sciencemag.org/cgi/content/full/289/5479/534.

15. Agenda Item 15 of the 23rd OEWG, Montreal, 2003.

16. E.U. delegation, 24th OEWG, Geneva, July 14, 2004, tape-recorded notes.

17. Ibid.

18. Nigerian delegation, 24th OEWG, Geneva, July 14, 2004, tape-recorded notes.

19. U.S. delegation, 24th OEWG, Geneva, July 14, 2004, tape-recorded notes.

20. Australian delegation, 24th OEWG, Geneva, July 14, 2004, tape-recorded notes.

21. Final report of the 16th MOP, Prague, 2004; UNEP/OzL.Pro.16/17.

22. Flannery, *The Weather Makers.*

23. Jonathan Banks, 23rd OEWG, Montreal, 2003, Synthesis Report Presentation, tape-recorded notes.

24. Ibid.

25. Australian delegation, 23rd OEWG, Montreal, 2003, tape-recorded notes.

26. Jopson, "Addiction."

27. UNEP, "Progress Report [2003]," 164.

28. Canadian delegation, 23rd OEWG, Montreal, 2003, tape-recorded notes.

29. U.S. delegation, 23rd OEWG, Montreal, 2003, tape-recorded notes.

30. Conversations with anonymous delegates from Western Europe, November 13, 2003.

31. Offner, "California Strawberries."

32. 1st ExMOP, Montreal, 2004, tape-recorded notes.

33. Ibid.

34. Ibid.

35. DuPuis and Gareau, "Neoliberal Knowledge"; see also Rose, *Powers of Freedom.*

36. 16th MOP, Prague, 2004, tape-recorded notes.

37. U.S. delegation, 16th MOP, Prague, 2004, tape-recorded notes.

38. Ibid.

39. Ibid.

40. IMF, "World Economic Outlook Database."

41. E.U. delegation, 16th MOP, Prague, 2004, tape-recorded notes.

42. U.S. delegation, 16th MOP, Prague, 2004, tape-recorded notes.

43. This section draws considerably from a group National Science Foundation research proposal. See Borrego et al., "Agents of Change."

44. Cf. M. Wells, *Strawberry Fields.*

45. National Agricultural Statistics Service, "Agricultural Statistics 2002"; Sances, "Ten Years"; and Wilhelm and Paulus, "How Soil Fumigation Benefits the California Strawberry Industry."

46. Shaw et al., "Genetic Variation."

47. Lopez, "Strangers in Their Own Land."

48. California Coastkeeper Alliance, "Notice of Call for Public Comment," 2; Harrison: "Abandoned Bodies" and *Pesticide Drift.*

49. USDA, Foreign Agricultural Service, "GAIN Report: Mexico Strawberries Annual 2005," 1–3.

50. Conversation with John Borrego regarding his research on strawberry production in Central Coast California and Spain, March 15, 2009.

51. TEAP, "Report."

52. Mezzetti and Simpson, *Proceedings;* UNIDO, "Ozone Friendly Industrial Development"; and Borrego, personal communication.

53. Conversation with John Borrego regarding his research on strawberry production in Central Coast California and Spain, March 15, 2009, and Pedreño: "Taylor y Ford" and "Construyendo la huerta de Europa."

54. USDA, Foreign Agricultural Service, "GAIN Report: China Frozen Strawberries."

55. USDA, Foreign Agricultural Service, "GAIN Report: China Strawberries Annual 2009." See also Carter, Chalfant, and Goodhue, "China's Strawberry Industry," and Fruitnet, "China's Strawberry Production Increase."

56. USDA, Foreign Agricultural Service, "GAIN Report: Strawberries in Poland," 4; FAO, "Fresh Strawberry Production Statistics"; Carter, Chalfant, and Goodhue, "China's Strawberry Industry"; California Strawberry Commission, "California Frozen Exports"; Borrego, "Models of Integration"; Borrego, Alvarez, and Jomo, *The State;* Arrighi, *Adam Smith in Beijing;* and Jomo, *Flat World.*

57. Chinese Association of Horticultural Science, "The Second National Conference of Strawberry Production"; Carter, Chalfant, and Goodhue, "China's Strawberry Industry," 9; USDA, Foreign Agricultural Service, "GAIN Report: China Strawberries Annual 2004"; Li and Gliessman, "A Comparative Study"; Muramoto et al., "Field-Scale Nutrient Cycling and Sustainability"; and Gareau and Borrego, "Global Environmental Governance."

58. See table 1 in Carter, Chalfant, and Goodhue, "China's Strawberry Industry," 7. In China, "Farmers are very keen. They even pick out worms by hand." Nakanishi, "Organic Farming Set to Boom in China."

59. 1st ExMOP, Montreal, 2004, tape-recorded notes.

60. Costa Rican delegation, 1st ExMOP, Montreal, 2004, tape-recorded notes.

61. Chilean delegation, 23rd OEWG, Montreal, 2003, tape-recorded notes.

62. Ugandan delegation, 23rd OEWG, Montreal, 2003, tape-recorded notes.

63. Dominican Republic delegation, 23rd OEWG, Montreal, 2003, tape-recorded notes, my emphasis.

64. Arrighi, *Adam Smith in Beijing;* Piana, "Hierarchy Structures"; and Wallerstein, "Whose Century Is the 21st Century?"

65. Chinese delegation, 23rd OEWG, Montreal, 2003, tape-recorded notes.

66. E.U. delegation, 23rd OEWG, Montreal, 2003, tape-recorded notes.

67. Twenty-fourth OEWG, Geneva, 2004, tape-recorded notes.

68. Ibid.

69. Ibid.

70. Ibid.

71. Ibid.

72. Ibid. See also Agenda Item 12a, CRP 1 of the 24th OEWG, Geneva, 2004.

73. Jonathan Banks, MBTOC co-chair, reporting on the MBTOC assessment of CUE nominations for MeBr, 24th OEWG, Geneva, 2004, tape-recorded notes.

74. Twenty-fourth OEWG, Geneva, 2004, tape recorded notes.

75. Ibid.

76. Paul Horwitz, U.S. delegation, 24th OEWG, Geneva, 2004, tape-recorded notes, and table 2, UNEP/OzL.Pro.WG.1/24/6.

77. Plenary co-chair at the 24th OEWG, Geneva, 2004, tape-recorded notes, my emphasis; and U.S. delegation, 24th OEWG, Geneva, 2004, tape-recorded notes.

78. Nigerian delegation, 24th OEWG, Geneva, 2004, tape-recorded notes; CRP 25 of the 24th OEWG, Geneva, 2004; and Chilean delegation, 24th OEWG, Geneva, 2004, tape-recorded notes.

79. E.U. delegation, 24th OEWG, Geneva, 2004, tape-recorded notes.

80. I.e., soil pathogens flourish without MeBr in conventional strawberry production. See Martin and Bull, "Biological Approaches"; Goud et al., "Long-Term Effect of Biological Soil Disinfestation on Verticillium Wilt"; and Schneider et al., "Pre-Plant and Post-Harvest."

81. Ezrahi, *The Descent of Icarus;* Jasanoff: *Designs on Nature* and *The Fifth Branch;* and Mukerji, *A Fragile Power.*

6

The Coproduction of Science/Knowledge and Politics

1. Jasanoff, *Designs on Nature,* 8–9. See also Mukerji, *A Fragile Power;* Jasanoff, *The Fifth Branch;* Ezrahi, *The Descent of Icarus;* Goldman, *Imperial Nature;* and Jasanoff et al., *Handbook.*

2. See Boykoff, *Who Speaks for the Climate?*

3. Cox, *Environmental Communication,* and Harrison, "Abandoned Bodies."

4. Faber, *Capitalizing on Environmental Injustice.*

5. Winner, *The Whale and the Reactor,* 27. See also Jasanoff, *States of Knowledge,* and Forsyth, *Critical Political Ecology.*

Notes to Pages 197–209

6. See Canan and Reichman, *Ozone Connections*.

7. Forsyth, *Critical Political Ecology*, 104.

8. Decision IX/6, in UNEP, "Report of the 9th Meeting."

9. Bodnar, "Annual Review," 916.

10. Ibid., 916–917.

11. Leahy, "Canada"; TEAP, "Report"; and Jasanoff, "Science, Politics and the Renegotiation of Expertise at EPA."

12. Krugman, "Salt of the Earth," and Beamish, "U.S. Pesticide Stockpile under Scrutiny."

13. Bodnar, "Annual Review," 908–909.

14. Litfin, *Ozone Discourses*, 51.

15. Jasanoff, *Designs on Nature*.

16. I am being purposely cryptic in order to protect the anonymity of the interviewees.

17. Discussed in chapter 6; also found in DeCanio and Norman, "Economics of the 'Critical Use' of Methyl Bromide."

18. Carter, Chalfant, and Goodhue, "China's Strawberry Industry," and Borrego et al., "Agents of Change."

19. Yet two pro-MeBr MBTOC members agreed that the MLF should not be simply viewed benevolently; they pointed out that the UNEP has spent more money on MeBr alternatives for tobacco than on any other substance grown in the LDCs: "This is a crazy expenditure on a terrible commodity," according to one of the members.

20. Sances, "Ten Years"; Sances and Ingham, "Conventional and Organic Alternatives"; FAO/UNEP, "Global Report"; National Agricultural Pesticide Impact Assessment Program, "Biologic and Economic Assessment of Methyl Bromide"; Schneider et al., "Pre-Plant and Post-Harvest"; California Department of Food and Agriculture, "California Agricultural Highlights 2005"; Thompson, "Methyl Bromide Critical Use Exemptions"; Duniway, "Status of Chemical Alternatives"; Ajwa et al., "Application of Alternative Fumigants"; and Carpenter, Lynch, and Trout, "Township Limits."

21. Muramoto, "Nutrient Dynamics"; Muramoto et al., "Maintaining Agroecosystem Health"; Shennan, "Biotic Interactions; Shetty et al., "Management of Verticillium Wilt"; Duniway et al., "Some Chemical, Cultural, and Biological Alternatives"; Eayre, "Alternatives"; Bull and Ajwa, "Yield of Strawberries"; Werner, Kluson, and Gliessman, "Colonization of Strawberry Roots"; Bull, "Factors"; Bull et al., "Strawberry Cultivars"; Sances and Ingham, "Conventional and Organic Alternatives"; Gordon et al., "Management of Verticillium Wilt"; Lazarovits, "Managing Soilborne Plant Diseases"; Arancon, Edwards, and Bierman, "Influences of Vermicomposts";

Millner, Ringer, and Maas, "Suppression of Strawberry Root Disease"; Sances, "Conventional and Organic Alternatives"; Walter et al., "Evaluation"; Shaw et al., "Genetic Variation"; Bull, Koike, and Shennan, "Performance"; Kabir et al., "Crop Rotation"; and Chellemi et al., "Evaluation."

22. DeCanio and Norman, "Economics of the 'Critical Use' of Methyl Bromide," and Sances, "Ten Years." This discussion of the chemical-based and nonchemical alternatives to MeBr benefits from a group NSF project: Borrego et al., "Agents of Change."

23. For example, at the 17th MOP in Dakar in 2005, Canada argued that the MBTOC's proposed cut for allowed quantities of MeBr to 150 kilograms per hectare was too extreme.

24. Verticillium wilt is a soil-borne disease that can damage a wide range of important crops in California. Potential host crops include lettuce, tomatoes, potatoes, apples, cotton, cauliflower, and strawberries. Bhat and Subbaro, "Host Range Specificity in *Verticillium dahliae.*" Due to its resistant structure, *Verticillium dahliae,* a pathogen that causes Verticillium wilt, can survive many years in soil without host plants. Koike et al., "Verticillium Wilt."

25. Recent studies demonstrate that a tarping technique that promotes soil disinfestation by stimulating anaerobic decomposition is quite viable and has considerable promise as a technique that could be readily adopted by both organic and conventional producers. Blok et al., "Control of Soilborne Plant Pathogens"; Goud et al., "Long-Term Effect of Biological Soil Disinfestation on Verticillium Wilt"; and Shinmura: "Causal Agent" and "Principle and Effect."

26. Jasanoff, *The Fifth Branch.*

27. Paul Horwitz, U.S. delegation, 24th OEWG, Geneva, 2004, tape-recorded notes.

28. Twenty-fourth OEWG, Geneva, 2004, tape-recorded notes.

29. Ibid.

30. Australian delegation, 24th OEWG, Geneva, 2004, tape-recorded notes.

31. Jonathan Banks, 24th OEWG, Geneva, 2004, tape-recorded notes.

32. Kenya, for example, submitted a "conference room paper" to the 24th OEWG that expressed worry that trade in its products treated with MeBr would be hampered by industrialized countries. The comment from the MBTOC member regarding E.U. labels for imported non-MeBr flowers indicates the reality of this issue. Commenting on its conference room paper, the Kenyan delegation stated:

Kenya is in full agreement with the international community
to phase out this very sweet but sour darling of developing
countries in the name of methyl bromide. How we do it is a
key issue. . . . The overriding principle should be to phase out
this lady in a manner that will not antagonize or be harmful to
the interests of those affected parties like Kenya. . . . Kenya's
economy largely depends on agriculture and as such derives a
significant portion of [its] foreign exchange from trade in
agricultural products. . . . This sector also employs the majority of the Kenyan population. . . . The flower industry, for
example, employs over a million Kenyans directly or indirectly.
. . . We continue to witness market bias on our products treated with or grown on soil treated with methyl bromide. The
stringent quality measures being imposed on our exports by
[industrialized] countries will no doubt have social, economic,
and political implications in our economy. . . . Kenya is in
compliance with the Montreal Protocol. . . . Hence, while we
are all protecting the ozone layer, we cannot overlook this
emerging scenario never seen before by a country like Kenya,
and when I say Kenya, I speak also for other developing countries under similar situations and conditions. . . . In the interest
of fair play, Kenya makes a strong plea to this august assembly
to agree that parties to the Protocol shall not restrict trade
in products or commodities from parties operating under
Article 5, para[graph] 1, solely because the commodities or
products have been treated with methyl bromide or because
the commodities have been produced or grown on soil treated
with methyl bromide as long as Kenya, or any other developing
party, is in compliance. (24th OEWG, tape-recorded notes.)

Many countries echoed Kenya's concerns, among them Egypt,
Uganda, Nigeria (on behalf of all of Africa), and Indonesia. The industrialized countries, such as Canada, Japan, and the United States, noted that
parties could not prevent private companies from purchasing or not
purchasing commodities produced with MeBr and that the Montreal
Protocol was in no position to discuss terms of trade. Canada added that
"we don't think that the Montreal Protocol or TEAP would perhaps be the
best location to undertake further work in this area. We think that perhaps
the work in this area should be undertaken under the World Trade Organization and one of its bodies—for example, the Trade and Environment

Committee or the Committee on Technical Barriers to Trade." The United States noted that "we could agree . . . that this issue might better be taken up in the context of the WTO." The point regarding the freedom of private companies, however, would still remain. Additionally, the Ozone Secretariat later reported at the 15th MOP that the WTO Committee on Trade and Environment would not be able to respond to the issue for some time because the 2003 WTO Ministerial Conference discussions (held in Cancun) had "collapsed" and that "the collapse of the Ministerial Council means that the Doha round may not end by the scheduled date of 1 January 2005" (UNEP/OzL.Pro.15/INF/4). It had not ended in January 2005, and as of November 2011 talks have still not resumed, let alone concluded. See BBC, "Davos 2011."

33. Jasanoff, *Designs on Nature.*

7
The Limited Influence of Global Civil Society

1. Compare, for example, Barnett and Finnemore, *Rules for the World;* Litfin, *Ozone Discourses;* Paterson, *Global Warming;* and Payne, "Persuasion."

2. See Bulkeley, "Reconfiguring Environmental Governance"; Bulkeley and Moser, "Responding to Climate Change"; Litfin, *The Greening of Sovereignty;* Newell: "The Political Economy of Global Environmental Governance" and *Climate for Change;* and Swyngedouw and Heynen, "Urban Political Ecology."

3. Olzak and Soule, "Cross-Cutting Influences"; Tarrow, "From Lumping to Splitting," 232; and Smith, "Global Civil Society?"

4. Brulle, "From Environmental Campaigns to Advancing the Public Dialog," 84. See also Johnston and Smith, *Globalization and Resistance;* Albrow et al., *Global Civil Society;* Newell, "The Political Economy of Global Environmental Governance"; and Bulkeley, "Reconfiguring Environmental Governance."

5. Keck and Sikkink, *Activists beyond Borders,* 128.

6. Greenpeace International, "Greenpeace Annual Report 2008."

7. Speth, *The Bridge.* See also Frank, Hironaka, and Schofer, "The Nation-State"; Conca and Dabelko, *Green Planet Blues;* Speth and Haas, *Global Environmental Governance;* and Park, Conca, and Finger, *The Crisis.*

8. Brenner and Theodore, "From the 'New Localism' to the Spaces of Neoliberalism"; McCarthy and Prudham, "Neoliberal Nature"; Harvey, *A*

Brief History of Neoliberalism; Gareau, "Dangerous Holes"; Goldman, *Imperial Nature;* Lipschutz, "Global Civil Society"; Eick, "Space Patrols"; B. Miller, "Modes of Governance"; Sending and Neuman, "Governance and Governmentality"; and Bartley, "How Foundations Shape Social Movements."

9. Cf. Keck and Sikkink, *Activists beyond Borders;* Rosenau, "Governance in a New Global Order"; and Price, "Transnational Civil Society."

10. Sending and Neuman, "Governance and Governmentality," 654

11. Sonnenfeld and Mol, "Globalization and the Transformation of Environmental Governance," 1325. See also Kaldor, *Global Civil Society,* and Anheier and Hawkes, "Accountability in a Globalising World."

12. Goldman, *Imperial Nature,* 184; Ebrahim, *NGOs;* Bartley, "How Foundations Shape Social Movements"; and Fernando, "The Power of Unsustainable Development."

13. Foucault, "Governmentality"; Dean, *Governmentality;* and Litfin, *Ozone Discourses,* ch. 2.

14. Sending and Neuman, "Governance and Governmentality," 657.

15. Bernstein, *The Compromise,* and Bakker, *Privatizing Water.*

16. B. Miller, "Modes of Governance," 226.

17. Cf. Okereke, Bulkeley, and Schroeder, "Conceptualising Climate Governance"; Ferguson, *The Anti-Politics Machine;* Luke, "Environmentality"; MacKinnon, "Managerialism"; Agrawal, *Environmentality;* and Goldman, *Imperial Nature.*

18. Foucault, *Power/Knowledge,* 93.

19. Bulkeley, "Reconfiguring Environmental Governance"; Liverman, "Who Governs?"; Peet and Watts, "Liberation Ecology"; and Watts, "Green Capitalism."

20. Cf. Scott, *Seeing like a State,* 13, and Foucault, *Power/Knowledge.*

21. Scott, *Seeing like a State,* and Agrawal, *Environmentality.*

22. Joseph, "Governmentality of What?," 414.

23. Brenner and Theodore, "Cities," 353.

24. Peck and Tickell, "Neoliberalizing Space."

25. Speth, *Red Sky at Morning,* and Bernstein, *The Compromise.*

26. EPA, "Essential Use Exemptions."

27. The three essential uses were (1) CFCs for MDIs, (2) methyl chloroform for cleaning rocket boosters on the U.S. space shuttle, and (3) some laboratory and analytical uses. Parson, *Protecting the Ozone Layer,* 226.

28. Decision IX/6, in UNEP, "Report of the 19th Meeting."

29. Vanessa Bogenholm, spokesperson for the CCOF, speaking at the 1st ExMOP, Montreal, 2004, tape-recorded notes.

30. EIA, 1st ExMOP, Montreal, 2004, tape-recorded notes.

31. Ibid.

32. Ibid., my emphasis.

33. Decision XVII/17 of the Montreal Protocol in UNEP, *Handbook of the Montreal Protocol.* It is interesting to note that in 2004 the E.U. delegate, Alistair McGlone, drew upon the same quote from the preamble in a Power-Point presentation on expedited procedures for amending the Montreal Protocol, as discussed in chapter 5 above. See http://www.powershow.com/view/7a4e-ZDA1O/EXPEDITED_PROCEDURE_FOR_AMENDING_THE_MONTREAL_PROTOCOL_flash_ppt_presentation.

34. Greenpeace at 2nd ExMOP, 2005, Montreal, tape-recorded notes.

35. EIA: "Top Awards" and "Best-of-the-Best."

36. Bogenholm, "Organic Strawberries"; and Sances, "Ten Years."

37. Norman, "Potential Impacts."

38. Department of Homeland Security, "Chemical Facility Anti-Terrorism Standard," and Nuckols et al., "Linkage."

39. Bondi and Laurie, "Introduction to Working the Spaces of Neoliberalism," 395.

40. Twenty-fourth OEWG, Geneva, 2004, tape-recorded notes.

41. Fifteenth MOP, Nairobi, 2003, tape-recorded notes.

42. Ibid.

43. Ibid. For links among neoliberalism, democracy, transparency, and accountability, see Guthman, "The Polanyian Way?"

44. Fifteenth MOP, Nairobi, 2003, tape-recorded notes.

45. Seventeenth MOP, Dakar, 2005, tape-recorded notes. The NRDC explained that under the Clean Air Act (how the U.S. implements the Montreal Protocol), any private or personal information (a "section 114 request") on issues related to international treaties may be requested. When the NRDC asked for stockpile data, the EPA said it would disclose them, but two companies (Ameribrom, and Hendrix and Dail) filed a lawsuit to keep the data confidential. Observations at the EIA/NRDC small-group session, 25th OEWG, Montreal, June 29, 2005.

46. Seventeenth MOP, Dakar, 2005, tape-recorded notes.

47. Ibid., tape-recorded notes and personal observations at the open-ended contact group held to discuss CUE nominations.

48. Seventeenth MOP, Dakar, 2005, tape-recorded notes.

49. EIA: "Strawberries Linked to Skin Cancer" and "California Strawberry Industry Defends Ozone-Depleting Chemicals."

50. Lipschutz and Rowe, *Globalization, Governmentality and Global Politics,* 768.

51. Brulle, "From Environmental Campaigns to Advancing the Public Dialog," 85.

52. Hacking, "Style."

53. Brulle, "From Environmental Campaigns to Advancing the Public Dialog," 85.

54. Sonnenfeld and Mol, "Globalization and the Transformation of Environmental Governance," 1331.

8

Conclusion

1. Cf. Andersen, Sarma, and Taddonio, *Technology Transfer*, and Norman, DeCanio, and Fan, "The Montreal Protocol at 20."

2. Bailey, "Neoliberalism," and Norman, DeCanio, and Fan, "The Montreal Protocol at 20."

3. Shindell, Rind, and Lonergan, "Increased Polar Stratospheric Ozone Losses."

4. Flannery, *The Weather Makers*, 44.

5. Chipperfield and Fioletov, "Global Ozone"; Andray, Hamid, and Torikai, "Effects"; van der Leun and Gruikl, "Climate Change"; Przeslawski, Davis, and Benkendorf, "Synergistic Effects"; van der Leun, "The Ozone Layer"; Le Quéré et al., "Saturation"; Cai and Cowan, "Trends"; and WMO, "Scientific Assessment of Ozone Depletion."

6. Preamble, in UNEP, *Handbook of the Montreal Protocol*; and Decision VCVI/2, in UNEP, *Handbook of the Vienna Convention*.

7. Marco Gonzalez, opening statement of the 25th OEWG, 2005, Montreal, tape-recorded notes. See also IPCC, "Safeguarding the Ozone Layer," and Agenda item 3(d) of the 25th OEWG.

8. Norman, DeCanio, and Fan, "The Montreal Protocol at 20," 4.

9. UNEP, "Report of the 19th Meeting." The revision allows continuing use of 2.5 percent of 2009 baseline levels of HCFCs for refrigeration and air-conditioning servicing until 2040. Caps on HCFC consumption do not take effect until 2013. World Bank Group, "Accelerated HCFC Phaseout."

10. Quoted in UNEP, "International Day for the Protection of the Ozone Layer."

11. ENB, "Summary of the Nineteenth Meeting."

12. Both James L. Connaughton and Dan Price are quoted in Myers, "Bush to Skip U.N. Talks on Global Warming."

13. Norman, DeCanio, and Fan, "The Montreal Protocol at 20," 6.

14. Bilefsky, "Europe Sets Ambitious Limits on Greenhouse Gases."

15. European Commission, "The E.U.'s Relations with the United States of America."

16. Bumiller and Broder, "McCain Differs with Bush on Climate Change," and Fisher, "COP-15 in Copenhagen."

17. Jonathan Banks, 17th MOP, Dakar, 2005, tape-recorded notes.

18. Chinese delegation, 17th MOP, Dakar, 2005, tape-recorded notes, my emphasis.

19. UNEP, "Arysta LifeScience."

20. Fisher, "COP-15 in Copenhagen."

21. Andersen and Zaelke, *Industry Genius*.

Afterword

1. Wollan, "Maker Pulls Pesticide."

2. Ibid.

3. EPA, "Retrospective Study of the Costs of EPA Regulations," 134; Mayfield and Norman, "Moving Away from Methyl Bromide."

4. EPA, "Retrospective Study," 134.

5. Quoted in Wollan, "Maker Pulls Pesticide."

6. Standen, "State Approves Pesticide despite Cancer Warning."

7. Philpot, "Methyl Iodide."

8. Fries and West, *Chemical Warfare*.

9. Mayfield and Norman, "Moving Away from Methyl Bromide"; U.S. Department of State, "Methyl Bromide Critical Use Nomination."

10. Mayfield and Norman, "Moving Away from Methyl Bromide"; see abstract, p. 93.

11. U.S. Department of State, "Methyl Bromide Critical Use Nomination," 8.

Appendix: Note on Methods

1. Bernard, *Research Methods in Anthropology*.

2. Canan and Reichman, *Ozone Connections;* Litfin, *Ozone Discourses;* Parson, *Protecting the Ozone Layer;* and Benedick, *Ozone Diplomacy*.

3. Weis, "The Five International Treaties"; Yearly, "The Environmental Challenge"; Jasanoff and Martello, *Earthly Politics;* and Goldman, *Imperial Nature*.

4. Canan and Reichman, *Ozone Connections.*

5. Informal discussions with the following also proved very helpful: (1) MBTOC co-chairs M. Marcott and I. Porter; (2) previous MBTOC co-chair Jonathan Banks (highly involved in earlier MeBr deliberations); (3) Stephen O. Andersen, co-chair of the TEAP; (4) David Doniger, policy director of the Climate Center, NRDC; and (5) representatives of Dow AgroSciences, the California Strawberry Commission, Greenpeace, and the EIA. Archival searches also were used to reveal patterns in research on MeBr alternatives.

6. Data sources included but were not limited to the following: (1) USDA Foreign Agricultural Service reports; U.N. International Labor Organization data on rural labor and poverty; California Agriculture Commissioner reports and factsheets; TEAP annual reports; (2) EPA data on MeBr use and alternatives; (3) reports from the annual International Research Conference on MeBr Alternatives; (4) WMO reports; (5) World Bank, IMF, and OECD data on levels of foreign direct investment in the three strawberry production regions over time, with a comparison of those levels to our analysis of the communities themselves. A great portion of this analysis was made possible by efforts orchestrated by a research team (of which I acted as a co-principal investigator) investigating the globalization of strawberry production; the team was centered at the University of California, Santa Cruz. Borrego et al., "Agents of Change."

Bibliography

Agee, Mark D., and Kenneth C. Fah. "Social Discount Rates from Stratospheric Ozone Control." *Economic Record* 71, no. 213 (1995): 191–196.

Agrawal, Arun. *Environmentality: Technologies of Government and the
Making of Subjects.* London: Sage, 2005.

Agricultural Research Service. "Excerpt of Remarks by David R. Riggs,
Chairman of the Crop Protection Coalition." Annual International
Research Conference on Methyl Bromide Alternatives and Emissions
Reductions, San Diego, CA, November 3–5, 1997. U.S. Department of
Agriculture, 1998. Available at http://www.ars.usda.gov/is/np/mba/
jan98/riggs.htm. Accessed December 20, 2002.

Ajwa, Husein A., T. Trout, J. Mueller, S. Wilhelm, S. D. Nelson, R. Soppe, and
D. Shatley. "Application of Alternative Fumigants through Drip
Irrigation Systems." *Phytopathology* 92, no. 12 (2002): 1349–1355.

Albrow, Martin, Helmut Anheier, Marlies Glasius, Monroe E. Price, and
Mary Kaldor, eds. *Global Civil Society 2007/8 Communicative Power
and Democracy.* Los Angeles: Sage, 2008.

American Cancer Society. "Cancer Facts and Figures 2010." American
Cancer Society, 2010. Available at http://www.cancer.org/acs/groups/
content/@epidemiologysurveilance/documents/document/
acspc-026238.pdf.

Ancarani, Vittorio. "Globalizing the World: Science and Technology in
International Relations." In Jasanoff, Markle, Petersen, and Pinch,
Handbook of Science and Technology Studies, 652–670.

Andersen, Stephen O., and K. Madhava Sarma. *Protecting the Ozone Layer:
The United Nations History.* London: Earthscan Publications, 2002.

Andersen, Stephen O., and Durwood Zaelke. *Industry Genius: Inventions
and People Protecting the Climate and Fragile Ozone Layer.* Sheffield,
U.K.: Greenleaf, 2003.

Andersen, Stephen O., K. Madhava Sarma, and Kristen N. Taddonio. *Technology Transfer for the Ozone Layer: Lessons for Climate Change.* Sterling: Earthscan, 2007.

Andray, Anthony L., Malim D. Hamid, and Ayako Torikai. "Effects of Climate Change and UV-B on Materials." *Photochemical and Photobiological Sciences* 2 (2003): 68–72.

Anheier, Helmut, and Amber Hawkes. "Accountability in a Globalising World: International Non-Governmental Organizations and Foundations." In Albrow, Anheier, Glasius, Price, and Kaldor, *Global Civil Society 2007/8,* 124–143.

Arancon, N. Q., C. A. Edwards, and P. Bierman. "Influences of Vermicomposts on Field Strawberries: 1. Effects on Growth and Yields." *Bioresource Technology* 93, no. 2 (2006): 145–153.

Arce M., Daniel G. "Leadership and Aggregation of International Collective Action." *Oxford Economic Papers* 53, no. 1 (2001): 114–137.

Arnault, Ingrid, Nathalie Mondy, Sabine Diwo, and Jacques Auger. "Soil Behaviour of Sulfur Natural Fumigants Used as Methyl Bromide Substitutes." *International Journal of Environmental and Analytical Chemistry* 84 (2004): 75–82.

Arrighi, Giovanni. *Adam Smith in Beijing: Lineages of the 21st Century.* New York: Verso, 2007.

———. *The Long Twentieth Century: Money, Power, and the Origins of Our Times.* New York: Verso, 1994.

Auffhammer, Maximilian, Bernard J. Morzuch, and John K. Stranlund. "Production of Chlorofluorocarbons in Anticipation of the Montreal Protocol." *Environmental and Resource Economics* 30, no. 4 (2005): 377–391.

Australian Bureau of Statistics. "Causes of Death 2009." Canberra Commonwealth of Australia 2009. Available at www.abs.gov.au.

Australian Institute of Health and Welfare (AIHW). "Health System Expenditures on Cancer and Other Neoplasms in Australia, 2000–2001." AIHW cat. no. HWE 29 (2005). Canberra: AIHW Health and Welfare Expenditure Series no. 22.

Australian Institute of Health and Welfare (AIHW) and Australasian Association of Cancer Registries (AACR). "Cancer in Australia: An Overview, 2006." Canberra: AIHW, 2007.

Babb, Sarah L. *Behind the Development Banks: Washington Politics, World Poverty, and the Wealth of Nations.* Chicago: University of Chicago Press, 2009.

———. *Managing Mexico: Economists from Nationalism to Neoliberalism.* Princeton, NJ: Princeton University Press, 2001.

Bailey, Ian. "Neoliberalism, Climate Governance and the Scalar Politics of EU Emissions Trading." *Area* 39, no. 4 (2007): 431–142.

Bailey, Ian, and G. A. Wilson. "Theorising Transitional Pathways in Response to Climate Change: Technocentrism, Ecocentrism and the Carbon Economy." *Environment and Planning A*, 41, no. 10 (2009): 2324–2341.

Bakker, Karen. *Privatizing Water.* Ithaca, NY: Cornell University Press, 2004.

———. *An Uncooperative Commodity: Privatising Water in England and Wales.* Oxford: Oxford University Press, 2004.

Bankobeza, Gilbert M. *Ozone Protection: The International Legal Regime.* The Hague: Eleven Publishing, 2005.

Banks, Jonathan. "Methyl Bromide Technical Options Committee." In *Protecting the Ozone Layer: Lessons, Models and Prospects,* ed. P. G. LePrestre, J. D. Reid, and E. T. Morehouse Jr., 167–172. Boston: Kluwer, 1998.

Barnett, Michael, and Martha Finnemore. *Rules for the World: International Organizations in Global Politics.* Ithaca, NY: Cornell University Press, 2004.

Barrett, Scott. "Self-Enforcing International Environmental Agreements." *Oxford Economic Papers* 46 (1994): 878–894.

Bartley, Tim. "How Foundations Shape Social Movements." *Social Problems* 54, no. 3 (2007): 229–255.

BBC. "An Animated Journey through the Earth's Climate History." British Broadcasting Corporation, 2009. Available at news.bbc.co.uk/2/hi/in_depth/sci_tech/2009/copenhagen/8386319.stm. Accessed December 10, 2009.

———. "Davos 2011: Doha Round 'Should Finish by End of Year.'" British Broadcasting Corporation, January 28, 2011. Available at http://www.bbc.co.uk/news/business-12309484. Accessed November 17, 2011.

———. "Ozone Hole 'Can Be Fixed by 2080.'" British Broadcasting Corporation, 2010. Available at http://news.bbc.co.uk/today/hi/today/news-id_8664000/8664292.stm. Accessed May 24, 2011.

———. "Whistle Blown on Illegal CFC Trade." BBC News, 2011. Available at http://news.bbc.co.uk/2/hi/science/nature/3442985.stm. Accessed May 30, 2011.

Beamish, Rita. "U.S. Pesticide Stockpile under Scrutiny." *Associated Press Online,* November 3, 2006.

Beck, Ulrich. *Risk Society: Towards a New Modernity.* Newbury Park, CA: Sage, 1992.

Becker, Gary S. *Accounting for Tastes.* Cambridge, MA: Harvard University Press, 1996.

Benedick, Richard Elliot. "The Diplomacy of Climate Change: Lessons from the Montreal Ozone Protocol." *Energy Policy* 19, no. 2 (1991): 94–97.
———. *Ozone Diplomacy: New Directions in Safeguarding the Planet.* Cambridge, MA: Harvard University Press, 1998.

Bernard, H. Russell. *Research Methods in Anthropology: Qualitative and Quantitative Approaches,* 2nd ed. Walnut Creek, CA: AltaMira Press, 1994.

Bernstein, Steven. *The Compromise of Liberal Environmentalism.* New York: Columbia University Press, 2002.

Beron, Kurt J., James C. Murdoch, and Wim P. M. Vijverberg. "Why Cooperate? Public Goods, Economic Power, and the Montreal Protocol." *Review of Economics and Statistics* 85, no. 2 (2003): 286–297.

Beukel, Erik. "Ideas, Interests, and State Preferences: The Making of Multilateral Environmental Agreements with Trade Stipulations." *Policy Studies* 24 (2003): 3–16.

Bhat, R. G., and K. V. Subbaro. "Host Range Specificity in *Verticillium dahliae.*" *Phytopathology* 89, no. 12 (1999): 1218–1225.

Bilefsky, Dan. "Europe Sets Ambitious Limits on Greenhouse Gases." *New York Times,* March 10, 2007.

Black, Richard. "Arctic Ozone Levels in Never-before-Seen Plunge." BBC, 2011. Available at http://www.bbc.co.uk/news/science-environment-12969167. Accessed May 24, 2011.

Blok, Wim J., Jan G. Lamers, Aad J. Termorshuizen, and Gerrit J. Bollen. "Control of Soilborne Plant Pathogens by Incorporating Fresh Organic Amendments Followed by Tarping." *Phytopathology* 90, no. 3 (2000): 253–259.

Bodansky, Daniel. "Prologue to the Climate Change Convention." In *Negotiating Climate Change: The Inside Story of the Rio Convention,* ed. Irving Mintzer and J. A. Leonard, 45–74. Cambridge: Cambridge University Press, 1994.
———. "The U.N. Framework Convention on Climate Change: A Commentary." *Yale Journal of International Law* 18 (1993): 451–458.

Bodnar, Alice L. "Annual Review of Environmental and Natural Resources Law: NRDC v. EPA: Testing the Waters of the Constitutionality of Delegation to International Organizations." *Ecology Law Quarterly* 895 (2007): 894–926.

Bogenholm, Vanessa. "Organic Strawberries: A Sweeter Choice." Paper presented at the 23rd Annual Ecological Farming Conference, Pacific Grove, CA, 2003.

Bolda, Mark, Laura Tourte, Karen Klonsky, and Richard L. De Moura. *Sample Costs to Produce Organic Strawberries: Central Coast, Santa*

Cruz and Monterey Counties. Davis, CA: University of California Cooperative Extension, 2006. ST-CC-06-O.

Boli, John, and George M. Thomas. "World Culture in the World Polity: A Century of International Non-Governmental Organization." *American Sociological Review* 62 (1997): 171–190.

Bonanno, Alessandro. "The Crisis of Representation: The Limits of Liberal Democracy in the Global Era." *Journal of Rural Studies* 16 (2000): 305–323.

Bondi, Liz, and Nina Laurie. "Introduction to Working the Spaces of Neoliberalism." *Antipode* 37, no. 3 (2005): 394–401.

Borrego, John. Conversation regarding Professor Borrego's research on strawberry production in Central Coast California and Spain, March 15, 2009.

——. "Models of Integration, Models of Development in the Pacific." *Journal of World Systems Research* 1, no. 11 (1995). Available at http://jwsr.ucr.edu/archive/vol1/v1_nb.php.

——. "The Restructuring of Frozen Food Production in North America and Its Impacts on Daily Life in Two Communities: Watsonville, California, and Irapuato, Guanajuato." In *New Frontiers of the 21st Century*, ed. N. Klahn, A. Alvarez, F. Manchon, and P. Castillo, 491–543. Mexico City: DEMOS, 2000.

Borrego, John, Alejandro Alvarez, and Kwame Sundaram Jomo, eds. *The State, Capital and Industrialization: Comparative Perspectives on the Pacific Rim*. Boulder, CO: Westview Press, 1996.

Borrego, John, Carol Shennan, Brian J. Gareau, Joji Muramoto, Stephen R. Gliessman, et al. "Agents of Change: Environmental Governance, Competition, and Sustainability in Global Strawberry Production: NSF Grant Proposal no. 0827330," Washington, D.C.: National Science Foundation, 2008.

Borrelli, Peter. *Crossroads: Environmental Priorities for the Future*. Washington, D.C.: Island Press, 1988.

Boswell, Terry, and Christopher Chase-Dunn. *The Spiral of Capitalism and Socialism: Toward Global Democracy*. Boulder, CO: Rienner, 2000.

Bourdieu, Pierre. *Distinction: A Social Critique of the Judgment of Taste*. London: Routledge and Kegan Paul, 1986.

——. "The Essence of Neoliberalism: Utopia of Endless Exploitation." *Le Monde Diplomatique*, December 1998. Available at http://mondediplo.com/1998/12/08bourdieu.

——. "The Forms of Capital." In *Handbook of Theory and Research for the Sociology of Education*, ed. J. G. Richards, 241–258. New York: Greenwood Press, 1985.

Boykoff, Maxwell T. *Who Speaks for the Climate? Making Sense of Media Reporting on Climate Change.* Cambridge: Cambridge University Press, 2011.

Breitmeier, Helmut, and Volker Rittberger. "Environmental NGOs in an Emerging Global Civil Society." In Chasek, *The Global Environment in the Twenty-First Century,* 130–163.

Brenner, Neil, and Nik Theodore. "Cities and the Geographies of 'Actually Existing Neoliberalism.'" *Antipode* 34, no. 3 (2002): 349–379.

——. "From the 'New Localism' to the Spaces of Neoliberalism." *Antipode* 34, no. 3 (2002): 341–347.

Brown, Lester. "Time Is Running Out on the Planet." *Earth Summit Times,* June 2, 1992.

Brulle, Robert J. "From Environmental Campaigns to Advancing the Public Dialog: Environmental Communication for Civic Engagement." *Environmental Communication* 4, no. 1 (2010): 82–98.

Bryk, Dale S. "The Montreal Protocol and Recent Developments to Protect the Ozone-Layer." *Harvard Environmental Law Review* 15, no. 1 (1991): 275–298.

Bulkeley, Harriet, "Reconfiguring Environmental Governance: Towards a Politics of Scales and Networks." *Political Geography* 24 (2005): 875–902.

Bulkeley, Harriet, and Susanne C. Moser. "Responding to Climate Change: Governance and Social Action beyond Kyoto." *Global Environmental Politics* 7 (2007): 1–10.

Bull, Carolee T. "Factors Influencing Integrated Methods for Control of Soilborne Diseases of Strawberry." Paper presented at the Annual International Research Conference on Methyl Bromide Alternatives and Emissions Reductions, San Diego, CA, November 1–4, 1999.

Bull, Carolee T., and Husein A. Ajwa. "Yield of Strawberries Inoculated with Biological Control Agents and Planted in Fumigated or Non-Fumigated Soil." Paper presented at the Annual International Research Conference on Methyl Bromide Alternatives and Emissions Reductions, Orlando, FL, December 7–9, 1998.

Bull, Carolee T., Steven T. Koike, and Carol Shennan. "Performance of Commercially Available Strawberry Cultivars in Organic Production Fields." Paper presented at the Annual International Research Conference on Methyl Bromide Alternatives and Emissions Reductions, San Diego, CA, September 1–2, 2001.

Bull, Carolee T., Joji Muramoto, Steven T. Koike, Jim Leap, Carol Shennan, and Polly Goldman. "Strawberry Cultivars and Mycorrhizal

Inoculants Evaluated in California Organic Production Fields." *Crop Management,* 2005. Doi:10.1094/CM-2005-0527-02-RS.

Bumiller, Elisabeth, and John M. Broder. "McCain Differs with Bush on Climate Change." *New York Times,* 2008. Available at http:////www. nytimes.com/2008/05/13/us/politics/13mccain.html. Accessed May 13, 2008.

Burawoy, Michael, ed. *Global Ethnography: Forces, Connections and Imaginations in a Postmodern World.* Berkeley: University of California Press, 2000.

Butler, J. H., J. W. Elkins, B. D. Hall, S. O. Cummings, and S. A. Montzka. "A Decrease in the Growth Rates of Atmospheric Halon Concentrations." *Nature* 359, no. 6394 (1992): 403–405.

Cai, Wenju, and Tim Cowan. "Trends in Southern Hemisphere Circulation in IPCC Ar4 Models over 1950–99: Ozone Depletion versus Greenhouse Forcing." *Journal of Climate* 20, no. 4 (2007): 681–693.

California Coastkeeper Alliance. "Notice of Call for Public Comment on Fumigant Iodomethane Petition (Methyl Iodide)." Fremont, California, Coastkeeper Alliance, 2011. Available at http://www. cacoastkeeper.org/document/protect-california-communities-and-ecosystems-from-methyl-iodide.pdf.

California Department of Food and Agriculture. "California Agricultural Highlights 2005," 2006. Available at http://www.cdfa.ca.gov/. Accessed August 16, 2006.

California Strawberry Commission. "California Delivers on Olympic Athlete's Request for Strawberries," 2008. Available at http://www. calstrawberry. com/commission/inthenews.asp?itnid=68. Accessed May 15, 2009.

———. "California Frozen Exports." 2006. Available at www.calstrawberry. com. Accessed February 8, 2006.

Campbell, John L., and Ove K. Pedersen. *The Rise of Neoliberalism and Institutional Analysis.* Princeton, NJ: Princeton University Press, 2001.

Canan, Penelope. "The Problem of Ozone Depletion: A Call for Sociological Action." *Sociological Practice Review* 3, no. 2 (1992): 67–73.

Canan, Penelope, and Nancy Reichman. "Montreal Protocol." In *Encyclopedia of Science, Technology, and Ethics,* ed. Carl Mitcham, 1232–1236. Detroit: Macmillan Reference USA, 2005.

———. *Ozone Connections: Expert Networks in Global Environmental Governance.* Sheffield: Greenleaf, 2002.

Capretta, Annette M. "The Future's So Bright, I Gotta Wear Shades: Future Impacts of the Montreal Protocol on Substances That Deplete the

Ozone Layer." *Virginia Journal of International Law* 29, no. 1 (1988): 211–248.

Carlowicz, Mike, and Kristyn Ecochard. "Arctic Ozone Loss: Image of the Day." 2011. Available at http://earthobservatory.nasa.gov/IOTD/view. php?id=49874. Accessed May 21, 2011.

Carpenter, Janet, Lori Lynch, and Tom Trout. "Township Limits on 1, 3-D Will Impact Adjustment to Methyl Bromide Phase-Out." *California Agriculture* 55, no. 3 (2001): 12–18.

Carter, Colin A., James A. Chalfant, and Rachael E. Goodhue. "China's Strawberry Industry: An Emerging Competitor for California?" *ARE Update* 9, no. 1 (2005): 7–15.

Carter, Colin A., James A. Chalfant, Rachael E. Goodhue, Frank M. Han, and Massimiliano DeSantis. "The Methyl Bromide Ban: Economic Impacts on the California Strawberry Industry." *Review of Agricultural Economics* 27, no. 2 (2005): 181–197.

Castells, Manuel. *The Rise of the Network Society*, vol. 1. Malden, MA: Blackwell Publishers, 1996.

Castree, Noel. "Neoliberalising Nature: Processes, Effects, and Evaluations." *Environment and Planning A* 40, no. 1 (2008): 153–171.

Center for Civil Society. "What Is Civil Society?" London School of Economics and Political Science Center for Civil Society, 2004. Available at http://www.lse.ac.uk/collections/CCS/what_is_civil_society.htm.

Chasek, Pamela S., ed. *The Global Environment in the Twenty-First Century: Prospects for International Cooperation*. New York: United Nations University Press, 2000.

Chellemi, D. O., J. Miruss, J. Nance, and K. Shuler. "Evaluation of Technology and Application Methods for Chemical Alternatives to Methyl Bromide." Paper presented at the Annual International Research Conference on Methyl Bromide Alternatives and Emissions Reduction, San Diego, CA, September 1–2, 2001.

Chemical Week 142, no.14 (April 16, 1988): 7.

Chinese Association of Horticultural Science. "The Second National Conference of Strawberry Production." Suan-Liu County, Chengdu, Sichuan Province, 2007.

Chipperfield, Martyn P., and Vitali E. Fioletov. "Global Ozone: Past and Present." In *Scientific Assessment of Ozone Depletion: 2006*, ed. World Meteorological Organization. Geneva: World Meteorological Organization, 2007.

Clark, Ezra. "Preventing Illegal Trade in ODS: Strengthening the Montreal Protocol Licensing System." Environmental Investigation Agency,

2007. Available at http://www.eia-global.org/PDF/reports--preventing illegaltrade--climate--May07.pdf. Accessed May 30, 2011.

Clarke, Jeanne Nienaber, and Hanna J. Cortner, eds. *The State and Nature: Voices Heard, Voices Unheard in America's Environmental Dialogue.* Upper Saddle River, NJ: Prentice Hall, 2002.

Cohen, Joseph N., and Miguel A. Centeno. "Neoliberalism and Macroeconomic Performance, 1980–2000." *Annals of the American Academy of Political and Social Science* 606 (2006): 32–67.

Coleman, James. "Social Capital in the Creation of Human Capital." *American Journal of Sociology* 94, supplement (1988): S95–S121.

Commoner, Barry. *The Closing Circle: Man, Nature, and Technology.* New York: Knopf, 1971.

Conca, Ken. *Governing Water: Contentious Transnational Politics and Global Institution Building.* Cambridge, MA: MIT Press, 2006.

——. "The WTO and the Undermining of Global Environmental Governance." *Review of International Political Economy* 7, no. 3 (2000): 484–494.

Conca, Ken, and Geoffrey D. Dabelko, eds. *Green Planet Blues: Environmental Politics from Stockholm to Kyoto,* 2nd ed. Boulder, CO: Westview Press, 2004.

Cox, Robert. *Environmental Communication and the Public Sphere.* Thousand Oaks, CA: Sage, 2006.

Dean, Mitchell. *Governmentality: Power and Rule in Modern Society.* Thousand Oaks, CA: Sage, 1999.

DeCanio, Stephen J. "Economic Analysis, Environmental Policy, and Intergenerational Justice in the Reagan Administration: The Case of the Montreal Protocol." *International Environmental Agreements* 3, no. 4 (2003): 299–321.

DeCanio, Stephen J., and Catherine S. Norman. "Economics of the 'Critical Use' of Methyl Bromide under the Montreal Protocol." *Contemporary Economic Policy* 23, no. 3 (2005): 376–393.

Dell'Amore, Christine. "First North Pole Ozone Hole Forming?" 2011. Available at http://news.nationalgeographic.com/news/2011/03/110321-ozone-layer-hole-arctic-north-pole-science-environment-uv-sunscreen/.

Department of Homeland Security. "Chemical Facility Anti-Terrorism Standard: Final Appendix A: Department of Homeland Security Chemicals of Interest." U.S. Department of Homeland Security, 2007. Available at http://www.dhs.gov/xlibrary/assets/chemsec_appendix-afinalrule.pdf. Accessed December 6, 2007.

320   Bibliography

Diaz-Bonilla, Eugenio, Soren Elkaer Frandsen, and Sherman Robinson, eds. *WTO Negotiations and Agricultural Trade Liberalization: The Effect of Developed Countries' Policies on Developing Countries.* Cambridge, MA: CABI, 2006.

Dinnage, Russell J. "Pesticides: Methyl Bromide Industry Seeks Changes in EPA's Phaseout Effort." *Greenwire*, 2007.

Doolittle, Diane M. "Underestimating Ozone Depletion: The Meandering Road to the Montreal Protocol and Beyond." *Ecology Law Quarterly* 16, no. 2 (1989): 407–441.

Dorfman, Robert, and Nancy S. Dorfman, eds. *Economics of the Environment*, 1st ed. New York: Norton, 1972.

———. *Economics of the Environment*, 2nd ed. New York: Norton, 1977.

———. *Economics of the Environment*, 3rd ed. New York: Norton, 1993.

Dryzek, John S., David Downes, Christian Hunold, David Scholsberg, and Hans-Kristian Hernes. "Ecological Modernization, Risk Society, and the Green State." In Mol, Sonnenfeld, and Spaargaren, *The Ecological Modernization Reader*, 226–253.

Duniway, John M. "Status of Chemical Alternatives to Methyl Bromide for Pre-Plant Fumigation of Soil." *Phytopathology* 92, no. 12 (2002): 1337–1343.

Duniway, John M., J. J. Hao, D. M. Dopkins, H. Ajwa, and G. T. Browne. "Some Chemical, Cultural, and Biological Alternatives to Methyl Bromide Fumigation of Soil for Strawberry." Paper presented at the Annual International Research Conference on Methyl Bromide Alternatives and Emissions Reduction, San Diego, CA, September 1–2, 2001.

Dunlap, Riley, and Angela Mertig, eds. *American Environmentalism: The U.S. Environmental Movement.* Bristol: Crane, Russak, 1992.

DuPuis, E. Melanie, and Brian J. Gareau. "Neoliberal Knowledge: The Decline of Technocracy and the Weakening of the Montreal Protocol." *Social Science Quarterly* 89, no. 5 (2008): 1212–1229.

Earthsky. "Record Depletion of Arctic Ozone in Past Few Days over Scandinavia." Earthsky.org, 2011. Available at http://earthsky.org/earth/record-depletion-of-arctic-ozone-in-past-few-days-over-scandinavia. Accessed June 16, 2011.

Eayre, Cynthia. "Alternatives to Methyl Bromide in Strawberries and Peaches." Paper presented at the Annual International Research Conference on Methyl Bromide Alternatives and Emissions Reduction, San Diego, CA, November 10–13, 2000.

Ebrahim, Alnoor. *NGOs and Organizational Change.* Cambridge: Cambridge University Press, 2003.

Eckersley, Robyn. *Environmentalism and Political Theory: Toward an Ecocentric Approach.* New York: State University of New York Press, 1992.

Edwards, Bob, and Michael W. Foley. "Social Capital and the Political Economy of Our Discontent." *American Behavioral Scientist* 40, no. 5 (1997): 669–678.

EIA. "California Strawberry Industry Defends Ozone-Depleting Cemicals as Children Face Unprecedented Skin Cancer Risks." Environmental Investigation Agency, 2006. Available at http://www.eia-international. org/cgi/news/news.cgi?t=templateanda=297. Accessed November 8, 2009.

———. "Montreal: Top Awards for Our Work Exposing Illegal Chemicals Trade." Environmental Investigation Agency, 2007. Available at http:// www.eia-international.org/index.shtml. Accessed September 8, 2007.

———. "Opportunity Wasted: Methyl Bromide: Our Best Chance to Reduce Ozone Depletion Now." Environmental Investigation Agency, 2006. Available at http://www.eia-international.org/files/reports123–1.pdf.

———. "Strawberries Linked to Skin Cancer during Melanoma Awareness Month." Environmental Investigation Agency, 2006. Available at http:// www.eia-international.org/cgi/news/news.cgi?t=templateanda=304. Accessed November 8, 2009.

Eick, Volker. "Space Patrols: The New Peace-Keeping Functions of Non-Profits: Contesting Neoliberalism or the Urban Poor?" In Leitner, Peck, and Sheppard, *Contesting Neoliberalism.*

Ekins, Paul, and Terry Barker. "Carbon Taxes and Carbon Emissions Trading." *Journal of Economic Surveys* 15, no. 3 (2001): 325–376.

ENB. "Summary of the Nineteenth Meeting of the Parties to the Montreal Protocol on Substances That Deplete the Ozone Layer: 17–21 September 2007." *Earth Negotiations Bulletin* 19, no. 60 (2007).

———. "20th Anniversary Seminar of the Montreal Protocol 'Celebrating 20 Years of Progress.'" *Earth Negotiations Bulletin,* 2007. Available at http:// www.iisd.ca/ozone/mop19/anniversary.htm. Accessed March 25, 2010.

Environment News Service. "Developing Countries Funded for Ozone Safe Technology." 2005. Available at http://www.ens-newswire.com/ens/ dec2005/2005–12–16–01.asp. Accessed October 13, 2006.

———. "South Pole Ozone Recovery 20 Years Later Than Expected." 2006. Available at http://www.ens-newswire.com/ens/jun2006/2006–06–30–05.asp. Accessed October 13, 2006.

———. "U.S. Demand for Methyl Bromide Blocks Ozone Accord." 2003. Available at http://www.ens-newswire.com/ens/nov2003/2003–11–14–02.asp. Accessed October 12, 2006.

EPA. "Essential Use Exemptions." U.S. Environmental Protection Agency, 2006. Available at http://www.epa.gov/ozone/title6/phaseout/mdi/. Accessed September 8, 2007.

———. "Fact Sheet: 25th Open-Ended Working Group, Second Extraordinary Meeting of the Parties." U.S. Environmental Protection Agency, 2006. Available at http://www.epa.gov/ozone/mbr/MeBr_FactSheet.html. Accessed October 15, 2006.

———. "Methyl Bromide (Bromomethane)." U.S. Environmental Protection Agency, 2000. Available at http://www.epa.gov//ttnatwo1/hlthef/methylbr.html. Accessed June 3, 2011.

———. "The Phaseout of Methyl Bromide." U.S. Environmental Protection Agency, 2006. Available at http://www.epa.gov/ozone/mbr/. Accessed October 12, 2006.

———. "Protection of Stratospheric Ozone: The 2006 Critical Use Exemption from the Phaseout of Methyl Bromide." Washington, D.C.: U.S. Environmental Protection Agency, 2006.

———. "Retrospective Study of the Costs of EPA Regulations: An Interim Report of Five Case Studies." White paper prepared for review by the EPA's Science Advisory Board– Environmental Economics Advisory Committee. March 2012.

———. "2007 Best-of-the-Best Stratospheric Ozone Protection Award Winners." Environmental Protection Agency, 2007. Available at http://www.epa.gov/spdpublc/awards/bestofthebest/2007_botb_winners.html. Accessed January 3, 2012.

———. "United States Nomination for Critical Use Exemptions from the 2008 Phaseout of Methyl Bromide." U.S. Environmental Protection Agency, 2006. Available at http://www.epa.gov/ozone/mbr/2008_nomination.html. Accessed October 15, 2006.

Esty, Daniel. *Greening the GATT: Trade, Environment, and the Future.* Washington, D.C.: Institute for International Economics, 1994.

Esty, Daniel C., and Andrew S. Winston. *Green to Gold: How Smart Companies Use Environmental Strategy to Innovate, Create Value, and Build Competitive Advantage.* New Haven: Yale University Press, 2006.

European Commission. "The EU's Relations with the United States of America: Environment." European Commission, 2006. Available at http://ec.europa.eu/external_relations/us/intro/environment.htm. Accessed May 8, 2008.

Evans, Peter. "Is an Alternative Globalization Possible?" *Politics and Society* 36 (2008): 271–305.

Expatica. "New Ozone Hole over Germany Poses Health Risks." Expatica, 2005. Available at http://www.expatica.com/de/news/local_news/new-ozone-hole-over-germany-poses-health-risk-21345.html. Accessed June 11, 2011.

Eyring, V., et al. "Multi-Model Assessment of Stratospheric Ozone Return Dates and Ozone Recovery in Ccmval-2 Models." *Atmospheric Chemistry and Physics* 10 (2010): 9451–9472.

Ezrahi, Yaron. *The Descent of Icarus: Science and the Transformation of Contemporary Democracy.* Cambridge, MA: Harvard University Press, 1990.

Faber, Daniel. *Capitalizing on Environmental Injustice: The Polluter-Industrial Complex in the Age of Globalization.* Lanham, MD: Rowman and Littlefield, 2008.

Faber, Daniel R., and Deborah McCarthy. "Neo-Liberalism, Globalization and the Struggle for Ecological Democracy: Linking Sustainability and Environmental Justice." In *Just Sustainabilities: Development in an Unequal World,* ed. Julian Agyeman, Robert D. Bullard, and Bob Evans, 38–63. London: Earthscan, 2003.

Fahey, David W., and Michaela I. Hegglin. "Twenty Questions and Answers about the Ozone Layer: 2010 Update, Scientific Assessment of Ozone Depletion: 2010." World Meteorological Organization, 2011. Available at http://ozone.unep.org/Assessment_Panels/SAP/Scientific_Assessment_2010/SAP-2010-FAQs-update.pdf.

FAO. "Fresh Strawberry Production Statistics," U.N. Food and Agriculture Organization, 2005.

FAO/UNEP. "Global Report on Validated Alternatives to the Use of Methyl Bromide for Soil Fumigation." Ed. R. Labrada and L. Fornasari. Rome: Food and Agriculture Association and U.N. Environmental Programme, 2001.

Farman, J. C., H. Gardiner, and J. D. Shanklin. "Large Losses of Total Ozone in Antarctica Reveal Seasonal CLO_x/NO_x Interaction." *Nature* 315 (May 16, 1985): 207–211.

Federal Register. "Protection of Stratospheric Ozone: Extension of the Laboratory and Analytical Use Exemption for Essential Class I Ozone-Depleting Substances." *Rules and Regulations* 76, no. 241 (December 15, 2011): 77909–77913.

Ferguson, James. *The Anti-Politics Machine: "Development," Depoliticization, and Bureaucratic Power in Lesotho.* Minneapolis: University of Minnesota Press, 1994.

Fernando, Jude L. "The Power of Unsustainable Development." *Annals of the American Political Science Society* 590, no. 1 (2003): 6–34.

Fest Grabiel, Danielle. "Crucial Crossroads." *Our Planet: The Magazine of the United Nations Environmental Programme*, September 2007:20–21.

Fine, Ben. "Callonistics: A Disentanglement." *Economy and Society* 32, no. 3 (2003): 478–484.

———. "Social Capital for Africa?." *Transformation* 53 (2003): 29–52.

———. *Social Capital versus Social Theory: Political Economy and Social Science at the Turn of the Millennium*. London: Routledge, 2001.

———. "They F**k You Up Those Social Capitalists." *Antipode* 24, no. 4 (2002): 796–799.

Fine, Ben, and Costas Lapavitsas. "Social Capital and Capitalist Economies." *South Eastern Europe Journal of Economics* 1 (2004): 17–34.

Fisher, Dana. "COP-15 in Copenhagen: How the Merging of Movements Left Civil Society Out in the Cold." *Global Environmental Politics* 10, no. 2 (2010): 11–17.

Fisher, Dana, Oliver Fritsch, and Mikael Skou Andersen. "Transformations in Environmental Governance and Participation." In Mol, Sonnenfeld, and Spaargaren, *The Ecological Modernisation Reader*, 141–155.

Flannery, Tim F. *The Weather Makers: How Man Is Changing the Climate and What It Means for Life on Earth*. New York: Atlantic Monthly Press, 2005.

Foley, Michael W., and Bob Edwards. "Escape from Politics? Social Theory and the Social Capital Debate." *American Behavioral Scientist* 40, no. 5 (1997): 550–561.

———. "Is It Time to Disinvest in Social Capital?" *Journal of Public Policy* 19 (1999): 141–173.

Forsyth, Tim. *Critical Political Ecology: The Politics of Environmental Science*. London: Routledge, 2003.

Foster, John Bellamy. "Marx's Theory of the Metabolic Rift: Classical Foundations for Environmental Sociology." *American Journal of Sociology* 105 (1999): 366–405.

Foucault, Michel. *Discipline and Punish: The Birth of the Prison*, 2nd ed. New York: Vintage Books, 1995.

———. "Governmentality." In *The Foucault Effect: Studies in Governmentality*, ed. G. Burchell, C. Gordon, and P. Miller, 87–104. Chicago: University of Chicago Press, 1991.

———. *The History of Sexuality: An Introduction*. Trans. Robert Hurley. New York: Vintage, 1990.

———. *Power/Knowledge: Selected Interviews and Other Writings, 1972–1977*. Ed. Colin Gordon. Trans. Colin Gordon, Leo Marshall, John Mepham, and Kate Soper. 1st American edition. New York: Pantheon Books, 1980.

———. "Truth and Power." In Foucault, *Power/Knowledge*, 109–133.

———. "Two Lectures." In Foucault, *Power/Knowledge*, 78–108.

Fourcade-Gourinchas, Marion, and Sarah Babb. "The Rebirth of the Liberal Creed: Paths to Neoliberalism in Four Countries." *American Journal of Sociology* 108, no. 3 (2002): 533–579.

Fox, Jonathan A. "The World Bank and Social Capital: Contesting the Concept in Practice." *Journal of International Development* 9, no. 7 (1997): 963–971.

Frank, David, Ann Hironaka, and Evan Schofer. "The Nation-State and the Natural Environment over the Twentieth Century." *American Sociological Review* 65 (2000): 96–116.

Franz, Neil. "Methyl Bromide Users Clamor for Alternatives." *Chemical Week*, February 16, 2000, 55.

Freudenburg, William R., and Robert Gramling. *Blowout in the Gulf: The BP Oil Spill Disaster and the Future of Energy in America*. Cambridge, MA: MIT Press, 2011.

Friedman, Milton. *Capitalism and Freedom*. Chicago: University of Chicago Press, 1962.

Friedman, Milton, and Anna J. Schwartz. *A Monetary History of the United States 1867–1960*. Princeton, NJ: Princeton University Press, 1963.

Fries, Amos Alfred, and Clarence Jay West. *Chemical Warfare*. New York: McGraw Hill, 1921.

Fruitnet. "China's Strawberry Production Increase," 2009. Available at://www.fruitnet.com/content.aspx?ttid=11andcid=3809. Accessed August 8, 2010.

Gareau, Brian J. "A Critical Review of the Successful CFC Phase-Out versus the Delayed Methyl Bromide Phase-Out in the Montreal Protocol." *International Environmental Agreements: Politics, Law, and Economics* 10, no. 3 (2010): 209–231.

———. "Dangerous Holes in Global Environmental Governance: The Roles of Neoliberal Discourse, Science, and California Agriculture in the Montreal Protocol." *Antipode* 40, no. 1 (2008): 102–130.

———. "Ecological Values amid Local Interests: Natural Resource Conservation, Social Differentiation, and Human Survival in Honduras." *Rural Sociology* 72, no. 2 (2007): 244–268.

———. "The Limited Influence of Global Civil Society: International Environmental Nongovernmental Organizations and the Methyl Bromide Controversy in the Montreal Protocol." *Environmental Politics* 21, no. 1 (2012): 88–107.

——. "We Have Never Been 'Human': Agential Nature, Actor-Network Theory (ANT), and Marxist Political Ecology." *Capitalism, Nature, Socialism* 16, no. 4 (2005): 128–140.

Gareau, Brian J., and John Borrego. "Global Environmental Governance, Competition, and Sustainability in Global Agriculture." In *Handbook of World-Systems Analysis: Theory and Research,* ed. Salvatore Babones and Christopher Chase-Dunn, ch. 51. New York: Routledge, 2012.

Gareau, Brian J., and E. Melanie DuPuis. "From Public to Private Global Environmental Governance: Lessons from the Montreal Protocol's Stalled Methyl Bromide Phase-Out." *Environment and Planning A* 41, no. 10 (2009): 2305–2323.

Gill, Stephen. "Constitutionalizing Inequality and the Clash of Globalizations." *International Studies Review* 4 (2002): 47–65.

Goldberg, Donald. "As the World Burns: Negotiating the Framework Convention on Climate Change." *International Environmental Law Review* 239 (1993): 244–251.

Goldman, Michael. *Imperial Nature: The World Bank and Struggles for Social Justice in the Age of Globalization.* New Haven: Yale University Press, 2005.

Goodhue, Rachael E., Steven A. Fennimore, and Husein A. Ajwa. "The Economic Importance of Methyl Bromide: Does the California Strawberry Industry Qualify for a Critical Use Exemption from the Methyl Bromide Ban?" *Review of Agricultural Economics* 27, no. 2 (2005): 198–211.

Goodland, Robert, and George Ledoc. "Neoclassical Economics and Principles of Sustainable Development." *Ecological Modeling* 38 (1987): 19–46.

Goodman, David, Bernardo Sorj, and John Wilkenson. *From Farming to Biotechnology.* Oxford: Basil Blackwell, 1987.

Gordon, Tom, Rob Webb, Steve Koike, and Krishna Subbarao. "Management of Verticillium Wilt in the Absence of Fumigation." Paper presented at the Annual International Research Conference on Methyl Bromide Alternatives and Emissions Reductions, Kissimmee, FL, November 13–16, 1994.

Goud, Jan-Kees C., Aad J. Termorshuizen, Wim J. Blok, and Ariena H. C. van Bruggen. "Long-Term Effect of Biological Soil Disinfestation on Verticillium Wilt." *Plant Disease* 88, no. 7 (2004): 688–694.

Greenpeace International. "Greenpeace Annual Report 2008." Amsterdam Greenpeace International, 2008. Available at http://www.greenpeace. org/raw/content/international/press/reports/international-annualreport-2008.pdf.

Grundmann, Reiner. "The Strange Success of the Montreal Protocol: Why Reductionist Accounts Fail." *International Environmental Affairs* 10, no. 3 (1998): 197–220.

——. *Transnational Environmental Policy: Reconstructing Ozone.* New York: Routledge, 2001.

Guston, David H. "Boundary Organizations in Environmental Policy and Science." *Science, Technology, and Human Values* 26, no. 4 (2001): 399–408.

Guthman, Julie. "The Polanyian Way? Voluntary Food Labels as Neoliberal Governance." *Antipode* 39, no. 3 (2007): 456–478.

Gutro, Rob. "NASA and NOAA Announce Ozone Hole Is a Double Record Breaker." NASA, 2006. Available at http://www.nasa.gov/vision/earth/lookingatearth/ozone_record.html. Accessed June 12, 2011.

Ha-Duong, Minh, Gerard Megie, and Didier Hauglustaine. "A Pro-Active Stratospheric Ozone Protection Scenario." *Global Environmental Change* 13, no. 1 (2003): 43–49.

Haas, Peter M. "Banning Chlorofluorocarbons." *International Organization* 46, no. 1 (1992): 187–224.

——. "Epistemic Communities and International Policy Coordination." *International Organization* 46, no. 1 (1992): 1–35.

Hacking, Ian. "'Style' for Historians and Philosophers." *Studies in History and Philosophy of Science* 23, no. 1 (1992): 1–20.

Hadekel, Peter. "Montreal Protocol Outshines Kyoto." *The Gazette,* September 12, 2007, B1.

Hahn, Robert W., and Albert M. McGartland. "The Political-Economy of Instrument Choice: An Examination of the United States Role in Implementing the Montreal Protocol." *Northwestern University Law Review* 83, no. 3 (1989): 592–611.

Hajer, Maarten. *The Politics of Environmental Discourse: Ecological Modernisation and the Policy Process.* Oxford: Oxford University Press, 1995.

Hammitt, James K. "Are the Costs of Proposed Environmental Regulations Overestimated? Evidence from the CFC Phaseout." *Environmental and Resource Economics* 16, no. 3 (2000): 281–301.

Hardin, Garrett. "Lifeboat Ethics: The Case against Helping the Poor." In *World Hunger and Moral Obligation,* ed. W. Aiken and H. La Follette. Englewood Cliffs, NJ: Prentice Hall, 1977.

——. "The Tragedy of the Commons." *Science* 162 (1968): 1243–1248.

Harris, John. *Depoliticizing Development: The World Bank and Social Capital.* London: Anthem Press, 2001.

Harris, Jonathan M. "Review of Duncan Brack's *International Trade and the Montreal Protocol.*" *Ecological Economics* 23, no. 3 (1997): 265–267.

Harrison, Jill. "Abandoned Bodies and Spaces of Sacrifice: Pesticide Drift Activism and the Contestation of Neoliberal Environmental Politics in California." *Geoforum* 39 (2007): 1197–1214.

———. *Pesticide Drift and the Pursuit of Environmental Justice.* Cambridge, MA: MIT Press, 2011.

Harvey, David. *A Brief History of Neoliberalism.* New York: Oxford University Press, 2005.

———. *The Limits to Capital.* Chicago: University of Chicago Press, 1982.

———. *The New Imperialism.* Oxford: Oxford University Press, 2003.

———. *Spaces of Hope.* Edinburgh: Edinburgh University Press, 2001.

Havel, Vaclav. "Democracy's Forgotten Dimension." *Journal of Democracy* 6, no. 2 (1995): 3–10.

Hayek, Friedrich A. von. *The Road to Serfdom.* London: Routledge, 2001.

Hayman, Gavin, and Steve Trent. "New Challenges to the Montreal Protocol." *CONNECT: UNESCO International Science, Technology and Environmental Education Newsletter* 22, no. 2 (1997).

Held, David. *Democracy and the Global Order.* Stanford, CA: Stanford University Press, 1995.

Helm, Dieter, and Cameron Hepburn, eds. *The Economics and Politics of Climate Change.* Oxford: Oxford University Press, 2009.

Henisz, Witold J., Bennet A. Zelner, and Mauro F. Guillen. "The Worldwide Diffusion of Market-Oriented Infrastructure Reform, 1977–1999." *American Sociological Review* 70, no. 6 (2005): 871–897.

Hepburn, Cameron. "Carbon Taxes, Emissions Trading, and Hybrid Schemes." In Helm and Hepburn, *The Economics and Politics of Climate Change,* 365–384.

Heynen, Nik, James McCarthy, Scott Prudham, and Paul Robbins, eds. *Neoliberal Environments: False Promises and Unnatural Consequences.* New York: Routledge, 2007.

Hobson, Art. "Gobal Warming: Lessons from Ozone Depletion." *Physics Teacher* 28, no. 8 (2010): 525.

Hoffman, Andrew J. "Institutional Evolution and Change: Environmentalism and the U.S. Chemical Industry." *Academy of Management Journal* 42, no. 4 (1999): 351–371.

Huber, Joseph. "Upstreaming Environmental Action." In Mol, Sonnenfeld, and Spaargaren, *The Ecological Modernisation Reader,* 334–355.

Hunter, David, James Salzman, and Durwood Zaelke. *International Environmental Law and Policy.* New York: Foundation Press, 2007. University Casebook Series.

IIED. "Reshaping Local Democracy through Participatory Governance." *Environment and Urbanization Brief* 9 (2004): 1–6.

IMF. "World Economic Outlook Database, April 2011 Edition: Nomical GDP List of Countries." International Monetary Fund, 2010. Available at http://www.imf.org/external/pubs/ft/weo/2011/01/weodata/index. aspx. Accessed June 14, 2011.

IPCC. "Climate Change 2007: Synthesis Report, Contribution of Working Groups I, II and III to the Fourth Assessment Report of the Intergovernmental Panel on Climate Change." Core writing team R. K. Pachauri and A. Reisinger. Geneva: Intergovernmental Panel on Climate Change, 2007.

——. "Safeguarding the Ozone Layer and the Global Climate System: Issues Related to Hydrofluorocarbons and Perfluorocarbons." Intergovernmental Panel on Climate Change (IPCC) and the Technology and Economic Assessment Panel (TEAP) on the invitation of the United Nations Framework Convention on Climate Change and the Montreal Protocol, 2005.

Jänicke, Martin, and Helge Jörgens. "New Approaches to Environmental Governance." In Mol, Sonnenfeld, and Spaargaren, *The Ecological Modernisation Reader,* 156–189.

Jasanoff, Sheila. *Designs on Nature: Science and Democracy in Europe and the United States.* Princeton, NJ: Princeton University Press, 2005.

——. *The Fifth Branch: Science Advisers as Policymakers.* Cambridge, MA: Harvard University Press, 1990.

——. "Science, Politics and the Renegotiation of Expertise at EPA." *Osiris* 7 (1992): 1–23.

——, ed. *States of Knowledge: The Co-Production of Science and Social Order.* New York: Routledge, 2004.

Jasanoff, Sheila, and Marybeth Long Martello, eds. *Earthly Politics: Local and Global in Environmental Governance.* Cambridge, MA: MIT Press, 2004.

Jasanoff, Sheila, Gerald E. Markle, James C. Petersen, and Trevor Pinch, eds. *Handbook of Science and Technology Studies.* Thousand Oaks, CA: Sage, 1995.

Johnston, Hank, and Jackie Smith, eds. *Globalization and Resistance: Transnational Dimensions of Social Movements.* Oxford: Rowman and Littlefield, 2002.

Jomo, Kwame Sundaram, ed. *Flat World, Big Gaps: Economic Liberalization, Globalization and Inequality.* London: Zed Books, 2007.

Jopson, Debra. "Addiction to Banned Fumigant Hard to Kick; Ozone Destroyer—Silent Killers—Special Investigation—Toxic Timebomb." *Sydney Morning Herald,* October 34, 2007, 18.

Joseph, Jonathan. "Governmentality of What? Populations, States and Organizations." *Global Society* 23, no. 4 (2009): 413–427.

Kabir, Z., K. V. Subbarao, F. N. Martin, and S. T. Koike. "Crop Rotation for Verticillium Wilt Management in Conventional and Organic Strawberries." *Phytopathology* 92, no. 6, supplement (2002): s40.

Kaldor, Mary. *Global Civil Society: An Answer to War.* Malden, MA: Polity, 2003.

Keck, Margaret E., and Kathryn Sikkink. *Activists beyond Borders: Advocacy Networks in International Politics.* Ithaca, NY: Cornell University Press, 1998.

Kegley, Susan, Anne Katten, and Marion Moses. "Secondhand Pesticides: Airborne Pesticide Drift in California." Pesticide Action Network North America, 2003.

Keith, Tamara. "Austrian School Economist Hayek Finds New Fans." *National Public Radio,* 2011. Available at http://www.npr.org/2011/11/15/142307737/austrian-school-economist-hayek-finds-new-fans. Accessed November 15, 2011.

Keynes, John Maynard. *The General Theory of Employment, Interest, and Money.* San Diego: Harcourt, Brace, Jovanovich, 1964.

Koike, Steven T., Krishna V. Subbarao, R. Michael Davis, Thomas R. Gordon, and Judith C. Hubbard. "Verticillium Wilt of Cauliflower in California." *Plant Disease* 78, no. 11 (1994): 1116–1121.

Krugman, Paul. "Salt of the Earth." *New York Times,* August 8, 2003.

Lazarovits, George. "Managing Soilborne Plant Diseases through Selective Soil Disinfestation by a Knowledge-Based Application of Soil Amendments: Guest Editorial." *Phytoparasitica* 32, no. 5 (2004): 427–432.

Leaf, Dennis. "Managing Global Atmospheric Change: A U.S. Policy Perspective." *Human and Ecological Risk Assessment* 7 (2001): 1211–1226.

Leahy, Stephen. 2007. "Canada: U.S. Demand for Exemption May Weaken Ozone Protocol." Global Information Network. Available at http://www.highbeam.com/doc/1G1-168936527.html. Accessed June 2, 2011.

Leinwand, Donna. "Farmers, Environmentalists Battle over Ban on a Chemical: Agriculture Interests Say They Need Methyl Bromide, Scientists Say It Depletes the Ozone." *Philadelphia Inquirer,* March 7, 1998, D05.

Leitner, Helga, Jamie Peck, and Eric S. Sheppard, eds. *Contesting Neoliberalism: Urban Frontiers*. New York: Guilford Press, 2007.

Lélé, Sharachchandra M. "Sustainable Development: A Critical Review." *World Development* 19 (1991): 607–621.

Le Quéré, Corinne, Christian Rödenbeck, Erik T. Buitenhuis, Thomas J. Conway, Ray Langenfelds, Antony Gomez, Casper Labuschagne, et al. "Saturation of the Southern Ocean CO_2 Sink Due to Recent Climate Change." *Science* 316, no. 5832 (2007): 1735–1738.

Li, Zhengfang, and Stephen R. Gliessman. "A Comparative Study of Energy and Economic Flows between Organic and Conventional Strawberry Production Systems in Nanjing, China." In *Proceedings, 10th IFOAM International Conference*, ed. R. A. Crowder, 145–146. Christchurch, New Zealand: Lincorn University, 1994.

Lipschutz, Ronnie. "Global Civil Society and Global Governmentality." In *Power in Global Governance*, ed. Michael Barnett and Raymond Duvall, 229–248. Cambridge: Cambridge University Press, 2005.

———. "Power, Politics and Global Civil Society." *Millennium: Journal of International Studies* 33, no. 3 (2005): 747–769.

Lipschutz, Ronnie, and Judith Mayer. *Global Civil Society and Global Environmental Governance*. Albany: State University of New York Press, 1996.

Lipschutz, Ronnie, and James Rowe. *Globalization, Governmentality and Global Politics: Regulation for the Rest of Us?* London: Routledge, 2005.

Litfin, Karen T., ed. *The Greening of Sovereignty in World Politics*. Cambridge, MA: MIT Press, 1998.

———. *Ozone Discourses: Science and Politics in Global Environmental Cooperation*. New York: Columbia University Press, 1994.

Liverman, Diana M. "Who Governs, at What Scale and at What Price? Geography, Environmental Governance, and the Commodification of Nature." *Annals of the Association of American Geographers* 94, no. 4 (2004): 734–738.

Liverman Diana M., and Silvina Vilas. "Neoliberalism and the Environment in Latin America." *Annual Review of Environment and Resources* 31, no.1 (2006): 327–363.

Lopez, Marcos. "Strangers in Their Own Land: Indigenous Farm Worker Politics and Organizing in Baja California." Paper presented at the 105th Annual Meeting of the American Sociological Association, Atlanta, 2010.

Lorente, J., Y. Sola, E. Campmany, X. de Cabo, and A. Redaño. "Climatology of Ozone 'Mini-Hole' Events and Their Influence on UV Solar

Radiation in Barcelona (Spain)." *American Institute of Physics Conference Proceedings* 1100 (2009): 65–68.

Lowenfeld, Andreas. *International Economic Law.* Oxford: Oxford University Press, 2002.

Lubchenco, Jane. "Entering the Century of the Environment." *Science* 279 (1998): 492.

Luke, Timothy W. "Environmentality as Green Governmentality." In *Discourses of the Environment,* ed. E. Darier. Malden, MA: Blackwell, 1999.

Luken, Ralph, and Tamas Grof. "The Montreal Protocol's Multilateral Fund and Sustainable Development." *Ecological Economics* 56, no. 2 (2006): 241–255.

MacKinnon, Danny. "Managerialism, Governmentality, and the State: A Neo-Foucauldian Approach to Local Economic Governance." *Political Geography* 19 (2000): 293–314.

Mansfield, Becky. "Rules of Privatization: Contradictions in Neoliberal Regulation of North Pacific Fisheries." *Annals of the Association of American Geographers* 94, no. 3 (2004): 565–584.

Marglin, Stephen A., and Juliet B. Schor, eds. *The Golden Age of Capitalism: Reinterpreting the Postwar Experience.* Oxford: Oxford University Press, 1992.

Martin, Frank N., and Carolee T. Bull. "Biological Approaches for Control of Root Pathogens of Strawberry." *Phytopathology* 92, no. 12 (2002): 1356–1362.

Marx, Karl. *Capital,* vol. 1. Trans. Ben Fowkes. New York: Vintage, 1977 [1867].

———. *Grundrisse.* Trans. Martin Nicolaus. New York: Vintage, 1973.

Mason, Robin, and Timothy Swanson. "A Kuznets Curve Analysis of Ozone-Depleting Substances and the Impact of the Montreal Protocol." *Oxford Economic Papers—New Series* 55, no. 1 (2003): 1–24.

Mayfield, Erin N., and Catherine S. Norman. 2012. "Moving Away from Methyl Bromide: Political Economy of Pesticide Transition for California Strawberries since 2004." *Journal of Environmental Management* 106 (September): 93–101.

McCarthy, James. "Privatizing Conditions of Production: Trade Agreements as Neoliberal Environmental Governance." *Geoforum* 35, no. 3 (2004): 327–341.

McCarthy, James, and Scott Prudham. "Neoliberal Nature and the Nature of Neoliberalism." *Geoforum* 35, no. 3 (2004): 275–283.

McKibbin, Warwick J., and Peter J. Wilcoxen. "The Role of Economics in Climate Change Policy." In Stavins, *Economics of the Environment,* 5th ed.

McMichael, Philip, ed. *Contesting Development: Critical Struggles for Social Change.* New York: Routledge, 2010.

Meadows, Donella H. *The Limits to Growth.* New York: Universe Books, 1972.

Meyer, John W. "The World Polity and the Authority of the Nation-State." In *Institutional Structure,* ed. George M. Thomas, John W. Meyer, Francisco O. Ramirez, and John Boli. Los Angeles: Sage, 1987.

Mezzetti, Bruno, and David W. Simpson, eds. *Proceedings of the Euro Berry Symposium, Cost 836 Final Workshop.* Ancona, Italy: International Society for Horticultural Science, 2004.

Miller, Byron. "Modes of Governance, Modes of Resistance: Contesting Neoliberalism in Calgary." In Leitner, Peck, and Sheppard, *Contesting Neoliberalism.*

Miller, Henry I. "Much Ado about MB." *Regulation* 29, no. 3 (2006): 10.

Millner, Patricia D., C. E. Ringer, and J. L. Maas. "Suppression of Strawberry Root Disease with Animal Manure Composts." *Compost Science and Utilization* 12, no. 4 (2004): 298–307.

Mitchell, Ronald B. "International Environment." In *Handbook of International Relations,* ed. Thomas Risse, Beth Simmons, and Walter Carlsnaes, 500–516. Thousand Oaks, CA: Sage, 2002.

———. "Of Course International Institutions Matter: But When and How?" In *How Institutions Change: Perspectives on Social Learning in Global and Local Environmental Contexts,* ed. Heiko Breit, Anita Engels, Timothy Moss, and Markus Troja, 35–52. Opladen, Germany: Leske and Budrich, 2003.

Mitchell, Ronald B., and Patricia M. Keilbach. "Situation Structure and Institutional Design: Reciprocity, Coercion, and Exchange." *International Organization* 55, no. 4 (2001): 891–917.

Mol, Arthur P. J. "Ecological Modernization and Industrial Reflexivity: Environmental Reform in the Late Modern Age." *Environmental Politics* 5 (1996): 302–323.

———. "The Environmental Movement in an Era of Ecological Modernization." *Geoforum* 31 (2000): 45–56.

Mol, Arthur. P. J., and Gert Spaargaren. "Ecological Modernization and the Environmental State." In *The Environmental State under Pressure,* ed. Arthur P. J. Mol and Fredrick H. Buttel, 33–55. Oxford: Elsevier Science, 2002.

Mol, Arthur P. J., David A. Sonnenfeld, and Gert Spaargaren, eds. *The Ecological Modernization Reader: Environmental Reform in Theory and Practice*. New York: Routledge, 2009.

Molina, Mario J., and S. Rowland. "Stratospheric Sink for Chlorofluoromethanes: Chlorine Atom Catalysed Destruction of Ozone." *Nature*, 1974:249.

Monbiot, George. *Heat: How to Stop the Planet from Burning*. Essex: Penguin Press, 2006.

Morrisette, Peter M. "The Evolution of Policy Responses to Stratospheric Ozone Depletion." *Natural Resources Journal* 29 (1989): 793–798.

———. "The Montreal Protocol: Lessons for Formulating Policies for Global Warming." *Policy Studies Journal* 19, no. 2 (1991): 152–161.

Moses, Jonathan W. "Abdication from National Policy Autonomy: What's Left to Leave?" *Politics and Society* 22, no. 2 (1994): 125–148.

Mukerji, Chandra. *A Fragile Power: Scientists and the State*. Princeton, NJ: Princeton University Press, 1989.

Mulder, Karel F. "Innovation by Disaster: The Ozone Catastrophe as Experiment of Forced Innovation." *International Journal of Environment and Sustainable Development* 4 (2005): 88–103.

Munasinghe, Mohan, and Kenneth King. "Accelerating Ozone-Layer Protection in Developing Countries." *World Development* 20, no. 4 (1992): 609–618.

———. "Implementing the Montreal Protocol to Restore the Ozone-Layer." *Columbia Journal of World Business* 27, no. 3–4 (1992): 136–143.

Muramoto, Joji. "Nutrient Dynamics in Organic Strawberries." Paper presented at the University of California Cooperative Extension Annual Central Coast Strawberry Meeting, Watsonville, CA, 2006.

Muramoto, Joji, Erle C. Ellis, Zhengfang Li, Rodrigo M. Machado, and Stephen R. Gliessman. "Field-Scale Nutrient Cycling and Sustainability: Comparing Natural and Agricultural Ecosystems." In *Agroecosystem Sustainability: Developing Practical Strategies*, ed. Stephen R. Gliessman, 121–134. Boca Raton, FL: CRC Press, 2001.

Muramoto, Joji, Stephen R. Gliessman, Steven T. Koike, Carol Shennan, Dan Schmida, Robert Stephens, and Sean L. Swezey. "Maintaining Agroecosystem Health in an Organic Strawberry/Vegetable Rotation System (Part 4): The First Four Years." Paper presented at the ASA-CSSA-SSSA International Annual Meetings, Section on Sustainable Cropping Systems: From Earthworms to Mapping Local Food Capacity, Salt Lake City, UT, November 8, 2005.

Murdoch, James C., and Todd Sandler. "The Voluntary Provision of a Pure Public Good: The Case of Reduced CFC Emissions and the Montreal Protocol." *Journal of Public Economics* 63, no. 3 (1997): 331–349.

Murphy, Joseph, and Andrew Gouldson. "Environmental Policy and Industrial Innovation: Integrating Environment and Economy through Ecological Modernisation." *Geoforum* 31 (2000): 33–44.

Murray, Louise. "Arctic Ozone Hole Moving South." Earth Times, 2011. Available at http://www.earthtimes.org/climate/arctic-ozone-hole-moving-south/669/. Accessed June 15, 2011.

Myers, Steven Lee. "Bush to Skip U.N. Talks on Global Warming." *New York Times,* September 24, 2007.

Næs, Tom. "The Effectiveness of the EU's Ozone Policy." *International Environmental Agreements* 4, no. 1 (2004): 47–63.

Nakanishi, Nao. "Organic Farming Set to Boom in China: Chinese Farmers Cash in on Need for Organic Food." *Reuters,* 2003. Available at http://www.organicconsumers.org/organic/china102703.cfm. Accessed June 19, 2003.

NAS. "Carbon Dioxide and Climate: A Scientific Assessment." Washington, D.C.: U.S. National Academy of Sciences, 1979.

National Agricultural Pesticide Impact Assessment Program. "Biologic and Economic Assessment of Methyl Bromide." Washington, D.C.: U.S. Department of Agriculture, 1993.

National Agricultural Statistics Service. "Agricultural Statistics 2002." Washington, D.C.: U.S. Department of Agriculture, 2002.

National Cancer Control Initiative. "The 2002 National Non-Melanoma Skin Cancer Survey, a Report by the NCCI Non-Melanoma Skin Cancer Working Group." Ed. M. P. Staples. Melbourne: NCCI, 2003.

Newell, Peter. *Climate for Change: Non-State Actors and the Global Politics of the Greenhouse.* Cambridge: Cambridge University Press, 2000.

———. "The Political Economy of Global Environmental Governance." *Review of International Studies* 34 (2008): 507–529.

Newell, Peter, and Matthew Patterson. "The Politics of the Carbon Economy." In *The Politics of Climate Change: A Survey,* ed. Maxwell T. Boykoff, 77–95. New York: Routledge, 2010.

Newman, Paul. "Annual Records." NASA, 2011. Available at http://ozonewatch.gsfc.nasa.gov/meteorology/ozone.html. Accessed June 12, 2011.

Ning, Liu. "Illegal Trade in Ozone Depleting Substances: Asia and Pacific Region." Nairobi: United Nations Environmental Programme, 2007.

Available at http://www.mea-ren.org/files/publications/Illegal%20 Trade%20in%20ODS.pdf.

Norman, Catherine S. "Potential Impacts of Imposing Methyl Bromide Phaseout on U.S. Strawberry Growers: A Case Study of a Nomination for a Critical Use Exemption under the Montreal Protocol." *Journal of Environmental Management* 75, no. 2 (2005): 167–176.

Norman, Catherine S., Stephen J. DeCanio, and Lin Fan. "The Montreal Protocol at 20: Ongoing Opportunities for Integration with Climate Protection." *Global Environmental Change* 18, no. 2 (2008): 330–340.

Norval, M., R. M. Lucas, A. P. Cullen, F. R. de Gruijl, J. Longstreth, Y. Takizawa, and J. C. van der Leun. "The Human Health Effects of Ozone Depletion and Interactions with Climate Change." *Photochemical and Photobiological Sciences* 10, no. 2 (2011): 199–225.

NRDC. "The Bush Record: USDA Rule Could Triple Use of Ozone-Depleting Pesticide." Natural Resources Defense Council, 2004. Available at http://www.nrdc.org/search/default.asp. Accessed February 3, 2005.

———. "Chemical Companies Rake in Millions Producing Unnecessary Ozone Depleting Chemicals." Natural Resources Defense Council, 2010. Available at http://www.nrdc.org/media/pressreleases/061030a. asp. Accessed June 7, 2011.

Nuckols, John R., Robert B. Gunier, Philip Riggs, Ryan Miller, Peggy Reynolds, and Mary H. Ward. "Linkage of the California Pesticide Use Reporting Database with Spatial Land Use Data for Exposure Assessment." *Environmental Health Perspectives* 115, no. 5 (2007): 684–689.

Oberthur, Sebastian. "Linkages between the Montreal and Kyoto Protocols: Enhancing Synergies between Protecting the Ozone Layer and the Global Climate." *International Environmental Agreements* 1, no. 3 (2001): 357–377.

O'Connor, James. "Capitalism, Nature, Socialism: A Theoretical Introduction." *Capitalism, Nature, Socialism,* 1, no. 1 (1988): 11–38.

———. *The Fiscal Crisis of the State,* 2nd ed. Piscataway, NJ: Transaction Publishers, 2002.

———. "Is Sustainable Capitalism Possible?" In *Is Capitalism Sustainable? Political Economy and the Politics of Ecology,* ed. Martin O'Connor, 152–175. New York: Guilford Press, 1994.

———. *Natural Causes: Essays in Ecological Marxism.* New York: Guilford Press, 1998. Democracy and Ecology Series.

———. "The Second Contradiction of Capitalism." In *The Greening of Marxism,* ed. Ted Benton. New York: Guilford Press, 1996.

OECD. "Multilateral Environmental Agreements and Private Investment: Business Contribution to Addressing Global Environmental Problems No 387." *OECD Papers* 5 (2005): 164–237.

Offner, Jim. "California Strawberries Poised for Another Record." The Packer, 2006. Available at http://www.thepacker.com/icms/_dtaa2/content/wrapper.asp?alink=2006–174552–941.asp#. Accessed January 17, 2006.

Ogden, Douglas H. "The Montreal Protocol: Confronting the Threat to Earth's Ozone-Layer." *Washington Law Review* 63, no. 4 (1988): 997–1018.

Okereke, Chukwumerije. *Global Justice and Neoliberal Environmental Governance: Ethics, Sustainable Development, and International Cooperation.* New York: Routledge, 2010.

Okereke, Chukwumerije, Harriet Bulkeley, and H. Schroeder. "Conceptualising Climate Governance beyond the International Regime." *Global Environmental Politics* 9, no. 1 (2009): 58–78.

Olzak, Susan, and Sarah A. Soule. "Cross-Cutting Influences of Environmental Protest and Legislation." *Social Forces* 88, no. 1 (2009): 201–226.

Ophuls, William. "Leviathan or Oblivion." In *Toward a Steady-State Economy,* ed. Herman Daley. San Francisco: W. H. Freeman, 1973.

———. "The Scarcity Society." In Conca and Dabelko, *Green Planet Blues,* 54–60.

Osteen, Craig. "Methyl Bromide Phaseout Proceeds: Users Request Exemptions." *Amber Waves* 1, no. 2 (2003): 22–28.

"Ozone Loss Hits Us Where We Live." *Science* 254 (1991): 645.

Palmer, Geoffrey. "New Ways to Make International Environmental Law." *American Journal of International Law* 86, no. 2 (1992): 259–283.

Park, Jacob, Ken Conca, and Matthias Finger. *The Crisis of Global Environmental Governance: Towards a New Political Economy of Sustainability.* London: Routledge, 2008. Environmental Politics Series.

Parson, Edward. *Protecting the Ozone Layer: Science and Strategy.* Oxford: Oxford University Press, 2003.

Paterson, Matthew. *Global Warming and Global Politics.* London: Routledge, 1996.

———. *Understanding Global Environmental Politics: Domination, Accumulation and Resistance.* London: Macmillan, 2000.

Patlis, Jason M. "The Multilateral Fund of the Montreal Protocol: A Prototype for Financial Mechanisms in Protecting the Global Environment." *Cornell International Law Journal* 25, no. 1 (1992): 181–230.

Payne, Rodger A. "Persuasion, Frames, and Norm Construction." *European Journal of International Relations* 7, no. 1 (2001): 37–61.

Peck, Jamie. "Geography and Public Policy: Constructions of Neoliberalism." *Progress in Human Geography* 28, no. 3 (2004): 392–405.

——. "Neoliberalizing States: Thin Policies/Hard Outcomes." *Progress in Human Geography* 25, no. 3 (2001): 445–455.

Peck, Jamie, and Adam Tickell. "Neoliberalizing Space." *Antipode* 34, no. 3 (2002): 380–404.

Pedreño, Andres. "Construyendo la 'huerta de Europa': Trabajadores sin ciudadania y nomadas permanentes en la agricultura murciana." *Migraciones* 5 (1999): 87–120.

——. "Taylor y Ford en los campos: Trabajo, genero y etnia en el cambio tecnológico y organizacional de la agricultura industrial murciana." *Sociologia del Trabajo* 35 (1999): 25–56.

Peet, Richard, and Michael Watts. "Liberation Ecology: Development, Sustainability, and Environment in an Age of Market Triumphalism." In *Liberation Ecologies: Environment, Development, Social Movements,* ed. Richard Peet and Michael Watts. New York: Routledge, 1996.

Pellow, David. "Review: Ozone Connections." *Contemporary Sociology* 33, no. 1 (2004): 67–69.

Peluso, Nancy Lee. "Coercing Conservation." In Conca and Dabelko, *Green Planet Blues,* 346–357.

Perreault, Thomas, and Patricia Martin. "Geographies of Neoliberalism in Latin America." *Environment and Planning A* 37, no. 2 (2005): 191–201.

Philpot, Tom. "Methyl Iodide: A Nasty Pesticide Explained." *Mother Jones,* 2011. Available at http://www.motherjones.com/tom-philpott/2011/09/methyl-iodide-pesticide-strawberries. Accessed May 1, 2012.

Piana, Valentino. 2004. "Hierarchy Structures in World Trade." Economics Web Institute, 2004. Available at http://www.economicswebinstitute.org/essays/tradehierarchy.htm#bas. Accessed January 3, 2007.

Polanyi, Karl. *The Great Transformation: The Political and Economic Origins of Our Time.* Boston: Beacon Press, 2001.

Portes, Alejandro. "Social Capital: Its Origins and Applications in Modern Sociology." *Annual Review of Sociology* 22, no. 1 (1998): 24.

Powell, Richard L. "CFC Phase-Out: Have We Met the Challenge?" *Journal of Fluorine Chemistry* 114, no. 2 (2002): 237–250.

Price, Richard M. "Transnational Civil Society and Advocacy in World Politics." *World Politics* 55, no. 4 (2003): 579–606.

Przeslawski, Rachel, Andrew R. Davis, and Kirsten Benkendorf. "Synergistic Effects Associated with Climate Change and the Development of Rocky Shore Molluscs." *Global Change Biology* 11, no. 3 (2005): 515–522.

Putnam, Robert D. "Bowling Alone: America's Declining Social Capital." *Journal of Democracy* 6, no. 1 (1995): 65–78.

Reagan, Ronald, "The American Sound." In Clarke and Cortner, *The State and Nature*, 310–315.

"The Right Time to Chop: Rich-Country Governments Must Ignore Special Pleading to Restrict Farm Trade." *The Economist* 387, no. 8578 (2008): 15–18.

Rittberger, Volker. "(I)NGOs and Global Environmental Governance: Introduction." In Chasek, *The Global Environment in the Twenty-First Century*, 83–86.

Rivas, M., M. C. Araya, V. Durán, E. Rojas, J. Cortes, and G. M. Cala. "Ultraviolet Light Exposure and Skin Cancer in the City of Arica, Chile." *Molecular Medicine Reports* 2, no. 4 (2009): 567–572.

Robbins, Paul. *Political Ecology*. Oxford: Blackwell, 2005.

Roscoe, Howard K., and Adrian M. Lee. "Increased Stratospheric Greenhouse Gases Could Delay Recovery of the Ozone Hole and of Ozone Loss at Southern Mid-Latitudes." *Advances in Space Research* 28, no. 7 (2001): 965–970.

Rose, Nikolas. *Powers of Freedom: Reframing Political Thought*. Cambridge: Cambridge University Press, 2004.

Rosenau, James T. "Governance in a New Global Order." In *Governing Globalization*, ed. D. Held and A. McGrew. Cambridge: Polity Press, 2002.

Rowland, Frank S., and Mario J. Molina. "Chlorofluoromethanes in the Environment." *Reviews of Geophysics and Space Physics* 13, no. 1 (1975): 1–35.

Ruggie, John Gerard. "International Regimes, Transactions, and Change: Embedded Liberalism in the Postwar Economic Order." *International Organization* 36, no. 2 (1982): 379–415.

Rutgeerts, Ann. "Trade and Environment: Reconciling the Montreal Protocol and the GATT." *Journal of World Trade* 33, no. 4 (1999): 61–86.

Saad, Lydia. "Increased Number Think Global Warming Is 'Exaggerated': Most Believe Global Warming Is Hapening, but Urgency Has Stalled." Gallup Poll, 2009. Available at http://www.gallup.com/poll/116590/Increased-Number-Think-Global-Warming-Exaggerated.aspx. Accessed December 9, 2009.

Sances, Frank V. "Conventional and Organic Alternatives to Methyl Bromide in California Strawberries." Paper presented at the Annual International Research Conference on Methyl Bromide Alternatives and Emissions Reduction, San Diego, CA, November 10–13, 2000.

———. "Ten Years of Methyl Bromide Alternatives Research and Develop-
    ment: Lessons Learned." Paper presented at the Annual International
    Research Conference on Methyl Bromide Alternatives and Emissions
    Reduction, San Diego, CA, October 30–November 3, 2005.
Sances, Frank V., and Elaine R. Ingham. "Conventional and Organic
    Alternatives to Methyl Bromide on California Strawberries." *Compost
    Science and Utilization* 5, no. 2 (1997): 23–37.
Schelling, Thomas. "The Cost of Combatting Global Warming: Facing the
    Tradeoffs." In Stavins, *Economics of the Environment*, 4th ed.
Schofer, Evan, and Ann Hironaka. "The Effects of World Society on
    Environmental Protection Outcomes." *Social Forces* 84, no. 1 (2005):
    25–47.
Schiermeier, Quirin. "Atmospheric Science: Fixing the Sky." *Nature* 460,
    no. 7257 (2009): 792–795.
Schneider, Sally M., Erin N. Rosskopf, James G. Leesch, Daniel O. Chellemi,
    Carolee T. Bull, and Mark Mazzola. "United States Department of
    Agriculture–Agricultural Research Service Research on Alternatives
    to Methyl Bromide: Pre-Plant and Post-Harvest." *Pest Management
    Science* 59, nos. 6–7 (2003): 814–826.
Scott, James C. *Seeing Like a State: How Certain Schemes to Improve the
    Human Condition Have Failed*. New Haven: Yale University Press,
    1998.
Sending, Ole J., and Iver B. Neuman. "Governance to Governmentality: Ana-
    lyzing NGOs, States, and Power." *International Studies Quarterly* 50,
    no. 3 (2006): 651–672.
Shaw, Douglas V., W. D. Gubler, Kirk D. Larson, and John Hansen. "Genetic
    Variation for Field Resistance to *Verticillium dahliae* Evaluated Using
    Genotypes and Segregating Progenies of California Strawberries."
    Journal of the American Society for Horticultural Science 121, no. 4
    (1996): 625–628.
Shende, Rajendra, and Steve Gorman. "Lessons in Technology Transfer un-
    der the Montreal Protocol." Paris: Ozone Action Programme, UNEP,
    Industry and Environment Office, 1997.
Shennan, Carol. "Biotic Interactions, Ecological Processes, and Agriculture."
    Philosophical Transactions of the Royal Society 363, no. 1492 (2008).
Shetty, K. G., K. V. Subbarao, Frank N. Martin, and Steve T. Koike. "Manage-
    ment of Verticillium Wilt in Strawberry Using Vegetable Crop Rota-
    tion." Paper presented at the Annual International Research Conference
    on Methyl Bromide Alternatives and Emissions Reduction, San Diego,
    CA, November 1–9, 1999.

Shindell, D. T., D. Rind, and P. Lonergan. "Increased Polar Stratospheric Ozone Losses and Delayed Eventual Recovery Owing to Increased Greenhouse-Gas Concentrations." *Nature* 392 (1998): 589–592.

Shinmura, A. "Causal Agent and Control of Root Rot of Welsh Onion." *PSJ Soilborne Disease Workshop Report* 20 (2000): 133–143 (in Japanese with English summary).

———. "Principle and Effect of Soil Sterilization Methods by Reducing the Redox Potential of Soil." *PSJ Soilborne Disease Workshop Report* 22 (2004): 2–12 (in Japanese with English summary).

Sideman, Roger. "Strawberry Growers Seek China Market." *Register-Pajaronian,* December 3, 2005. Available at http://www.register-pajaronian.com/view_zrs_article.php?index=0.

Sims, Holly. "The Unsheltering Sky: China, India, and the Montreal Protocol." *Policy Studies Journal* 24, no. 2 (1996): 201–214.

Skin Cancer Foundation. "Ozone and UV: Where Are We Now?" Skin Cancer Foundation, 2011. Available at http://www.skincancer.org/pdf/ozone-and-uv-where-are-we-now.pdf. Accessed June 1, 2011.

Smith, Jackie. "Global Civil Society? Transnational Social Movement Organizations and Social Capital." *American Behavioral Scientist* 42, no. 1 (1998): 93–107.

Sonnenfeld, David A., and Arthur P. J. Mol. "Ecological Modernization, Governance, and Globalization: Epilogue." *American Behavioral Scientist* 45, no. 9 (2002): 1456–1461.

———. "Globalization and the Transformation of Environmental Governance: An Introduction." *American Behavioral Scientist* 45, no. 9 (2002): 1318–1339.

Speth, James Gustave. *The Bridge at the End of the World: Capitalism, the Environment, and Crossing from Crisis to Sustainability.* New Haven: Yale University Press, 2008.

———. *Red Sky at Morning: America and the Crisis of the Global Environment.* New Haven: Yale University Press, 2005.

Speth, James Gustave, and Peter M. Haas. *Global Environmental Governance.* St. Louis: Island Press, 2006.

Staehelin, Johannes, Neil R. P. Harris, Cristof Appenzeller, and J. Eberhard. "Ozone Trends: A Review." *Reviews of Geophysics* 39, no. 2 (2001): 231–290.

Standen, Amy. 2010. "State Approves Pesticide despite Cancer Warning." *California Watch,* December 2, 2012. Available at http://californiawatch.org/dailyreport/state-approves-pesticide-despite-cancer-warning-7152. Accessed May 1, 2012,

Staples, Margaret P., Mark Elwood, Robert C. Burton, Jodie L. Williams, Robin Marks, and Graham G. Giles. "Non-Melanoma Skin Cancer in Australia: The 2002 National Survey and Trends since 1985." *Medical Journal of Australia* 184, no. 1 (2006): 6–10.

Stavins, Robert N., ed. *Economics of the Environment,* 4th ed. New York: W. W. Norton, 2000.

——. *Economics of the Environment,* 5th ed. New York: W. W. Norton, 2005.

Stigson, Björn. "Walking the Talk: The Business Case for Sustainable Development." In Conca and Dabelko, *Green Planet Blues.*

Swain, Nigel. "Social Capital and Its Uses." *Archives Européennes de Sociologie* 44, no. 2 (2003): 185–212.

Swanson, Timothy. "Negotiating Effective International Environmental Agreements: Is an Objective Approach to Differential Treatment Possible?" *International Environmental Agreements* 1, no. 1 (2001): 125–153.

Swyngedouw, Erik, and Nikolas C. Heynen. "Urban Political Ecology, Justice and the Politics of Scale." *Antipode* 35, no. 5 (2003): 898–918.

Szasz, Andrew. *Ecopopulism: Toxic Waste and the Movement for Environmental Justice.* Minneapolis: University of Minnesota Press, 1994.

Tarrow, Sidney. "From Lumping to Splitting: Specifying Globalization and Resistance." In Johnston and Smith, *Globalization and Resistance,* 229–249.

TEAP. "Report of the Technology and Economic Assessment Panel: Evaluations of 2010 Critical Use Nominations for Methyl Bromide and Related Matters." Nairobi: United Nations Environmental Programme, 2010.

Thompson, John E. "Methyl Bromide Critical Use Exemptions for Preplant Soil Use for Strawberries Grown for Fruit in Open Fields." 2006. Available at http://www.epa.gov/ozone/mbr/CUN2005/CUN2005/StrawberryFruitUSA.pdf. Accessed February 22, 2009.

Tickell, Adam, and Jamie Peck. "Making Global Rules: Globalization or Neoliberalization?" In *Remaking the Global Economy,* ed. Jamie Peck and Henry Wai-Chung Yeung. Thousand Oaks, CA: Sage, 2003.

Tietenberg, Thomas. "Transferable Discharge Permits and the Control of Stationary Source Air Pollution." In Dorfman and Dorfman, *Economics of the Environment,* 3rd ed., 241–270.

Tilly, Charles. *Durable Inequality.* Berkeley: University of California Press, 1999.

Trask, Jeff. "Montreal Protocol Noncompliance Procedure: The Best Approach to Resolving International Environmental Disputes." *Georgetown Law Journal* 80, no. 5 (1992): 1973–2001.

Turner, Mark Holman. "Building an Ecosystem from Scratch." *Bioscience* 39, no. 3 (1989): 147–150.

UNEP. "Arysta LifeScience—Methyl Iodide Comparison to Methyl Bromide." Meeting Documents of the 22nd Meeting of the Parties to the Montreal Protocol. United Nations Environmental Programme, 2010. Available at http://ozone.unep.org/Meeting_Documents/mop/22mop/conf-ngo-pubs/MeI_MeBr_Comparison%20FINAL_2010%2011%2003.pdf.

———. "Brief Primer on the Montreal Protocol." Nairobi: United Nations Environmental Programme, 2007. Available at http://ozone.unep.org/Publications/MP_Brief_Primer_on_MP-E.pdf. Accessed August 20, 2007.

———. "Case Studies on Alternatives to Methyl Bromide: Technologies with Low Environmental Impact." Ed. Tom Batchelor. Nairobi: United Nations Environmental Programme, 2000.

———. "Earth Report (TVE): Global Environmental Governance in 2050." *The Environment in the News,* November 30, 2004.

———. "Economic Instruments for Environmental Protection." *UNEP Briefs on Economics, Trade, and Sustainable Development,* July 2002.

———. *Environmental Effects Panel Report: Report of the Environmental Effects Panel of the Montreal Protocol.* Nairobi: United Nations Environmental Programme, November 1991.

———. *Handbook of the Montreal Protocol on Substances That Deplete the Ozone Layer,* 7th ed. Nairobi: Secretariat of the Vienna Convention for the Protection of the Ozone Layer and the Montreal Protocol on Substances That Deplete the Ozone Layer. Nairobi: United Nations Environmental Programme, 2006. Available at http://ozone.unep.org/Publications/MP_Handbook/Section_4/index.shtml.

———. *Handbook of the Vienna Convention for the Protection of the Ozone Layer,* 7th ed. Nairobi: Secretariat of the Vienna Convention for the Protection of the Ozone Layer and the Montreal Protocol on Substances That Deplete the Ozone Layer, United Nations Environmental Programme, 2006.

———. "International Day for the Preservation of the Ozone Layer, 19th Meeting of the Parties, HCFCs Accelerated Phaseout, Compilation of Relevant Articles from the Press Worldwide." 2007. Available at http://www.unep.org/ozonaction/News/MontrealPressArticles/CompilationofRelevantArticlesStatements/tabid/51972/Default.aspx. Accessed June 20, 2011.

———. "Progress Report of the UNEP Technology and Economics Assessment Panel." Nairobi: United Nations Environmental Programme,

2003. Available at http://www.unep.org/ozone/pdfs/teap-2003-report.pdf.

———. "Progress Report of the UNEP Technology and Economic Assessment Panel." Nairobi: United Nations Environmental Programme, 2009. Available at http://www.unep.org/ozone/teap/Reports/TEAP_Reports/.

———. *Protecting the Ozone Layer: The United Nations History.* Nairobi: United Nations Environmental Programme, 2002.

———. "Report of the Methyl Bromide Technical Options Committee, 1995 Assessment." Nairobi: United Nations Environmental Programme, 1994.

———. "Report of the Nineteenth Meeting of the Parties to the Montreal Protocol on Substances That Deplete the Ozone Layer." Nairobi: United Nations Environmental Programme, 2007.

———. "Report of the Ninth Meeting of the Parties to the Montreal Protocol on Substances That Deplete the Ozone Layer." Nairobi: United Nations Environmental Programme, 1997.

———. "Report of the Seventh Meeting of the Parties to the Montreal Protocol." Nairobi: United Nations Environmental Programme, 1995.

———. "Scientific Assessment of Ozone Depletion: 1994. Report of the Scientific Assessment Panel of the Montreal Protocol. WMO Global Research and Monitoring Project." Geneva: WMO/UNEP, United Nations Environmental Programme, 1995.

———. "Statement by Dr. Klaus Töpfer, the Executive Director of the United Nations Environmental Programme." At the United Nations Conference on Trade and Development, Sao Paulo, Brazil, June 17, 2004. Available at http://www.un.org/webcast/unctadxi/speeches/17une_eng.pdf.

———. "Synthesis of the 2002 Reports of the Scientific Assessment Panel (SAP), Environmental Effects Assessment Panel (EEAP) and the Technology and Economic Assessment Panel (TEAP) of the Montreal Protocol." Montreal: United Nations Environmental Programme. Available at http://www.unep.org/ozone, 2002.

UNIDO. "Ozone Friendly Industrial Development: 10 Years of UNIDO in the Montreal Protocol." Vienna: United Nations Industrial Development Organization, 2002.

U.S. Committee on Agriculture. *The Implications of Banning Methyl Bromide for Fruit and Vegetable Production.* U.S. House of Representatives, second session, July 13, 2000. Washington, D.C.: Government Printing Office, 2000.

USDA (U.S. Department of Agriculture), Foreign Agricultural Service. "GAIN Report: China Frozen Exports." 2005.

———. "GAIN Report: China Frozen Strawberries." 2002.

———. "GAIN Report: China Strawberries Annual 2004." 2004.

———. "GAIN Report: China Strawberries Annual 2009." 2009.

———. "GAIN Report: Mexico Strawberries Annual 2005." 2005.

———. "GAIN Report: Spain Strawberries Annual 2002." 2002.

———. "GAIN Report: Strawberries in Poland: Anti-Dumping Protective Measures against the Chinese." 2006.

USDA/ERS (Economic Research Service). "Economic Implications of the Methyl Bromide Phaseout." 2000.

U.S. Department of State. "Methyl Bromide Critical Use Nomination for Preplant Soil Use for Strawberry Fruit Grown in Open Fields (Submitted in 2012 for the 2014 Use Season)." File Name: USA CUN14 Soil Strawberry Fruit Open Field. Washington, D.C.: Bureau of Ocean and International Environmental and Scientific Affairs, 2012.

van der Leun, Jan C. "The Ozone Layer." *Photodermatology, Photoimmunology and Photomedicine* 20, no. 4 (2004): 159–162.

van der Leun, Jan C., and Frank R. Gruikl. "Climate Change and Skin Cancer." *Photochemical and Photobiological Sciences* 1, no. 5 (2002): 324–326.

van der Leun, Jan C., and H. van Weelden. "Light-Induced Tolerance to Light in Photodermatoses." *Journal of Investigative Dermatology* 64, no. 4 (1975): 280.

Walker, Bill. "California Study Admits Methyl Bromide Safety Standards Inadequate." Environmental Working Group, 1997. Available at http://www.ewg.org/files/dpr.pdf. Accessed June 16, 2011.

Walker, Richard. *Conquest of Bread: 150 Years of Agribusiness in California.* New York: New Press, 2004.

Wallerstein, Immanuel. *The Modern World-System.* New York: Academic Press, 1974.

———. "Whose Century Is the 21st Century?" Fernand Braudel Center, Binghamton University, 2006. Available at http://fbc.binghamton.edu/commentr.htm. Accessed December 12, 2006.

Walter, Monika, Cath Snelling, Kirsty S. H. Boyd-Wilson, Graeme Williams, and Geoff I. Langford. "Evaluation of Organic Strawberry Runner Production." *Horttechnology* 15, no. 4 (2005): 787–796.

Wapner, Paul. *Environmental Activism and World Civic Politics.* Albany: State University of New York Press, 1996.

——. "The Transnational Politics of Environmental NGOs: Governmental, Economic, and Social Activism." In Chasek, *The Global Environment in the Twenty-First Century*, 87–108.

Watts, Michael. "Green Capitalism, Green Governmentality." *American Behavioral Scientist* 45, no. 9 (2002): 1313–1317.

Weber, Max. *Economy and Society: An Outline of Interpretive Sociology*. Ed. Guenther Roth and Claus Wittich. New York: Bedminster, 1968.

Weis, Edith Brown. "The Five International Treaties: A Living History." In *Engaging Countries: Strengthening Compliance with International Environmental Accords*, ed. Edith Brown Weis and Harold Jacobson. Cambridge, MA: MIT Press, 1998.

Wells, Miriam J. *Strawberry Fields: Politics, Class, and Work in California Agriculture*. Ithaca, NY: Cornell University Press, 1996.

Wells, Scott. "Ozone Depletion: The Problem with the Ozone Layer." Articles-Base, 2009. Available at http://www.articlesbase.com/environment-articles/ozone-depletion-the-problem-with-the-ozone-layer-1350703.html#axzz1Q8QAtcGX. Accessed June 22, 2011.

Werner, Matthew R., R. A. Kluson, and Stephen R. Gliessman. "Colonization of Strawberry Roots by VA Mycorrhizal Fungi in Agroecosystems under Conventional and Transitional Organic Management." *Biological Agriculture* 7, no. 2 (1990): 139–151.

Whitney, Craig R. "20 Nations Agree to Join Ozone Pact." *New York Times*, March 8, 1989.

Wilhelm, Stephen, and Alburt O. Paulus. "How Soil Fumigation Benefits the California Strawberry Industry." *Plant Disease* 64, no. 3 (1980): 264–270.

Williams, William Appleman. *The Roots of the Modern American Empire: A Study of the Growth and Shaping of Social Consciousness in a Market-place Society*. New York: Random House, 1969.

Winner, Langdon. *The Whale and the Reactor: A Search for Limits in an Age of High Technology*. Chicago: University of Chicago Press, 1986.

WMO. "Record Stratospheric Ozone Loss in the Arctic in Spring of 2011." 2011. Available at http://www.wmo.int/pages/mediacentre/press_releases/pr_912_en.html. Accessed June 20, 2011.

——. "Scientific Assessment of Ozone Depletion: 2006, Global Ozone Research and Monitoring Project—Report no. 47." Geneva: World Meteorological Organization, 2007.

WMO/UNEP. "Executive Summary, Scientific Assessment of Ozone Depletion: 2002." Geneva: United Nations Environmental Programme and World Meteorological Organization, 2002. Prepared by the Scientific Assessment Panel of the Montreal Protocol on Substances That Deplete the Ozone Layer.

Wollan, Malia. "Maker Pulls Pesticide amid Fear of Toxicity." *New York Times,* March 21, 2012. Available at http://www.nytimes.com/2012/03/22/us/pesticide-pulled-from-us-market-amid-fear-of-toxicity.html. Accessed March 22, 2012.

World Bank Group. "Accelerated HCFC Phaseout." World Bank, 2011. Available at http://go.worldbank.org/8PWRMO4SO0. Accessed June 20, 2011.

World Commission on Environment and Development. *Our Common Future.* New York: Oxford University Press, 1987.

Wozniacka, Gosia. "Neighbors Oppose Strawberry Farms' Fumigant Use." *Mercury News,* 2011. Available at http://www.mercurynews.com/ci_18055926?IADID=Search-www.mercurynews.com-www.mercurynews.com. Accessed June 3, 2011.

Yamin, F., J. Burniaux, and A. Nentjes. "Kyoto Mechanisms: Key Issues for Policy Makers for COP-6." *International Environmental Agreements* 44, no. 1 (2001): 187–218.

Yearly, Steven. "The Environmental Challenge to Science Studies." In Jasanoff, Markle, Petersen, and Pinch, *Handbook of Science and Technology Studies,* 457–479.

———. *Sociology, Environmentalism, Globalization: Reinventing the Globe.* Thousand Oaks, CA: Sage, 1996.

Yeates, Nicola. "Social Politics and Policy in an Era of Globalization: Critical Reflections." *Social Policy and Administration* 33, no. 4 (1999): 372–393.

Yokouchi, Y., D. Toom-Sauntry, K. Yazawa, T. Inagaki, and T. Tamaru. "Recent Decline of Methyl Bromide in the Troposphere." *Atmospheric Environment* 36, no. 32 (2002): 4985–4989.

Young, Oran. *Global Governance: Drawing Insights from the Environmental Experience.* Cambridge, MA: MIT Press, 1997.

———. *International Governance: Protecting the Environment in a Stateless Society.* Ithaca, NY: Cornell University Press, 1994.

———. "Political Leadership and Regime Formation: On the Development of Institutions in International Society." *International Organization* 45, no. 3 (1991): 281–308.

Young, Oran, Mark A. Levy, and Gail Osherenko. "The Effectiveness of International Environmental Regimes." In *The Effectiveness of International Environmental Regimes: Causal Connections and Behavioral Mechanisms,* ed. Oran Young. Cambridge, MA: MIT Press, 1996.

Index

and freedoms, 25–26, 41–42, 45,
162–163, 240–241
industrialized countries: versus
less-developed countries,
tensions over MeBr phaseout,
145–146, 176–183; methyl
bromide (MeBr) phaseout
schedule, 86–87. See also *specific
countries*
Intergovernmental Panel on
Climate Change (IPCC), 11, 13,
253–254, 256
*International Environmental Law
and Policy*, 11
international environmental
NGOs. *See* IENGOs
International Institute for
Environment and Development
(IIED), 113
International Monetary Fund
(IMF), 40, 41
international relations, 47, 103,
111, 145
IPCC. *See* Intergovernmental
Panel on Climate Change
(IPCC)
Israel, MeBr producers, 86, 87,
147, 179
Issa, Darrell, 201

Japan: on MeBr alternatives, 189;
MeBr usage, 94, 145; and
Protocol ratifications, 152, 154;
on U.S. MeBr exemptions,
114–115
Jasanoff, Sheila, 195–196
Johannesburg Earth Summit
(2002), 42, 54, 57
Johnson, Stephen, 271

*Journal of Environmental
Management*, 272

Kenya, 187–188, 242, 303n.32
Keynes, John Maynard, 40
knowledge. *See* science/
knowledge
knowledge brokers, 134–135
Kyoto Protocol, 11, 54, 253–254,
254–255, 256–257

Lee-Bapty, Steve, 118
less-developed countries
(LDCs): future MeBr
phaseouts by, 155, 184–188,
189–190; and MeBr alternatives,
206–207; and MLF, 108; status
of, 132–133; and tensions over
MeBr phaseout, 145–146,
176–183; and U.S. attempts
at multi-year exemptions,
188–194; and U.S. MeBr
exemptions, 115, 125. See also
specific countries
Lewis, C. S., 272
Litfin, Karen, 23, 77, 105, 134–135,
135–136, 202
London Amendment (1990),
82, 87, 108, 151
London School of Economics
Center for Civil Society, 67
Lucas, Frank, 201

marine organisms, 252
market-based logic/solutions, 3,
25–26, 27, 48, 51–52, 55, 56–58,
115–116
market disruption, 91–93,
129–130
Mayfield, Erin, 269, 272, 273